India in Africa

Changing Geographies
of Power

Through the voices of the peoples of Africa and the global South, Pambazuka Press and Pambazuka News disseminate analysis and debate on the struggle for freedom and justice.

Pambazuka Press – www.pambazukapress.org

 A Pan-African publisher of progressive books and DVDs on Africa and the global South that aim to stimulate discussion, analysis and engagement. Our publications address issues of human rights, social justice, advocacy, the politics of aid, development and international finance, women's rights, emerging powers and activism. They are primarily written by well-known African academics and activists. Most books are also available as ebooks.

Pambazuka News – www.pambazuka.org

 The award-winning and influential electronic weekly newsletter providing a platform for progressive Pan-African perspectives on politics, development and global affairs. With more than 2,500 contributors across the continent and a readership of more than 660,000, Pambazuka News has become the indispensable source of authentic voices of Africa's social analysts and activists.

Pambazuka Press and Pambazuka News are published by Fahamu (www.fahamu.org)

India in Africa

Changing Geographies of Power

Edited by Emma Mawdsley
and Gerard McCann

Pambazuka Press
An imprint of Fahamu

Published 2011 by Pambazuka Press, an imprint of Fahamu
Cape Town, Dakar, Nairobi and Oxford

www.pambazukapress.org www.fahamubooks.org www.pambazuka.org

Fahamu, 2nd floor, 51 Cornmarket Street, Oxford OX1 3HA, UK
Fahamu Kenya, PO Box 47158, 00100 GPO, Nairobi, Kenya
Fahamu Senegal, 9 Cité Sonatel 2, BP 13083, Dakar Grand-Yoff,
Dakar, Senegal
Fahamu South Africa, c/o 19 Nerina Crescent, Fish Hoek,
7975 Cape Town, South Africa

British Library Cataloguing in Publication Data
A catalogue record for this book is available from the British Library

ISBN: 978-1-906387-65-5 paperback
ISBN: 978-1-906387-66-2 ebook – pdf
ISBN: 978-0-85749-061-2 ebook – epub
ISBN: 978-0-85749-062-9 ebook – Kindle

Manufactured on demand by Lightning Source

Contents

Contributors   vii

Introduction: Towards a re-evaluation of contemporary India–Africa relations   1
Emma Mawdsley and Gerard McCann

Part 1 India–Africa relations in context   11

1   India–Africa relations in the 21st century: genuine partnership or a marriage of convenience?   12
Fantu Cheru and Cyril Obi

2   India and the 'Asian drivers' in Africa   30
Pádraig Carmody

3   Upping the ante in Africa: India's increasing footprint across the continent   48
Sanusha Naidu

Part 2 Contemporary India–East Africa engagements   69

4   The impact of India–Kenya trade relations on the Kenya garment industry   70
Paul Kamau and Dorothy McCormick

5   Chinese and Indian entrepreneurs in the East African economies   88
Aleksandra W. Gadzala

6   Diaspora, political economy and India's relations with Kenya   108
Gerard McCann

7   Offshore healthcare management: medical tourism between Kenya, Tanzania and India   125
Renu Modi

8   *AwaaZ*: a personal and collective journey   140
Zarina Patel and Zahid Rajan

9   Fragile fortunes: India's oil venture into war-torn Sudan   153
Luke Patey

Part 3 A wider picture of India–Africa partnership   165

10 The rhetorics and rituals of 'South–South' development
   cooperation: notes on India and Africa   166
   Emma Mawdsley

11 India's security concerns in the western Indian Ocean   187
   Alex Vines

12 India goes over to the other side: Indo-West African relations
   in the 21st century   203
   Simona Vittorini and David Harris

Index   218

Contributors

Pádraig Carmody is a senior lecturer in geography at Trinity College Dublin, where he coordinates the TCD-UCD masters in development practice. Recent books include *Globalisation in Africa: Recolonisation or Renaissance?* (Lynne Reinner 2010) and the *New Scramble for Africa* (Polity 2011).

Fantu Cheru is research director at the Nordic Africa Institute in Uppsala, Sweden and Emeritus Professor of African and Development Studies at American University in Washington, DC. Dr Cheru served as a member of UN Secretary-General Kofi Annan's Panel on Mobilising International Support for the New Partnership for African Development (2005–07) and also served as the UN's Special Rapporteur on Foreign Debt and Structural Adjustment for the UN Commission for Human Rights in Geneva from 1998 to 2001. Professor Cheru's publications include co-editorship with Cyril Obi of *The Rise of China and India in Africa* (2010).

Aleksandra W. Gadzala is a doctoral candidate in politics at the University of Oxford and a consultant with London-based political risk firm, Control Risks Group. Previously she worked as editorial assistant to the *Journal of Eastern African Studies* and an aid effectiveness policy analyst with the UNDP based in New York. Her research focuses on relations between the Horn of Africa, China and the United States.

David Harris is a senior teaching fellow in the Politics Department at the School of Oriental and African Studies, London. He is a specialist in African politics, in particular Sierra Leone and Liberia, which are the focus of a book to be published in 2011.

Paul Kamau is a research fellow at the Institute for Development Studies, University of Nairobi, Kenya. He holds a PhD in development studies, and a BA and MSc in economics. His research interests are on international trade and industrial development in Africa. He has published on global value chains in textile and clothing industries and on Asian drivers. His recent book is *Upgrading and Technical Efficiency in Kenya Garment Firms: Does Insertion in Global Value Chains Matter?* (Lambert Academic 2010).

Emma Mawdsley is a senior lecturer in the Geography Department, Cambridge University and a fellow of Newnham College. She has written on critical development politics, including accounts of knowledge and power in transnational NGO networks, and on the World Development Reports and Millennium Challenge Account. She has also written extensively on environmental issues and politics in India. Recent publications include work on China and Africa, and she is currently writing a book on the (re-)emerging development cooperation partners (Zed Books).

Gerard McCann is a lecturer in international history at the University of York, before which he was the Mellon Fellow in Transnational History at Oxford University. His book on India–Africa relations, to be published as part of Zed Books' African Arguments series, will be published in 2012.

Dorothy McCormick is a professor at the Institute for Development Studies, University of Nairobi. She has a long history of research and teaching in the area of industrialisation and enterprise development in Africa. Her work has dealt with the institutions and enterprise development, enterprise clusters and value chains. A theme in her recent research has been the impact on Africa of the rise of China and India. Professor McCormick holds MA and PhD degrees in international studies from Johns Hopkins University, an MBA from the Wharton School of the University of Pennsylvania and a BA from Trinity University, Washington, DC.

Renu Modi is a senior lecturer and director of the Centre for African Studies, University of Mumbai. She served as the social development consultant with the Inspection Panel of the World Bank in 2005. She has published on issues of India–Africa economic relations from a historical and a contemporary perspective. Her recent edited book is titled, *Beyond Relocation: the Imperative of Sustainable Resettlement* (Sage 2009).

Sanusha Naidu is a senior researcher with the Democracy, Governance and Service Delivery Programme based at the Human Sciences Research Council (HSRC), Cape Town, South Africa. Ms Naidu, who holds an MA in international relations from Staffordshire University (UK), has worked on international relations and strategic issues for more than a decade. She has published widely in various international journals including the

Review of African Political Economy. Her latest co-edited volume is entitled: *African and Chinese Perspectives on China in Africa* (Pambazuka Press 2010). She is a regular commentator for international and national media, and was formerly the research director of the Emerging Powers in Africa Programme based with Fahamu, in Cape Town, South Africa.

Cyril Obi is a senior researcher and leader of the research cluster on Conflict, Displacement and Transformation at the Nordic Africa Institute, Uppsala, Sweden. Together with Fantu Cheru, he recently co-edited a book on *The Rise of China and India in Africa* (Zed Books 2010).

Zarina Patel is an author and historian as well as a human rights activist and environmentalist with a long-term interest in Kenyan-South Asian affairs. She is the granddaughter of Alibhai Mulla Jeevanjee, known as the father of South Asian politics in Kenya. She is the author of three books and a multitude of writings in mainstream media on politics, culture and gender mainstreaming. She is the managing editor of *AwaaZ*.

Luke Patey is a project researcher at the Danish Institute for International Studies. He is currently writing a book on the rise of Asian national oil companies from China, India and Malaysia and their investment in Sudan. His work has been published in *African Affairs*, *The Journal of Modern African Studies* and *Third World Quarterly*.

Zahid Rajan is a printer by profession. He has participated in civil society activism since 1992. He has been involved in the publishing of South Asian history in Kenya and is the executive editor of *AwaaZ*. Presently he is the chairman of the Eastern Action Club for Africa, a lobby group for minority rights whose motto is 'Equity and Equality for all'. He is the moderator of Solidarity Network Kenya, which publicises material on South–South Solidarity.

Alex Vines is director of regional and security studies and head of the Africa Programme at Chatham House. He is also a part-time lecturer at the Department of International Studies and Social Science, Coventry University.

Simona Vittorini is a senior teaching fellow in the Politics Department at the School of Oriental and African Studies, London. As a specialist in Indian politics, she has published widely in English and Italian.

 # Introduction

Towards a re-evaluation of contemporary India–Africa relations

Emma Mawdsley and Gerard McCann

In 2003 a report by Goldman Sachs, the global investment bank, made the startling claim that the 'BRIC' economies of Brazil, Russia, India and China would surpass the combined gross domestic product of the G6 by 2040 (Wilson and Purushothaman 2003). Beyond the magic four, a whole host of other emerging economies are also contributing to a changing global geography of wealth and power, including nations as diverse as Mexico, South Africa and Indonesia. However this transition actually unfolds in practice, there is no question that the world is witnessing the beginnings of very major changes – although those with a long view point out that it is the rise of western hegemony, following the great divergence of the 17th to 19th centuries, that is the historical anomaly.

Not surprisingly, these trends and shifts are under intense scrutiny by governments, academics, state-led and private sector firms, and militaries and the media, who are observing, commenting on and shaping trade, investment, finance, diplomatic relations, military capacities and development cooperation. India–Africa relations, the subject of this volume, are therefore couched within a dynamic and arguably increasingly complex world system. But cautioning us against too confident a set of predictions about the future, the world also confronts a host of uncertainties – climate change, disease pandemics, nuclear proliferation and religious fundamentalism of all hues, to name just a few. The challenges to human rights, sovereignties and just sustainable development – themes with which this book tentatively

1

grapples – are merely some of the critical issues to be faced by the global community in the coming century.

This book is a contribution to a growing literature on the so-called emerging or rising powers. It arises out of a grant we were awarded by the British Academy in 2007. At the time, interest in contemporary India–Africa relations was eclipsed by a strong focus on China and Africa. China is certainly a more potent player in most African countries and sectors than India at present, so in part this very uneven interest simply responded to an accurate assessment of their relative material powers and impacts. But media and (to some extent) policy concern with Sino-African relations was also the product of a long-standing anxiety about China in the world, neuroses amplified by distorting images and discourses (Pan 2004; Mawdsley 2008). Although some authors have been assiduous in producing field-based observations, empirical evidence and nuanced analysis of the complex nature of the challenges and opportunities raised by current China–Africa relationships (notably Brautigam 1998, 2009; Manji and Marks 2007; Alden et al 2008; Mohan and Power 2008; Carmody 2009), others still trade in simplistic and sweeping caricatures.

By developing a modest research project exploring India–Africa interactions we sought to address a number of problems. First, as noted above the changing contours of contemporary India–Africa relations were, with some honourable exceptions, being overlooked in favour of China. Second, of the available literature, some tended to make rather comfortable but untested assumptions about India's growing role in Africa based on a somewhat idealised construction of their historical relations and present-day declarations of continued solidarity. Although we are extremely sensitive to the historical conditioning of contemporary relations, we believe that older tensions are not always being acknowledged, while newer differences are on occasions obscured. Some of the current circuits of trade and investment, for instance, are not working through historical Indian diasporic communities in Africa, as is widely assumed (see McCann, Chapter 6 in this volume). Third – and bringing us back to the predominance of China–Africa studies – we felt that by going beyond China and Africa and broadening the analysis of the different emerging powers, a more helpful comparative lens might be held up to China.

To take just one example, examining India's investment in Sudanese oil provides a more structural understanding of the conflicts (global and domestic) and the opportunities that confront would-be players in this field. Previously, much western media and policy commentary had roundly criticised China's complicity in Sudanese human rights violations, driven by what was viewed as its irresponsible hydrocarbon investments. These criticisms frequently overlooked the wider range of actors engaged in parallel activities. Among others, democratic and liberal India was not subjected to the same scrutiny or condemnation.

We suggest then that by locating China as one among many actors with a growing interest in African markets and resources, including other emerging powers, but also North American and European countries, the dangers of asserting a caricatured singularity are moderated. Indeed, although this collection of India–Africa studies makes some contribution to that endeavour, we are aware of the continued relative neglect of many other countries with a growing footprint in different parts of Africa, including the United Arab Emirates, Malaysia, Iran, Russia and Japan, to name but a few.

The relationship between India and Africa during the 20th century has been previously charted by a number of authors, most of who were preoccupied with highlighting instances of Indo-African cooperation in the struggle against colonialism, apartheid and other instances of political oppression. There is also a very rich literature examining South Asian diasporas in East and South Africa, a corpus of work which has often sought to celebrate Indian Ocean cosmopolitanism and assert the legitimate place of South Asian communities within African polities. Since 2007, when we started this project, there has also been a modest surge in writing on more contemporary interactions between Africa and India, most notably the collection edited by Fantu Cheru and Cyril Obi (2010).

In this collection we aim to contribute in two particular ways. First, we have tried to collect field-based research, including certain chapters grounded in specific case studies. There continues to be an empirical lag in the field of India–Africa studies, especially in comparison with China–Africa work. Moreover, much of the writing that exists on India–Africa relations has focused on the panoramic – addressing issues of geopolitics, international relations, resource security and trade and investment within sub-Saharan Africa generally (although with passing reference to specific regions, nations and sectors). This 'big picture' thinking is a natural and desirable point of departure for the profound and very recent changes affecting the India–Africa relationship – that guarded and complex transition from the paramount political solidarities of the colonial and cold war eras to the contemporary partnerships based more obviously, though not exclusively, on commercial imperatives. In many ways, this macro bias is unavoidable given the resources available for the study of such disparate locales. That said, there is certainly an overtly repetitive feeling in much of the India–Africa literature, which might be gradually overcome.

Some associated methodological questions must also be addressed. For instance, a more conspicuous scepticism about the accuracy and provenance of the internet sources on which these studies are necessarily based is needed. Again, it is more local fieldwork that is required. Some of the chapters in this collection therefore have a preliminary feel to them – individual case studies that indicate the need for larger analyses. In other cases we have been fortunate to get chapters from contributors who have undertaken extensive fieldwork. It is in the detail of specific events and relationships that we begin to test our assumptions and claims – allowing us to reach for more nuanced understandings of the wider picture. We hope this book contributes in some small degree to such an endeavour.

The second contribution we have sought to make is a more critical analysis of India–Africa relations. Some of the media and policy assertions, and indeed some academic writing, posits an unproblematic win-win relationship between India and Africa, based on those historical third worldist solidarities and India's own seemingly instructive post-liberalisation development model. We are sympathetic and in agreement with many of the optimistic and positive predictions of the unfolding benefits that the emerging set of relationships might bring. However, we are also cautious, and concur with the formulations of the Asian drivers model in recognising the direct and indirect competitive and zero-sum outcomes of greater trade, investment, development cooperation, peacekeeping and diplomatic relations. Future research on India in Africa, it is hoped, can depart from unproblematic normative assumptions about India's place within the developing world, and bring due recognition to the agency of African actors in the formation of these new partnerships.

In this latter regard, we are struck by the relative shortage of African authors engaged in the study of India–Africa, a state of affairs that is unfortunately reflected in this book. Although several African scholars, politicians, journalists, businesspersons and activists have grappled with issues surrounding local South Asian communities and their contested place within post-colonial African societies, fewer have thus far devoted their energies to unpacking India's transformed relationships with a range of African players (and indeed its own diaspora) in recent years. This is, in part, a function of troubled social relations between Africans and South Asians in certain regions, East Africa especially, where essentialist local discourses about the Asian presence have not, by and large, been marked by analytical rigour.

More importantly, the paucity of African commentary on India reflects the wider fascination with China's African exploits, which are so visibly transforming an enormously wide range of urban and rural African environments. There have been a number of published works dealing with African perspectives on China in Africa (see Manji and Marks 2007), and it is to be hoped that parallel works might emerge in reference to a wider range of emerging partners. More African-driven analyses and approaches would help to re-orientate some of the early Asian-driver literature, which implies a certain unidirectional power flow and underplays the potency of African agency. This represents one of the most vital avenues going forward, to which several of the case studies in this book are aligned.

Because of the initial nature of the collaboration, which was set up between the British Association of South Asian Studies (BASAS) and the British Institute in Eastern Africa (BIEA), the collection leans toward East Africa. However, we also solicited chapters on other regions, as well as critical synoptic analyses of the India–Africa relationship as a whole. Part 1 aims to frame the canvas on which more specific pictures will be painted. Fantu Cheru and Cyril Obi set out a broad analysis of the wide spectrum of India–Africa relations in the 21st century, concluding that ultimately the prospects of India–Africa engagements facilitating worthwhile African development lie in the hands of Africa's political and economic elites. Pádraig Carmody considers India as an Asian driver within the 'new scramble for Africa', drawing on statist and private sector examples to explore India's globalisation slipstreaming behind China, and further unpacking India's specific engagements in a range of African contexts. Finally, Sanusha Naidu also covers the widening general impact of India's footprint in Africa, analysing the ways in which India is strategically positioning itself as an alternative development partner to other southern actors, particularly China.

Part 2 turns to consider India's relations with East Africa through a number of original national and sectoral case studies and represents the core of the British Academy project in which this book has its genesis. Kamau and McCormick set out a detailed account of the opportunities and costs within the textile industry in Kenya. What their analysis demonstrates is that the actual and potential benefits and costs must be seen as both highly differentiated (depending on which part of the textile industry one inhabits) and dynamic. Various external and internal factors – from the US's African Growth and Opportunity Act to government decisions about national investment or tariff strategies – can and will change the playing field. Certain actors will be in a position to take advantage of these opportunities, while others will find themselves on the ropes.

Aleksandra W. Gadzala's chapter on Sino-Indian competition is welcome in utilising a very different scale of analysis to those employing standard geopolitical and macroeconomic lenses. She addresses the lacuna in studies of small-scale enterprises with her examination of Indian and Chinese entrepreneurs in contemporary urban East African economies, posing the question as to whether Chinese businesspersons are becoming the 'new dukawallahs', a loaded north Indian moniker denoting local South Asian-origin (mainly Gujarati) traders. These historical South Asian communities in East Africa provide one of the most apparently relevant Indo-African linkages across the Indian Ocean.

Gerard McCann explores the location of South Asians in East Africa and notes that, although Indian investors in Kenya are becoming increasingly prominent, few are utilising India's supposed new-found conviviality with its diaspora to drive their projects and agendas. Indeed, he argues that East African Asian networks could actually create obstacles to India–Africa partnership in the context of Kenya's historically ethnicised political economy. Renu Modi offers a useful initial foray into health tourism between Kenya, Tanzania and India, pointing to older diasporic ties, as well as new enabling factors, such as cheap flights and communications and new medical technologies.

Although most of these chapters take on questions of politics and the economy, we also include the first-ever published account of the history and development of *AwaaZ*, a remarkable Kenyan publication founded by social activists Zarina Patel and Zahid Rajan. The challenges they have faced and questions they have had to ask themselves on their journey provide a very personal insight into some of the difficult issues of Asian identity in East Africa.

Lastly in Part 2, Luke Patey provides a lucid and highly informative account of India's investments into Sudan's oil sector, demonstrating that, contrary to popular opinion, Chinese private and state-owned firms do not always out-compete their Indian rivals. He shows that deft diplomatic manoeuvring in New Delhi and Khartoum has enabled diversification of Asian investment in Sudan, but that certain challenges await all foreign players in specific African contexts, no matter their domestic characteristics, relative diplomatic power and overseas ambitions.

The third and final part of the book provides a wider thematic and geographical optic. In her chapter, Emma Mawdsley eschews a standard account of India–Africa development cooperation (of which there are plenty of strong examples), and offers instead a critical evaluation of the contrasting symbolic and performative regimes between western and non-western donors in Africa, focusing of course on India. At the other end of the spectrum, Alex Vines examines in some detail India's strategic interests in the Indian Ocean, and its overtures to and collaborations with different African states in projecting its military power in its traditional backyard. He clearly demonstrates that economic considerations are not the sole motives for India's renewed interest in Africa. To round off the book, Simona Vittorini and David Harris take us to West Africa, a crucial new frontier in Indian diplomatic and corporate global strategy, and a comparison of Indian engagements with two very different African political and investment environments – Liberia and Ghana.

We have a very large debt of gratitude to a number of institutions and individuals. The project was funded by the British Academy, for which we are very grateful. Newnham College, Cambridge also very kindly contributed to the costs of publication of this book. Our warm thanks to Justin Willis, Humphrey Mathenge and all the staff at the BIEA who did so much to help organise the conference in Nairobi in April 2009, especially in rushing through the completion of their new facilities for the event. Many thanks are due to Professor Kunal Sen and the other committee members of British Association for South Asian Studies for their support. We are also appreciative of the research assistance of Grace Puliyel in Nairobi. We have of course benefited from the intellectual stimulation and stellar scholarly examples of numerous colleagues. We would particularly like to thank Deborah Brautigam, Dan Large, Chris Alden, David Anderson and Giles Mohan in this regard. Our next debt of gratitude is to Firoze Manji and the Pambazuka Press team who have been supportive throughout, even in the face of repeated delays in publication. We also appreciate the patience of all our contributors. We are particularly grateful to all the participants at our British Academy workshop in London in November 2008 and conference in Nairobi the following year. The latter was opened by Rob Macaire, the British high commissioner to Kenya and Dr Ketan Shukla, the deputy Indian high commissioner to Kenya, whom we also thank for their presence and contributions. The event proved to be a highly stimulating occasion, one which was hopefully a harbinger of things to come within the field of India–Africa relations.

References

Alden, C, Large, D. and Soares de Oliveira, R (eds) (2008) *China Returns to Africa: A Continent and a Rising Power Embrace*, London and New York, Hurst Publishers and Columbia University Press

Brautigam, D. (1998) *Chinese Aid and African Development: Exporting Green Revolution*, London, Macmillan Press

—— (2009) *Dragon's Gift: The Real Story of China in Africa*, Oxford, Oxford University Press

Carmody, P. (2009) 'An Asian-driven economic recovery in Africa? The Zambian case', *World Development*, vol. 37, no. 7, pp. 1197–1207

Cheru, F. and Obi, C. (eds) (2010) *The Rise of China and India in Africa*, London, Zed Books

Manji, F. and Marks, S. (eds) (2007) *African Perspectives on China in Africa*, Oxford, Fahamu

Mawdsley, E.E. (2008) 'Fu Manchu versus Dr Livingstone in the dark continent? Representing China, Africa and the West in British broadsheet newspapers', *Political Geography*, vol. 27, no. 5, pp. 509–29

Mohan, G. and Power, M. (2008) 'New African choice? The politics of Chinese engagement in Africa and the changing architecture of international development', *Review of African Political Economy*, vol. 35, no. 1, pp. 23–42

Pan, C. (2004) 'The "China" threat in American self-imagination: the discursive construction of the other as power politics', *Alternatives*, vol. 29, no. 3, pp. 305–31

Wilson, D. and Purushothaman, R. (2003) 'Dreaming with BRICs: the path to 2050', Global Economics paper 99, Goldman Sachs

Part 1
India–Africa relations in context

1

India–Africa relations in the 21st century: genuine partnership or a marriage of convenience?

Fantu Cheru and Cyril Obi

Introduction

From most indications, India and China, two leading emerging economies in the world, are competing with each other, as well as Africa's traditional western trading partners, to build a stronger relationship with Africa. Both Asian giants have contributed to the increase in the volume and value of African exports, bringing in more revenue to resource-rich African countries. This has provided African countries with an opportunity also to diversify the destination of exports, creating some room for greater flexibility, as well as an alternative to the condition-laden, asymmetrical relations into which African countries had been hitherto locked with their western trading partners and financial institutions.

By the same logic, India and China have provided Africa with cheaper imports, investments and low-cost technology, while their resource diplomacy has provided the continent with new and visible forms of development cooperation and aid that are largely free of the terms imposed by western partners. It would appear that this competition between India and China is underscored by the quest for oil, markets, minerals, raw materials and influence.

Although the growing presence of India and China in Africa is creating some concern in western capitals, particularly in the context of a 'new' scramble for Africa's resources and the implications of such ties for democracy and accountability in Africa, it is rather too early to tell whether this renewed interest in Africa by China and India will constitute a new dimension of South–South relations, or alternatively, if it will produce new forms of asymmetrical relations. What is clear, however, is that the rise of both India and China in Africa certainly will have significant implications for the future of Africa's development and its international relations. Trade between China and Africa grew from $20 billion in 2001 to more than $120 billion in 2009. Similarly, India's trade with Africa (excluding oil) also surged from $914 million in 1991 to between $25 billion and $30 billion in 2008.

Despite official Indian denial that there is no competition between the two Asian giants (*The Economic Times* 2010) in Africa, India's foreign policy swings between attempting to catch up with the Chinese, who have made major inroads in Africa over the past decade, and accommodating the aspirations of China, India and the western world in the context of India's enduring relations with the continent. Thus, we argue that what we see is an emerging trend of competition sometimes moderated by accommodation. This competition centres on three major issues: energy security, access to Africa's untapped markets and diplomatic influence (National Intelligence Council 2004; Martin 2008).

Also of note is the reality that India cannot match China's 'deep pockets' when it comes to resource diplomacy, state backing for private sector investments, and the provision of credit and aid to African countries. India compensates for this with its rhetoric of being a true friend and equal partner of Africa that is keen to facilitate development on the continent, as defined by Africans themselves, in the spirit of solidarity and mutual benefit. However, India's policy toward Africa is different from China's more in terms of its form/degree than of its intent (Mawdsley and McCann 2010). It is important to note that when stripped of its rhetoric, it is hard to ignore the similarities between the African strategies of India and China, which Naidu rightly observes is found in 'their demands for resource security, trade and investment opportunities, forging of strategic partnerships, African–Asian solidarity and South–South solidarity' (Naidu 2010, p. 34).

The other aspect that relates to the expansion of Indian influence in Africa is framed in the context of an Indo-Africa renaissance, which can act both for economic partnership and a voice in shaping the emerging world order (Sharma 2009). In this regard, India has doubled its lines of credit (LOC), opened up niches in the areas of human resource development, technical training and capacity building, energy cooperation, investments, a pan-African e-network and the transfer of low-cost appropriate technology. Although the evidence strongly indicates that 'India has lagged behind China's aggressive courting of African nations to secure rights to energy as well as raw materials' (Redvers 2010), India's competition with China in Africa will serve as an interesting window on the way in which these three issues affect Indian policy.

India's race to catch up with the Chinese

It is important to establish from the outset that India is not a newcomer to Africa and the relationship dates back to the pre-colonial period. It became stronger during the period of anti-colonial struggle and later, at the height of the cold war, when India, under the leadership of Jawaharlal Nehru, took an instrumental role in the establishment of the Non-Aligned Movement (NAM) to demand for a just international order. The principle of non-alignment and South–South cooperation became the centrepiece of Indian foreign policy until the late 1980s.

With the economic liberalisation in the 1990s, India's foreign policy objectives became more pragmatic, with the aim of promoting India's economic ambitions on the world stage. Just as China had done under Premier Deng Xiaoping in the late 1970s, India began to strengthen its external relations with Europe, the United States and its closest neighbours in Asia to fully realise its political and economic ambitions. Among India's more recent foreign policy initiatives were the decisions to enter into a strategic dialogue with the US, open new economic relations with the countries of Latin America and Asia, ease tensions with China and pursue a deliberate policy to collaborate with them in key international organisations, such as the World Trade Organisation. Yet, engagement with the African continent did not peak in India's ambitious globalisation strategy until 2008, almost a decade after Beijing's well-coordinated penetration of the African market.

There are a number of reasons why New Delhi is increasingly courting the African continent. At the forefront of India's foreign policy priorities is energy security (Patey, Chapter 9 in this volume; Obi 2010; Vines and Campos 2010). The Indian economy has grown rapidly from the 1990s, and securing cheap energy and other strategic raw materials from the African continent on a long-term basis has become an economic and political imperative. It is projected that by 2030 India will be the world's third-largest consumer of energy (Madan 2006). Currently, 75 per cent of India's oil imports come from the politically volatile Middle East. Because India possesses few proven oil reserves, diversifying the sources of its energy supply by developing stronger economic ties with the African continent tops the political agenda (Sharma and Mahajan 2007). With projections suggesting that India will depend on oil for almost 90 per cent of its energy needs by the end of this decade, it is little wonder that energy security through the diversification of supplies is a key priority. Given Africa's position as the last oil frontier, it is only strategic that India engages the continent in pursuit of its energy security interests. This urgency is further elevated by the increasing scramble for African resources by both China and the industrialised countries.

Second, Africa has emerged as an important market for Indian goods and services, as well as a vital element in India's quest for strategic minerals and other natural resources needed to feed its burgeoning economy. In this regard, the Indian private sector, with some government support, has been active in expanding trade and investment in Africa and to capture Africa's untapped market potential. Accordingly, India's trade with Africa expanded by 500 per cent, from $5.2 billion in 2003 to an estimated $26 billion in 2008. The most recent figures for 2009 indicate that India's trade with Africa has grown to an estimated 'US$39 billion, compared to China–Africa trade of US$109 billion' (Indiainteracts 2010), showing a continuous growth in Indo-African trade, but also indicating the gap between India and China's trade with Africa. India is working hard, however, as suggested by agreements reached at the March 2010 India–Africa Conclave meeting in New Delhi attended by 400 African delegates from 34 countries, 'to scale up its bilateral trade with Africa to US$70 billion by 2015' (Thaindian News 2010).

Similarly, African countries have been interested in acquiring cost effective and intermediate technology from India in the fields of information technology, agriculture, health and pharmaceuticals (Modi 2010). Only half a million Africans have access to the internet, and there is thus a pressing need to narrow the digital divide. Africans also want to gain more knowledge and expertise from India's successful green revolution experience in order to attain food self-sufficiency. In the field of health, African consumers are interested to have access to affordable drugs as well as treatment in India's highly sophisticated health delivery system (Beri 2008).

Third, as its economic power grows, India also has decided to project its military power in the Indian Ocean region, which it has long considered to be within its sphere of influence. Given the existence of extremist organisations and criminal syndicates that traffic drugs, arms and people, as well as pirates in the Indian Ocean region, India has begun to dramatically expand its military presence in the Horn of Africa and the Indian Ocean, through which the oil tankers that carry nearly all of India's oil imports must travel (Volman 2009).

In October 2008, Indian warships began conducting patrols off the Somali coast to protect ships from pirate attacks. India has also established a listening post in northern Madagascar, which consists of a radar surveillance station equipped with a high-tech digital communications system and which is intended, at least in part, to monitor Chinese activities. In 2003, India signed a defence cooperation agreement with Seychelles and in 2006 signed a defence agreement with Mozambique to provide arms and to conduct regular naval patrols off Mozambique's coast (Vines, Chapter 11 in this volume; Vines and Oruitemeka 2008).

Development assistance

The Indian government has launched a number of initiatives to strengthen economic cooperation between Africa and India. This engagement takes three forms: development assistance, foreign direct investment and trade, and diplomacy. There are two instruments through which India extends development assistance: the LOC extended by the Export-Import (Exim) Bank of India and the traditional technical assistance predominately managed by the country's ministry of external affairs. Overall,

Indian development assistance has grown from Rs.9.2 billion in 2000 to Rs.25 billion in 2009 (Ministry of Finance 2009). Needless to say, it is difficult to ascertain precisely the volume and types of India's development assistance to Africa because complete and disaggregated data is hard to find (Jobelius 2007; Kragelund 2008; Rowlands 2008). The available data does not make a distinction between what the OECD's (Organisation for Economic Cooperation and Development) development action committee would define as aid and what is export credit, a problem that also holds true to Chinese aid to Africa (Brautigam 2009). As will be made clear later in this chapter, a large part of what India spends on development assistance in Africa is nothing more than an export subsidy scheme for surplus Indian goods (Agrawal 2007; Mawdsley and McCann 2010).

The share of India's official development assistance going to Africa is relatively small compared with aid going to India's Asian neighbours (Mawdsley 2010). In the fiscal year 2009–10, a mere Rs.20.53 billion was allocated to the whole of Africa, compared to

Table 1.1 Destination of India's aid programme (in $)*

Country	2005–06	2006–07	2007–08
Bhutan	251.36	120.4	162.44
Bangladesh	11.56	4.44	13.33
Nepal	14.67	46.67	22.22
Sri Lanka	5.56	6.23	6.22
Myanmar	4.89	8.89	4.44
Maldives	2.93	1.33	4.33
African countries	13.55	4.44	11.11
Afghanistan			96.44
Central Asia			4.44
Latin America			0.34
Other developing countries	111.96	98.94	53.35

*excluding lines of credit

(Source: Ministry of External Affairs, Annual Reports 2006-07)

the Rs.400.00 billion allocated to Afghanistan. The bulk of Indian development assistance to Africa is devoted to training, capacity building, project-related consultancy services, deputation of experts, study tours and other 'soft' investments, although the country also supports a number of capital projects financed by export credit extended through the Exim Bank (Katti et al 2009; Sinha 2010).

Among the most important technical assistance programmes are the Indian Technical and Economic Cooperation (ITEC) Programme and the Special Commonwealth African Assistance Programme for Africa (SCAAP). Under ITEC and SCAAP, some 1,000 African experts are given short-term training in India every year in a number of technical fields — from public administration to agricultural research and computer literacy. In addition, the ITEC programme provides scholarships to African students who take regular academic courses in India (Katti et al 2009).

Increasingly, however, commercial interests have become embedded in India's foreign policy. As India faces a potential energy crisis, Africa has entered centre stage in India's foreign policy priorities and development assistance is channelled to achieve this goal (Mawdsley and McCann 2010; Obi 2010; Vines and Campos 2010). Currently, about 24–30 per cent of India's crude oil imports is sourced from Africa (Obi 2009). Consequently, India has stepped up its diplomatic offensive in West Africa's Gulf of Guinea, where 70 per cent of African oil is extracted. Indian oil companies, such as the Oil and Natural Gas Corporation Videsh Limited (OVL), have invested heavily in equity assets in Sudan, Ivory Coast, Libya, Egypt, Nigeria, Gabon and Angola. India has also recently completed a $200 million project to lay pipeline from Khartoum to Port Sudan on the Red Sea. Indian companies have invested in exploration and production blocks in Madagascar and Nigeria (the latter currently accounts for between 10 per cent and 15 per cent of India's total oil imports, estimated at 400,000 barrels per day and is the second largest source of Indian imports).

During a visit to Abuja the Nigerian capital city, as part of a four-nation Africa tour in January 2010, Murli Deora, India's Minister of Petroleum and Natural Gas, announced the country's commitment to invest $360 million to develop two oil blocs (Oil Prospecting Licenses 279 and 285). Also included in the package was a deal between ONGC (Oil and Natural Gas Corporation) Mittal and the Nigerian National Petroleum Corporation (NNPC) to establish a refinery and explore the possibility of cooperation between GAIL (India) and India Oil Corporation in the Nigerian liquefied natural gas sector (Ezigbo 2010). Deora's tour marked the latest endeavour of India's burgeoning African petro-diplomacy. For example, it represented a follow-up to the second India–Africa Hydrocarbon conference in New Delhi in December 2009, and underscored the industry of the Indian state in pursuing India's energy security interests in Africa in the face of competition from China and western oil-import dependent countries.

The Focus Africa Programme launched in 2002 by the Ministry of Commerce and administered by the Exim Bank of India aims to provide financial assistance to various trade promotion organisations and export promotion councils. The programme now covers some 24 African countries and has been instrumental in encouraging and assisting the tremendous growth in Indian exports to sub-Saharan African countries. The programme has particularly targeted regional economic blocks, such as the Economic Community of West African States (ECOWAS) and the Common Market for Eastern and Southern Africa as critical nodes to expand Indian exports to the sub-regions by extending to them LOC.

Two years later, the Techno-Economic Approach for Africa–India Movement (TEAM-9) for cooperation between India and eight West and Central African countries situated in the oil-rich Gulf of Guinea was initiated to promote trade and investment (Beri 2008). This is essentially a credit facility with a volume of $500 million for Burkina Faso, Chad, Côte d'Ivoire, Equatorial Guinea, Ghana, Guinea Bissau, Mali and Senegal. The aim is to promote economic development in these countries through access to Indian technology. Some of the projects established under this initiative include $30 million for rural electrification in Ghana, a $4 million bicycle plant in Chad, a $12 million tractor assembly plant in Mali and a $15 million potable drinking water project in Equatorial Guinea (see Vittorini and Harris, Chapter 12, this volume).

Another novel initiative by India has been the launch of the Pan-African e-Network in February 2009. The aim of the project is to bridge the digital divide and accelerate development on the African continent. The project, which is expected to cost

$1 billion, supports tele-education, tele-medicine, resource mapping and e-commerce. For example, major hospitals in many African countries are now connected through the e-network with the leading Indian hospitals and receiving real-time instructions and assistance to provide advanced medical services to their patients (Modi 2009). State-owned Telecommunications Consultants India Ltd will implement the network, which India will manage for five years before turning it over to the Africa Union (AU).

In April 2008, the first official India–Africa Summit was held in New Delhi, indicating the coming of age of India's relations with the African continent. Among the many initiatives that India announced at the summit were:

- An increase of the existing level of credit to Africa from about $2 billion to $5.4 billion by 2013.
- A duty-free tariff preference scheme for 34 least developed African countries. The scheme will cover 94 per cent of total tariff lines and products, such as cotton, cocoa, aluminium ores, copper ores, cashew nuts, cane sugar, clothing and non-industrial diamonds.
- The doubling of trade from $25 billion to $50 billion by 2011.
- A $500 million budget allocation for capacity building and human resource development, expanding existing training programmes for African students and technocrats.
- Support to Africa's regional integration efforts and provision of financial support to the AU and the New Partnership for Africa's Development (NEPAD). This includes a $200 million line of credit to NEPAD.

The second India–Africa Summit will take place in the spring of 2011 and is expected to review implementation of the agreed goals of the first summit and promote new initiatives to expand the economic and political relationship between Africa and India. The picture emerging thus far is that, despite a slow start, India's strategy toward Africa is becoming more focused, and policy coherence between the activities of various Indian economic agents and the Indian state has improved significantly during the past three years. With a huge Indian diaspora in Africa, English as the principal working language for the Indian private sector and the government bureaucracy, and given its proximity to the continent, India is steadily consolidating its expanding and much closer ties with Africa. In the medium to long term, it could conceivably close the gap with China on the continent.

The Indian private sector

Unlike the predominantly state-driven approach of China, India's entry into Africa is spearheaded by private companies covering sectors such as telecommunications, agriculture, hotels, mining, rail and road infrastructure and pharmaceuticals. Buoyed by the economic boom in India, the easy availability of capital and the search for new markets, Indian companies such as Kirloskar Brothers Limited, the Tata Group, Mahindra and Mahindra, Fortis, Escort and Apollo have begun looking to the continent of Africa as a source of raw materials and markets. There are long-established trade relations between Africa and India, yet according to many commentators and businesspersons African nations are interacting with a renewed wave of Indian exporters in sectors in which Indian light engineering products, consumer goods and intermediate products can compete on price and are well adapted to local conditions. Indian companies are also seeking to mine gold, diamonds, manganese, bauxite, iron ore and chrome, either by operating new mines or by forming local partnerships with local firms to exploit existing ones.

The dramatic growth of the Indian private sector in Africa has taken place under the stewardship of the Confederation of Indian Industries (CII), the publicly owned Exim Bank of India and the captains of major Indian companies. Between 2004 and 2011, the CII and Exim Bank have jointly organised seven major meetings that brought together key Indian and African private sector organisations and government representatives to discuss and review the progress made in deepening economic engagement between India and Africa (Bhattacharya 2010; Modi 2010).

In addition to the Indian private sector, Indian state-owned corporations, such as the Indian Telecom Industries, Rail India Technical and Economic Services (Rites), Konkan Railways, the ONGC and many others are also very active in the extractive sector as well as in large-scale construction projects, such as roads, railways, telecommunications and the building construction sectors. For example, although Rites and IRCON, the two large state-owned infrastructure and engineering companies have been engaged in construction of rail networks and the leasing of locomotives in Sudan, Tanzania, Kenya and Mozambique, companies such as Kalapaaru Power Transmission Ltd have secured major contracts to build power transmission sites. In general, the state-owned enterprises work very closely with the Indian private enterprise and operators in both sectors draw a great deal of support from the Exim Bank through its LOC programme.

The Exim Bank has been a key institution and has played a critical role in facilitating the entry of Indian private sector companies into Africa, including the financing of major capital projects on the continent (Mawdsley and McCann 2010). It has done this through its LOCs to African governments, parastatal boards, regional entities such as the Eastern and Southern African Trade and Development Bank, the West African Development Bank, and the East Africa Development Bank to promote Indian exports and consultancy services to Africa. According S.R. Rao, the Chief General Manager of the Exim Bank of India, some 30 LOCs were in operation in Africa in 2006 alone, totalling about $1 billion (Rao 2006, p. 21).

At the end of March 2009, almost $2.27 billion (or 60 per cent of total Exim LOCs of $3.75 billion) went to African countries. In the financial year 2008–09 alone, the Exim Bank extended 25 LOCs worth $479 million to Africa (Exim Bank 2008). Total LOCs are expected to reach $5.4 billion over the next five years. Examples of funded projects in Africa executed by Indian companies include: supply of pharmaceuticals (Uganda, Ghana); building of transmission lines (Kenya); telecom projects (Malawi); a railway construction project (Tanzania); the erection of a sugar plant (Nigeria); and a sewerage study (Ethiopia) (Rao 2006).

Although the increasing volume of LOCs to individual African countries, regional multilateral bodies by the Exim Bank is a good indication of the private sector-led thrust of India's Africa policy, there is a risk of adding to Africa's debt burden. Great care must be taken to balance credits destined to promote mere consumption of Indian luxury goods versus credits to support investment aimed at raising African productivity, increasing income and reducing poverty in the long term.

Furthermore, the OECD has been extremely critical of both India and China's approach to trade with Africa, arguing that both the Asian giants are mainly interested in securing raw materials and energy from Africa and finding new markets for their cheap goods and services. Because this could lead to 'Dutch disease' in African countries, it is not to their advantage in the long term (Goldstein et al 2006). This conclusion has already been assigned to Chinese investments in Africa and India will not be able to escape the same criticism if it fails to heed African concerns.

In addition to providing export credits, the Exim Bank has bought equity stake in the Africa Export-Import Bank (Afreximbank), the West African Development Bank and the Development Bank of Zambia. It also has a strong relationship with the African Development Bank (AfDB), and as a non-regional member of this bank has been able to assist Indian companies to bid successfully in AfDB-financed infrastructure projects in Africa. It also influences private sector development in Africa through its consultancy and advisory services to numerous African governments and the World Bank Group, resulting in the participation of Indian companies in projects financed by the International Finance Corporation under its Africa project development facility, the Africa Enterprise Fund and the Technical Assistance and Trust Fund in a number of African countries (Rao 2006).

Diplomacy

On the diplomatic front, both India and China compete fiercely to win the hearts and minds of African leaders for their respective foreign policy goals. The big prize for China is winning the support of Africans for its 'one China' policy over Taiwan; for India, the big prize is securing a seat at the UN Security Council (Schaffer and Mitra 2005; Suri 2007). As noted earlier, India's pitch has been to underscore its long-standing relationship with the continent, its track record of solidarity with Africa in struggles of decolonisation and the quest for development. Indian diplomats and government officials are quick to emphasise that far from being a fair-weather friend, India offers a unique model of engagement with the continent based on equality, mutual respect and benefits. As Tharoor recently asserted, 'we do not wish to go and demand certain rights or impose certain rights or projects or impose our ideas in Africa. But we want to contribute to Africa's development objectives' (Indiainteracts 2010). However, like China, India has hosted African summits, which have been (at least partially) concerned with the promotion of Indian business and hydrocarbon interests.

There is also the fact that India is a multiparty democracy, which acts as a form of leverage and legitimacy in its dealings with Africa but also constitutes a bureaucratic bottleneck preventing quick and timely decisions with regard to its interests in a rather competitive African scene. But the recent upsurge in visits by Indian high-ranking officials to strategic African countries and the engagement of Africa's regional organisations point to greater Indian presence and influence on the continent. By seeking to differentiate its model of engagement with Africa from that of China and the western powers, India is no doubt attempting to carve an image for itself as an alternate and beneficial partner as it seeks to out-manoeuvre a more endowed and aggressive China that has so far outpaced it in the 'new' scramble for Africa.

Another aspect of India's Africa diplomacy that deserves some attention is its role in the training of Africa's militaries and peacekeepers. India continues to be one of the largest contributors to peacekeeping missions in Africa (Singh 2007). According to Singh (2007), India has been a part of all UN peacekeeping missions in Africa. Although Indian peacekeepers had to be withdrawn from Sierra Leone, reports of India's involvement in peacekeeping operations on the continent have been largely positive. India is also the third-largest troop contributor to UN African peace operations (Singh 2007), and its efforts in supporting peace operations on the continent cannot be separated from its efforts to promote peace and its influence in Africa, while also playing a positive role in world affairs.

Following the lead of many European donors, India has also been supporting African regional institutions, such as the AU and NEPAD, ECOWAS and the Southern African Development Community (SADC) as stated above. Indeed, the India–South African relationship was formalised through the formation of the SADC-Indian Forum in 2003, and within the context of the tripartite India–Brazil–South Africa institution. India has contributed $200 million for the implementation of various projects under NEPAD. Also the Indian Chambers of Commerce and Industry (FICCI) have signed a memorandum of understanding with ECOWAS on trade relations (Afrique en ligne 2010).

To underscore its strategic partnership with Africa, India and the AU have recently 'finalised a Plan of Action of the Framework for Cooperation of the Indian African Forum Summit' (NetIndian 2010). The framework is both to guide the implementation of the agreements reached at the first India–Africa Forum Summit and set the stage for the second summit planned for the spring of 2011. In this regard, the programme sets out the details for establishing several institutions to promote Indo-African relations. These include the India Africa Institute for Foreign Trade, India Africa Diamond Institute, India Africa Institute of Educational Planning and Administration, India Africa Institute of Information Technology, and the Pan African Stock Exchange (NetIndian 2010).

Prospects for India–Africa relations

India is moving fast to consolidate its growing footprint in Africa as it competes with China and with developed countries to secure energy, raw material resources, and markets to fuel its growing economy and export its manufactured goods and services. India's active engagement with Africa is motivated by a general desire to exert greater influence in global affairs and more specifically to secure African diplomatic support in New Delhi's quest to gain a permanent seat on the UN Security Council. Although China currently dominates the African market, India will more likely gain the comparative advantage in the medium to long term: its strong diasporic community on the ground in Africa, its proximity to the continent, its use of historical ties and special niches to promote its cause of African friendship, its first-class education system and its enduring democratic tradition will contribute towards making it more competitive than China (Modi 2010).

For the Indian private sector to succeed in doing business in Africa, it requires elaborate and proactive state guidance. At the moment, such guidance does not exist in a coordinated way and is only just being constructed. The democratic setup of India, which will be an advantage in the long term, can in the short term also fetter business process because of the bureaucratic state machinery. Furthermore, with an aggressive free press, transparency in business contracts needs to be maintained. The challenge for the government is how to actively support India's private business in Africa while staying firm on the need to uphold the principles of democratic practice and corporate social responsibility in the areas of labour standards, environment sustainability and respect for human rights.

Needless to say, there is a growing concern in Africa that the increasing engagements of the Asian giants in their search for energy, minerals, markets and influence, if not managed properly could turn out to be just as bad as the scramble for resources that led to the colonisation of the continent during the second half of the 19th century. Some of the risks include:

- Increasing 'securitisation' of African international relations (Volman 2009)
- Weak governance standards and misallocation of receipts from high raw material prices
- A weakening of the still low local standards and regulations on environment and labour
- The destruction of local economies unable to compete with China and India's hyper-competitive manufacturing sectors
- Political support to African regimes that are not open to democratic governance (Goldstein et al 2006; Cheru and Obi 2010).

Unless India is prepared to address these critical African concerns, the red carpet rolled out to welcome it to the continent will quickly be rolled up and taken away, and the stigma of India as a new coloniser will take decades to erase. In the final analysis, the prospects for India–Africa relations contributing positively to African development ultimately lie in the hands of Africa's political and economic elites, their fulfilment (or betrayal) of the visionary and transformative potential that the diversification of African production and exports represents in the context of an emergent shift in post-cold war global power from the West to the East.

References

Afrique en ligne (2010) 'ECOWAS, India business group sign MOU', 19 March, http://www.afriquejet.com/news/africa-news/ecowas,-india-business-group-sign-mou-2010011542075.html, accessed 19 March 2010

Agrawal, Subhash (2007) 'Emerging donors in international development assistance: the India case', IDRC-CRDI Report, December

Bhattacharya, Sanjukta (2010) 'Engaging Africa: India's interest in the African continent, past and present', in Cheru, F. and Obi, C. (eds) *The Rise of China and India in Africa*, London and Uppsala, Zed Books and The Nordic Africa Institute

Beri, Ruchita (2003) 'India's Africa policy in post-Cold War era', *Strategic Analysis*, April–June

—— (2008) 'India woos Africa', IDSA Strategic Comments, Institute for Defense Studies and Analysis, 19 March, http://www.idsa.in/idsastrategiccomments/IndiaWoosAfrica_RBeri_190308, accessed 19 March 2010

Brautigam, Deborah (2009) *The Dragon's Gift: The Real Story of China in Africa*, Oxford, Oxford University Press

Cheru, Fantu and Obi, Cyril (eds) (2009) *The Rise of China and India in Africa,* London and Uppsala, Zed Books and The Nordic Africa Institute

The Economic Times (2010) 'India was not competing with China or any other country to expand its influence in Africa', 15 March, http://economictimes.indiatimes.com/news/politics/nation/India-not-competing-with-China-to-expand-its-sway-over-Africa-Tharoor/articleshow/5686844.cms, accessed 19 March 2010

Ezigbo, Onyebuchi (2010) 'Nigerian crude oil export to India hits $10 bn', This Day, 26 January, http://www.thisdayonline.com/nview.php?id=165081, accessed 19 March 2010

Goldstein, A. et al (2006) The Rise of China and India: What's in it for Africa?, Paris: OECD.

Indiainteracts (2010) 'Tharoor unveils Indian model of engagement with Africa', 15 March, http://indiainteracts.in/news/2010/03/15/Tharoor-unveils-Indian-model-of-engagement-with-Africa.html, accessed 19 March 2010

Jobelius, Matthias (2007) 'New powers for global change? International development cooperation: the case of India', FES briefing paper 5–07, http://library.fes.de/pdf-files/iez/global/04718.pdf, accessed 17 May 2010

Katti, V., Chahoud, T. and Kaushik, A. (2009) 'India's development cooperation: opportunities and challenges for international development cooperation', briefing paper, no. 3, German Development Institute

Kragelund, Peter (2008) 'The return of non-DAC donors to Africa: new prospects for African development', *Development Policy Review*, vol. 26, no. 5, pp. 555–84

Madan, Tanvi (2006) 'India', Energy Security Series, Brookings Foreign Policy Series, November, http://www.brookings.edu/~/media/Files/rc/reports/2006/11india_fixauthorname/2006india.pdf, accessed 19 March 2010

Martin, W. (2008) 'Africa's futures: from North–South to East–West?', *Third World Quarterly*, vol. 29, no. 2, pp. 339–56

Mawdsley, Emma (2010), 'The non-DAC donors and the changing landscape of foreign aid: the (in)significance of India's development cooperation with Kenya', *Journal of Eastern African Studies*, vol. 4, no. 2, pp. 361–79

Mawdsley, Emma and McCann, Gerard (2010) 'The elephant in the corner? Reviewing India–Africa relations in the new millennium', *Geography Compass*, vol. 4, no. 2, pp. 81–93

Ministry of Finance, Government of India (2009) *Annual Report 2008–09*, New Delhi, Ministry of Finance, http://finmin.nic.in/reports/AnnualReport2008-09.pdf, accessed 12 February 2011

Modi, Renu (2009), 'Pan-African e-network: a model of South–South cooperation', *African Quarterly*, vol. 49, no. 1

—— (2010) 'The role of India's private sector in the health and agricultural sectors of Africa', in Cheru, Fantu and Obi, Cyril (eds) *The Rise of China and India in Africa*, London and Uppsala, Zed Books and The Nordic Africa Institute

Naidu, Sanusha (2010) 'India's African relations: in the shadow of China?' in Cheru, Fantu and Obi, Cyril (eds) *The Rise of China and India in Africa*, London and Uppsala, Zed Books and The Nordic Africa Institute

National Intelligence Council (2004) 'Mapping the global future', report of the National Intelligence Council's 2020 Project, NIC 2004–13, Washington DC

NetIndian (2010) 'India and the African Union (AU) have finalised a plan of action of the framework for cooperation of the Indian Africa Forum Summit', 12 March, http://netindian.in/news/2010/03/12/0005736/india-african-union-finalise-plan-cooperation, accessed 19 March 2010

Obi, Cyril (2009) 'Oil: a curse or a catalyst for African resurgence', in Lahiri, D., Schultz, J. and Chand, M. (eds) *Engaging with a Resurgent Africa*, New Delhi, Observer Research Foundation, in association with Macmillan Publishers India, pp. 27–39

—— (2010) 'African oil in the energy security calculations of China and India', in Cheru, Fantu and Obi, Cyril (eds) *The Rise of China and India in Africa*, London and Uppsala, Zed Books and The Nordic Africa Institute

Rao, S.R. (2006) 'Exim Bank: partnership in Africa's development', presentation made at the Organisation for Economic Cooperation and Development (OECD), Paris, 16–17 March

Redvers, Louise (2010) 'India steps up scramble with China for African energy', Pambazuka News, 4 February, http://www.pambazuka.org/en/category/africa_china/61982, accessed 19 March 2010

Rowlands, Dane (2008) 'International development assistance executive summary report: the case of Brazil, China, India and South Africa', Ottawa, International Development Research Centre (IDRC)

Schaffer, T.C. and Mitra, P. (2005) 'India as a global power?', Deutsche Bank Research, Frankfurt, 16 December

Sharma, Anand (2009) 'India and Africa: sharing a robust partnership', in

Beri, Ruchita and Sinha, Uttam (eds) *Africa and Energy Security: Global Issues, Local Responses*, New Delhi, Academic Foundation

Sharma, Devika and Mahajan, Deepti (2007) 'Energising ties: the politics of oil', *South African Journal of International Affairs*, vol. 14, no. 2, pp. 37–52

Singh, Sushant (2007) 'Peacekeeping in Africa: a global strategy', *South African Journal of International Affairs*, vol. 14, no. 2, pp. 71–85

Sinha, Pranay (2010) 'Indian development cooperation with Africa', in Cheru, Fantu and Obi, Cyril (eds) *The Rise of China and India in Africa*, London and Uppsala, Zed Books and The Nordic Africa Institute.

Suri, Navdeep (2007) 'India and Africa: contemporary perspectives', in Sinha, Atish and Moharta, Madhup (eds) *Indian Foreign Policy: Challenges and Opportunities*, New Delhi, Foreign Service Institute, Academic Foundation Press

Thaindian News (2010) 'India–Africa business conclave to firm up $9bn deals', http://www.thaindian.com/newsportal/business/india-africa-business-conclave-to-firm-up-9-bn-deals-lead_100333867.html, accessed 17 May 2010

Vines, Alex and Campos, Indira (2010) 'China and India in Angola', in Cheru, Fantu and Obi, Cyril (eds) *The Rise of China and India in Africa*, London and Uppsala, Zed Books and The Nordic Africa Institute

Vines, Alex and Oruitemeka, B. (2008) 'India's engagement with the Africa Indian Ocean rim states', AFP briefing paper P1/08, London, Chatham House

Volman, Daniel (2009) 'China, India, Russia and the United States: the scramble for African oil and the militarisation of the continent', *Current African Issues*, no. 43

2

India and the 'Asian drivers' in Africa

Pádraig Carmody

> God forbid that India should ever take to industrialism after the
> manner of the West. The economic imperialism of a single tiny
> island kingdom [Britain] is today keeping the world in chains.
> If an entire nation of 300 million took to similar economic
> exploitation, it would strip the world bare like locusts.
>
> (Mahatma Gandhi, in Shiva 2008, p. 62)

> The commerce between India and Africa will be of ideas and
> services, not of manufactured goods against raw materials after
> the fashion of the western exploiters.
>
> (Mahatma Gandhi, in Bhattacharya 2010, p. 63)

These two opening quotes reflect on the process of globalisation.
As they show, Gandhi was not opposed to the idea of globalisation, but was in favour of an alternative globalisation to that pro-
moted during the colonial era: one based on ideas and services
rather than the unequal trade of raw materials for manufactured
goods. On the other hand his political comrade and competitor,
Jawaharlal Nehru, had a high modernist vision of an industrialised India. To some extent his vision would now seem to be
unfolding, although he might not have approved of the distributional consequences of India's current growth model.

Although Chinese interests and engagement in Africa have
dominated the media and academic literature recently, India is
also becoming an important economic and political player in
Africa. The Indian economy is only about one-sixth the size of
China's, but it is still substantial and growing fast and consequently exerts considerable demand for natural resources. It was
once commonly believed that China was a global manufacturing

hub and India a service hub, but the picture is more complicated. India is also home to major manufacturing companies, such as Tata and ArcelorMittal[1] – the world's largest steel company. These companies, along with major Indian global service suppliers, such as the well-known information technology company InfoSys, require natural resources for their growth. Thus Gandhi was only partly correct. Although services are an increasingly important part of India's relations with Africa, raw materials and manufacturing are also key sectors.

Much empirical work and theorising to date has focused on China's engagement in Africa. As many of the largest Chinese companies operative in Africa are state-owned it is easier to examine the links between the government's geo-economic strategy and state-owned corporates, although it is very important to pay attention to context and detail in examining these relationships (Brautigam 2009). The Indian case is more difficult because there is generally a clearer separation between state and corporate interests, although there are also Indian state-owned corporations engaged in Africa. Consequently Indian engagements with Africa appear somewhat more 'messy' or uncoordinated than those of the Chinese, although there is substantial variation within and between cases.

Much of the incipient literature on India's engagements with Africa details different resource and infrastructure deals, but in this chapter, while making reference to some of these, the broader goal is to examine the drivers and some of the impacts of increased Indian state and corporate involvement and investment in Africa.

Who and what drives the 'drivers' in Africa? The case of India

Although it began the process of economic reform later, like China's, the Indian political economy has undergone a fundamental restructuring in the past 20 years. This began in earnest with the economic liberalisation programme of 1991. The architect of this programme, Manmohan Singh, was then Minister of Finance and is now India's prime minister. India moved towards economic liberalisation and free market policies because it faced a balance of payments crisis, with very little foreign exchange left to pay for imports (although this can be interpreted as a storyline captured by the elites to help legitimate radical change: Corbridge and Harriss 2000). If you do not have enough foreign exchange to buy fuel and other essential economic inputs the economy grinds to a halt. Prior to this programme of liberalisation India had been characterised by its famous, but slow, 'Hindu rate of growth' (of between 3 and 4 per cent per annum), although some dispute this interpretation (Sen 2007). Once the economy was liberalised it began to grow quickly, particularly as foreign investors were attracted by the highly educated scientific workforce that had been developed through the Indian institutes of technology and the elite universities that had developed under India's more statist architecture.

Outsourcing of basic back-office functions led to the establishment of call centres in India, with operators sometimes adopting English or American names and briefed on the plots of western soap operas so that callers from the West would not know they were Indians – a kind of veiled globalisation, with echoes of India's current relations with Africa. Liberalisation also enabled Indian conglomerates, which had focused on domestic markets, to grow and expand overseas and more easily access technology.

The fruits of India's growth, however, have been highly unevenly distributed with certain social classes and areas continuing to be mired in deepening poverty (Patnaik 2008; Shiva 2008). For example, farmer suicides have caused outrage for many in India, as distressed individuals have apparently been driven to despair by the declining productivity and profitability of agriculture. This private-sector driven, unplanned, polarising and chaotic model of economic development is in evidence in Indian economic relations with Africa. However, there are signs that the Indian government is beginning to awake slowly in Africa from its previous 'sleepwalking' and is now devoting serious diplomatic and economic resources to the continent (Naidu 2010).

Indian trade and investment in Africa

Indian trade with Africa amounted to $35 billion in 2008, about one-third of the figure for China. In 2006, India imported 12 per cent of its gold imports, 79 per cent of its phosphates, 91 per cent of its nuts and 16 per cent of its copper from the continent (Naidu 2009). Nine out of every ten rough diamonds around the world are cut and polished in India and they are the country's single most profitable export, at around $14 billion a year (AsiaPulse News 2008). Of the $10 billion in rough diamonds imported each year into India, about 80 per cent are thought to come from Africa and the Indian government is keen to source these directly rather than through traders in Europe. The Indian government is reportedly keen to disrupt De Beers' near monopoly of the global diamond trade and to source them directly from Botswana, for example (Benza 2010). In Angola it has reportedly been promised that the Indian government will sponsor a diamond cutting and polishing centre in order to retain more of the 'value added' locally (Bhattacharya 2010). As part of the first India–Africa Forum Summit in 2008 it was announced that India, like China, would allow duty-free imports for selected products from the 34 African countries with which it has trade agreements. These products include mineral ores and gems which can be further processed in India and the added value consequently captured there.

Indian trade with Africa almost doubled to 7.7 per cent of its total trade between 1990/1 and 2006/7 (Naidu 2010), in contrast to China's current 3 per cent. Thus, Africa is proportionately a more important trading partner for India than it is for China, a fact often neglected in the current literature. Trade promotion is supported through the Export-Import (Exim) Bank Focus Africa Programme. The bank has about half-a-billion dollars in lines of credit (LOC) operative in Africa under this programme, which is very small compared to the Chinese Exim Bank operations. However, when all India's Exim LOCs are included, those active in sub-Saharan Africa amounted to more than $2 billion in 2009. This represents 60 per cent of the bank's total (Bhattacharya 2010), again showing the strategic priority that is attached to the region. These loans are at concessional interest rates, which mean that for low-income countries the grant or aid element amounts to 41 per cent of the loan. Some of these LOCs aim to develop information and communication technology infrastructure, which may be relatively inexpensive when compared to massive Chinese loans for road and rail infrastructure, for example.

Despite the relatively small scale of India's Exim Bank operations in Africa it was Indian firms that topped the list of greenfield foreign direct investment sites in Africa at 48, compared to 32 from China between 2002 and 2005 (United Nations Conference on Trade and Development 2007), although this is now likely to have changed. Data from the Zambian Development Agency shows that as a result of large-scale mining and mineral processing projects, Chinese investment in that country is much more capital-intensive when compared to Indian investment, at $80,145 per job versus $34,782 respectively (Carmody and Hampwaye 2010). Nonetheless, India is the second largest investor in Uganda and the largest in Ghana by number of projects (Bhattacharya 2010). These are two countries with very liberal foreign investment regimes. Ironically, given some hostile accounts of the Asian 'scramble for Africa', it was the western-sponsored economic liberalisation in Africa in the 1980s and 1990s that opened up the continent's economies to Asian investment (Kragelund 2009).

In contrast to China, India does not have a stated 'go global' policy for its corporations to encourage them to enter international markets. The absence of such a formal stated policy might mean Indian investment draws less attention and actually conforms more closely to the Chinese foreign policy of 'be good at keeping a low profile, never become the leader and make some contributions'. China's leadership position in Africa means that India attracts less attention around its oil investments, in Sudan for example. Because China has a permanent seat on the United Nations Security Council, which has been used at times to shelter the Sudanese government, and because it has also sold substantial amounts of arms there, its involvement in Sudan has been much more controversial. India, then, is arguably engaged in a kind of 'globalisation slipstreaming' behind China in Africa.

Resource access

Oil is arguably of even greater strategic importance for India than it is for China, as the former has only 0.4 per cent of the world's proven reserves (Naidu 2008). Consequently it imports 75 per cent of its oil needs, compared to only one-third for China (McCormick 2008). To maintain an 8 per cent average economic growth rate India needs to increase its primary energy supply by three to four times its 2003/4 levels (Naidu 2010). It is also estimated that India will run out of coal in the next 40 years. Consequently it currently needs to import the majority of its energy needs and it is projected that by 2030 India could be the world's third-largest consumer of energy after the US and China (Naidu 2009). India now imports 11 per cent of its oil from Africa, partly to fuel its rapidly growing car fleet (Arnold 2009). Shiva (2008) estimates that in Delhi alone, 200,000 cars are added to the streets every year.

In 2005, India offered $1 billion in LOCs to West African petro-states in exchange for oil exploration rights (Frynas and Paulo 2007), and new lines have been negotiated since. Energy, and resource security more broadly, is then an important driver of Indian engagement with Africa. This can be achieved through state-owned corporations, in addition to private enterprise (see Patey, Chapter 9 in this volume; Singh 2007).

Indian companies have been very active in resource deals in Africa. For example, in 2003 OVL – the overseas arm of India's state-owned energy company, Oil and Natural Gas Corporation (ONGC) – bought a 25 per cent stake in the Greater Nile Petroleum Operating Corporation in Sudan for $250 million from the Canadian Talisman company, which had been forced to relinquish its stake by US sanctions applied against the regime there (Arnold 2009). The ONGC also has major investments in Nigeria, Côte d'Ivoire and other countries, while the private conglomerate ArcelorMittal had expressed an interest in buying the Port Harcourt Refinery in Nigeria.

But in 2008 the new Nigerian government revoked its contracts to run a number of steel plants in the country, because it was felt they were overly favourable to ArcelorMittal. Although Indian oil and gas companies have sometimes been outbid by their cash-rich Chinese rivals for oil and mineral concessions in Africa, in 2006 the governments of these two Asian powers reached an agreement not to bid against each other for energy resources in an effort to contain spiralling energy prices (Obi 2010).

In Zambia, the country's most important copper mine (Konkola), accounting for 65 per cent of mineral production, was sold to Vedanta Resources, which is an Indian company in origin. In order to attract investment and on the insistence of the World Bank the mineral royalty rate was set at 0.6 per cent, giving the Zambian government $12 million in 2006 off the $2 billion in copper extracted that year (Arnold 2009). When tax write-offs for new investment were included, the World Bank estimated that the effective rate of taxation on copper in Zambia was zero – a shocking statistic given that it is by far the country's dominant export (Fraser and Lungu 2007).

Although there has been new investment and some associated job creation as a result of this investment, there have also been environmental costs. The Konkola Copper Mine polluted one of the rivers in Copperbelt province. An environmental assessment noted: 'The contamination from this latter plant area is, at least periodically, very severe, with ph sometimes as low as 2.2 being experienced in the South Uchi steam' (Zambia Consolidated Copper Mines 2005), which flows into the Kafue River.

ArcelorMittal, now the world's largest steel producer, has also signed a major iron ore deal with Liberia, although the government of Ellen Sirleaf Johnson renegotiated the unfavourable terms (Vittorini and Harris, Chapter 12 in this volume; Alden 2007). Global Witness had previously criticised ArcelorMittal for the extractive nature of the deal in post-conflict Liberia and for setting up a 'state within a state'. ArcelorMittal had previously abrogated sovereign power unto itself in Liberia controlling 'company and capital structure, taxation, royalties, transfer pricing, rights to minerals and confidentiality' (Global Witness quoted in Arnold 2009, p. 86). This quasi-sovereignty is something which is arguably replicated in Chinese-built special economic zones in Africa and American oil-compounds where the phone lines are sometimes in Texas, for example, rather than any African calling code area (Maass 2009).

But the resource boom that lasted through 2008 gave greater bargaining power to African states, which they have asserted in the two cases detailed above with ArcelorMittal. Perhaps because it is a private company it is felt that renegotiating deals ex post is less likely to damage relations with the home country government (India), than if the same were to be attempted with Chinese state-owned corporations. Also the fact that Indian aid and loans are on a much smaller scale than those emanating from China makes the trade-off easier. Nonetheless, Indian conglomerates have continuing structural power, depending on context. Arcelor-Mittal is South Africa's largest steel producer for example (Cheru and Obi 2010).

Other economic sectors and the legacy of migration

From 1961 to 2007, 56 per cent of Indian foreign direct investment in Africa was in the manufacturing sector, 26 per cent in the service sector and 18 per cent in the primary sectors (Pradhan 2008). However, this seemingly high level of manufacturing investment is undoubtedly boosted by mineral processing activities.

There has also been investment in pure manufacturing and other sectors, however. 'Zambia ha[s] been declared a major investment destination under the Tata Group expansion programme in Africa' (Republic of Zambia 2006) with investments in the agricultural sector and in hydropower. Yet, a manager at the Indo-Zambian Bank, which was set up after an agreement between Indira Gandhi and Kenneth Kaunda, noted that 'I don't see assembly lines' (interview April 2007), although there has been some foreign investment in the production of juices, a source of competition for local companies, such as Manzi (Nordic/SADC 2005, in Fick 2006). Tata has also opened a new bus and truck assembly plant in Ndola in Zambia (*India News* 2006), although according to a World Bank economist (interview October 2007), this project would not have taken place without government incentives, and the government will be the major buyer of the few hundred buses and trucks assembled each year. Some Indian companies have also been active in the tourism sector. For example, Tata invested $8 million in the renovation of the Taj Pamodji Hotel in Lusaka (Naidu 2009).

India–Africa investment flows are not all one way, however.

For example, Mauritius, whose population is largely of Asian extraction, was the largest single foreign investor in India during the June quarter of 2007, with investments of $1.9 billion (Reuters 2007). In fact, from 2000 to 2009, Mauritian-based companies invested more than $40 billion in India, making it the single largest foreign investor there (IBEF 2010a). In contrast to common assumptions, African investment is sometimes being used to develop India's infrastructure. For example in March 2010 the India Infrastructure Development Fund (Mauritius) received Indian cabinet approval for a fund which it was thought would bring $163.8 million for infrastructure investment into the country (IBEF 2010b). There has also been substantial South African investment in the tourism and manufacturing sectors in India in recent years.

India is now digitally linked to East Africa through the East African Submarine Cable (EASSY) and to Mauritius, South Africa and West African countries through the new or South Atlantic 3/West Africa Submarine Fibre Optic Cable (SAT-3/WASC). This latter project undoubtedly facilitates joint ventures between Indian and Mauritian companies. For example, the joint venture of Nextcell – an Indian mobile phone company – and AquaSan – a Mauritian company specialising in water and sanitation – to set up Nextcell Mauritius (IBEF 2010c), demonstrates the recursive nature of globalisation. The venture, it is hoped, will capture mobile phone market share in Africa.

India is thus seeking not only the extraction of natural resources from Africa, but also capital resources and investment. Although the Indian state might be paying increasing attention to resource-rich African states, the fact that there is an extensive Indian diaspora in Mauritius and that there is a potential strategic coupling of their economies based on information technology makes it somewhat of an exception. This deepening South–South economic globalisation also has security implications discussed in more detail later in this chapter. There were earlier forms of South–South globalisation, although they were often previously directed at the North. Nonetheless these earlier forms of interconnection put in place flows of dependency which structure current interactions – through diasporas for example.

There is a substantial Indian-origin diaspora in Africa. Many

Indians came to Africa during the colonial period to work as indentured labourers and as 'free' traders and some of their descendants maintain close connections with their areas of origin. In some colonies they served as an ethnicised intermediate class, with European countries controlling the commanding heights of large-scale commercial agriculture, banking, manufacturing and mining, and indigenous Africans, for the most part, supplying manual labour. After their periods of indenture or other official contracts were up many stayed on and became involved in trading. Moreover, these pioneer networks of migration were soon taken up independently by various trading groups. A commonly held assumption is that this diaspora provides India with an automatic entrée into Africa. However, there is not necessarily the coincidence of interests that intuition might suggest (see McCann, Chapter 6 in this volume).

According to a senior official in the Indian Ministry of Commerce, East African countries, where along with South Africa the diaspora is concentrated, are in the process of being eclipsed in India's strategy of engagement with the continent in favour of West African oil producers (Vittorini and Harris, Chapter 12 in this volume; Mawdsley and McCann 2010). Even Central Africa will arguably be of greater economic interest in the future, they argued, because of its rich mineral resources. The first India–Central Africa Trade Forum was held in Congo-Brazzaville in 2009, for instance.

In countries such as Kenya, where there is a substantial Indian diaspora, Indian engagement is largely private-sector driven and market seeking (Mawdsley and McCann 2010). Indian investment in non-resource rich countries has concentrated in areas such as mobile phones. The Mumbai-based Essar group, for example is active in this area and also acquired a 50 per cent stake in Kenya Petroleum Refineries in 2009. This is the sole petrol refinery in East Africa. Indian trade with Kenya reached almost half-a-billion dollars in 2004–5, which was an increase of more than 55 per cent over two years and meant that Indian trade with Kenya was only slightly below that of China. India's main exports to Kenya are engineering products, cotton and pharmaceuticals, while the principal imports are gemstones and inorganic chemicals (Vines and Oruitemeka 2008).

Indian overseas assistance to Africa

Somewhat controversially, given acute poverty at home and the fact that there are proportionately more malnourished children in India than in Africa for example, India also gives aid to Africa. Indeed, average incomes across Africa are about $200 a head per year higher than India (Southall and Melber 2009). The motivation for this is surely primarily political and economic, rather than humanitarian.

India donated food to Namibia, Chad and Lesotho in 2003/4 and several hundred thousand mosquito nets to the Republic of Congo (Naidu 2009), in addition to being involved in UN peace-keeping missions on the continent (Singh 2007). According to Naidu 'this use of soft power for humanitarian purposes is possibly intended to downplay India's image of scrambling in Africa and instead project New Delhi as a development partner' (Naidu 2009, p. 130). According to the minister of state for commerce 'the first principle of India's involvement in Africa [is] unlike that of China. China says go out and exploit the natural resources, our strategy is to go out there and add value' (Dawes 2008, in Naidu 2009, p. 134). However, she argues that ultimately it will be how African governments engage with India that will determine whether it is a 'scrambler' or a development partner. As Chris Alden (2007) has pointed out in relation to China however, the two are not incommensurable and international relations contain elements of both self and mutual interest.

India's aid relations are also tied up with its own self-image. For example, despite the fact that it ranks seven places below South Africa on the United Nations Human Development Index (number 127), in 2003 the Indian government announced it would suspend taking bilateral development assistance from 22 donor countries (McCormick 2008). This was a symbolic statement that the country was independent and could begin to assert itself as a great power. As Alex Wendt has noted, ideas are what drive the creation of social structures, so states do not necessarily only follow their material interests, but also may undertake seemingly irrational actions, such as wars, for this reason (Wendt 1999). In the 2007/8 budget speech the government of India asserted its intention to establish its own overseas aid agency – the India

International Development Cooperation Agency, an endeavour informed by these broader ideological concerns.

As a poor country India does not see itself as giving substantial grants-in-aid, but instead concentrates its aid in Africa on technical training and assistance (McCormick 2008; Mawdsley 2010). Much of India's aid is delivered through the Indian Technical and Economic Cooperation (ITEC), which was set up in 1964 to examine ways of improving cooperation with Africa (Naidu 2010). For example India initiated the Pan-African e-Network project, which will connect African countries to Indian institutions and each other through satellite and fibre optics to facilitate tele-medicine and tele-education programmes. This network might also facilitate communication between African heads of state and perhaps Indian politicians.

According to a professor of African studies in Delhi, India needs African votes to get a permanent seat on the UN Security Council but does not have the money of the Chinese, or the US's military might. Consequently, India has to rely on cooperation in information technology, agriculture and engineering, where it has experience (Arnold 2009), although this opportunity has now arguably passed for a variety of geopolitical reasons, including lack of Chinese support for a permanent Indian seat. For Sanusha Naidu 'the launch of the Pan-African e-Network reflects the first step towards strengthening the ICT partnership before losing out to the Chinese, designed perhaps to enable India's telecom giants to become industry-shapers in the continent' (Naidu 2010, p. 47), although empirical support for this statement is lacking currently.

There are also some high-level initiatives worth examining, for example the TEAM-9, which was initiated in 2004. The '9' describes the partnership between India and eight resource-rich West African states. The goal of the programme is to improve healthcare, food security, transport and telecommunications through a focus on technology (Mawdsley and McCann 2010). India has, however, also cancelled the bilateral debt of some African countries such as Mozambique and Tanzania, which are less well endowed with natural resources (Vines and Oruitemeka 2008; Mawdsley 2010). The Indian government does not have the same economic weight behind it as the Chinese government, in terms of access to foreign exchange reserves or indeed granting access to its domestic market. Consequently the Indian government has gone for the direct approach in its dealings with African governments.

The Pan-African e-Network, noted earlier, was launched in 2007 in Addis Ababa, Ethiopia – the site of the headquarters of the African Union. The e-network provides facilities for tele-medicine and education, but perhaps more importantly from a political point of view it allows videoconferencing for all 53 heads of state in the AU. According to the e-Network website this is the VVIP (very, very important people's network). Undoubtedly African heads of state will be flattered if they don't already know this. This overt support for sitting heads of state is more 'top down' than China's approach, because India does not have the same economic resources to bring to bear in its African relations. Consequently it must rely more on the goodwill of African elites, because it can exercise less hard or coercive power over them.

The geopolitics of economic engagement

According to Cheru and Obi (2010), although attempts by India's foreign ministry to support private-sector engagement in Africa are small compared to the resources Chinese state-owned corporations can draw on, over the longer-term India will have a comparative advantage over China in Africa as a result of its diaspora, strong education system, its proximity to the continent and its democratic tradition. Whether this is the case remains to be seen, but India is using a variety of strategies to cooperate and compete with China. One of these is balancing through alliances with other middle powers.

In part to offset the influence of China, India has been involved in the India, Brazil, South Africa (IBSA) group, which was launched in 2003. South–South globalisation thus has a variable geometry to it. A host of agreements have been signed between the participating parties on issues such as health and wind resources, but despite proclamations by IBSA of a desire to move towards a free trade area, little progress has been made on tariff reductions. China, with the support of South Africa, requested to be included in the IBSA dialogue forum on commercial issues. However, fearing a loss of influence, India blocked this on the basis that China is not a democracy (Vines and Oruitemeka 2008).

The Indian navy has patrolled Mauritius's exclusive economic zone since 2003 and has a similar agreement with the Seychelles (Vines and Oruitemeka 2008). India has also signed defence agreements with other countries on Africa's east coast, such as Mozambique, Madagascar and Kenya and has had joint training exercises with other African naval forces (Vines, Chapter 11 in this volume). These defence agreements are also reportedly driven by fears of Chinese expansion.

India is keen to protect its shipping routes, and its enhanced military capabilities also signal its emergence as a great power (Vines and Oruitemeka 2008). This preoccupation might be a reflection of the fact that 90 per cent of India's trade by volume and almost three-quarters of its value is by sea (Bhattacharya 2010). This regional geo-economy finds institutional expression through the Indian Ocean Rim Association for Regional Cooperation, which meets every two years. This organisation has assumed greater salience recently as result of heightened economic engagements.

According to Rao Inderjit Singh, India's Minister of State for Defence 'if India and Africa are able to synergise energies and initiatives and adapt to a changing world, the 21st century could surely belong to them' (Singh, in Naidu 2008, p. 116). The rhetoric of Indo-African relations follows closely that of the Chinese, with an emphasis on win-win relationships. The first Indo-African conclave was held in 2005 and the India–Africa partnership launched. Many potential economic development projects were discussed at this meeting.

As noted earlier, Manmohan Singh, the Indian Prime Minister, announced at the 2008 Forum Summit, the scheme to allow preferential market access to India for exports of 50 of the world's least developed countries, of which 34 are in Africa. At this meeting he also announced half a billion dollars of new aid for Africa and an increase in LOCs to the continent to $5.4 billion by 2013 (Mawdsley and McCann 2010).

Indian state governments have also signed agreements with African governments. For example, Andhra Pradesh signed a letter of intent with Kenya and Uganda to send five hundred farmers from India to cultivate land in those countries (Naidu 2009), although this has not been put into practice. Although some people argue that China will be eclipsed by India in Africa in the long-term as a result of the fact that it is a democracy, its engagement to date on the continent has been much more limited and less coordinated than that of China.

Conclusion

The difference between the first and the second 'scrambles' for Africa is the difference between colonialism and globalisation. Although China's influence in Africa is much more prominent and powerful than that of India (see Carmody and Taylor 2010), India is nonetheless an important emerging actor on the continent. Indian relations with China are characterised by competition and collaboration. India subscribes to the principle of non-interference in the sovereign affairs of other nation states, as does China. This is in contrast to the western promotion of good governance on the continent. Non-interference serves to placate African political elites and thereby aid or ensure continued resource access.

As this chapter has noted, Africa is arguably of greater strategic importance for India than for China, given the structure of trade between the two and the importance of particular commodities such as diamonds, gold and cashew nuts, in addition to oil and minerals. Through the principle of non-interference, India and other BRIC (Brazil, Russia, India and China) countries are status-quo powers in Africa. But India is distinct from China in that its engagements in Africa are still largely below the radar of the international media. It is engaged in 'globalisation slipstreaming', perhaps with a view to overtaking China when, and if, the time is appropriate.

Notes

1. This company was formed from the merger of Arcelor and Mittal in 2006 and is now headquartered in Luxembourg, but Lakshimi Mittal is the chairman of the board. This then is an example of transnational capital in terms of its ownership, management and corporate operations, but with strong Indian connections and associations.

References

Alden, C. (2007) *China in Africa: Partner, Competitor or Hegemon?*, London, Zed Books

Arnold, G. (2009) *The New Scramble for Africa*, London, North South Books

AsiaPulse News (2008) 'India seeks African diamonds: Ramesh to visit Angola, Namibia', 24 March

Benza, B. (2010) 'Botswana and India in diamond trade deal-report', Mmegionline, 3 December, http://www.mmegi.bw/index. php?sid=4&aid=16&dir=2010/January

Bhattacharya, S. (2010) 'Engaging Africa: India's interest in the African continent, past and present', in Cheru, F. and Obi, C. (eds) *The Rise of China and India in Africa*, London and Uppsala, Zed Books and The Nordic Africa Institute

Brautigam, D. (2009) *Dragon's Gift: The Real Story of China in Africa*, Oxford and New York, Oxford University Press

Carmody, P. and Hampwaye, G. (2010) 'Inclusive or exclusive globalisation? Asian investment and Zambia's economy', *Africa Today*, vol. 56, no. 3, pp. 84–102

Carmody, P. and Taylor, I. (2010) 'Flexigemony and force in China's resource diplomacy in Africa: Sudan and Zambia compared', *Geopolitics*, vol. 15, no. 3, pp.496–515

Cheru, F. and Obi, C. (2010) 'Introduction – Africa in the 21st century: strategic and development challenges', in Cheru, F. and Obi, C. (eds) *The Rise of China and India in Africa*, London and Uppsala, Zed Books and The Nordic Africa Institute

Corbridge, S. and Harriss, J. (2000) *Reinventing India: Liberalisation, Hindu Nationalism and Popular Democracy*, Cambridge and Malden, MA, Polity and Blackwell Publishers

Fick, D. (2006) Africa: Continent of Economic Opportunities, Johannesburg, STE Publishers

Fraser, A. and Lungu, J. (2007) For Whom the Windfalls? Winners and Losers in the Privatisation of Zambia's Copper Mines, Lusaka, Civil Society Trade Network of Zambia

Frynas, J.G. and Paulo, M. (2007) 'A new scramble for African oil? Historical, political, and business perspectives', *African Affairs*, vol. 106, no. 423, pp. 229–51

India Brand Equity Foundation (IBEF) (2010a) 'Foreign direct investment', http://www.ibef.org/economy/fdi.aspx, accessed 10 February 2011

—— (2010b) 'Govt approves plan of IIDF', http://www.ibef.org/artdisplay. aspx?cat_id=60&art_id=25400&utm_source=newsletter&utm_ medium=email&utm_campaign=http://www.ibef.org, accessed 10 February 2011

—— (2010c) 'Nextcell forms JV with African firm', http://www.ibef.org

India News (2006) 'President Mwanawasa commissions Tata Zambia assembly plant', vol. 3, no. 3, p. 7

Kragelund, P. (2009) 'Knocking on a wide-open door: Chinese investments in Africa', *Review of African Political Economy*, vol. 122, pp. 479–97

Maass, P. (2009) *Crude World: The Violent Twilight of Oil*, London, Allen Lane, Penguin Books.

Mawdsley, E. (2010) 'The Non-DAC donors and the changing landscape of foreign aid: the (in)significance of India's development cooperation with Kenya', *Journal of Eastern African Studies*, vol. 10, no. 1

Mawdsley, E. and McCann G. (2010) 'The elephant in the corner? Reviewing India–Africa relations in the new millennium', *Geography Compass*, vol. 4, no. 2, pp. 81–93

McCormick, D. (2008) 'China and India as Africa's new donors: the impact of aid on development', *Review of African Political Economy*, vol. 115, pp. 73–92

Naidu, S. (2008) 'India's growing African strategy', *Review of African Political Economy*, vol. 35, no. 115, pp. 116–28

—— (2009) 'India's engagements in Africa: self-interest or mutual partnership?' in Southall, R. and Melber, H. (eds) *A New Scramble for Africa? Imperialism, Investment and Development*, Durban, University of KwaZulu-Natal Press

—— (2010) 'India's African relations: in the shadow of China?' in Cheru, F. and Obi, C. (eds) *The Rise of China and India in Africa*, London and Uppsala, Zed Books and The Nordic Africa Institute

Nordic/SADC (Norsad) (2005) http://www.norsad.org, accessed 16 February 2011

Obi, C. (2010) 'African oil in the energy security calculations of China and India', in Cheru, F. and Obi, C. (eds) *The Rise of China and India in Africa*, London and Uppsala, Zed Books and The Nordic Africa Institute

Patnaik, U. (2008) 'Imperialism, resources and food security with reference to the Indian experience', *Human Geography: A New Radical Journal*, vol. 1, no. 1

Pradhan, J. (2008) 'Indian direct investment in developing countries: emerging trends and development impacts, Munich Personal PePEc Archive, http://mpra.ub.uni-muenchen.de/12323

Republic of Zambia (2006) 'Levy commissions bus, truck plant', http://allafrica.com/stories/200609080412.html, accessed 10 February 2011

Reuters (2007) 'India says June qtr FDI inflows rise to $4.9 billion', 17 August

Sen, Kunal (2007) 'Why did the elephant start to trot? India's growth acceleration re-examined', *Economic and Political Weekly*, vol. 42, no. 43, pp. 37–47

Shiva, V. (2008) *Soil not Oil: Environmental Justice in a Time of Climate Crisis*, Cambridge, South End Press

Singh, S. (2007) *India and West Africa: A Burgeoning Relationship*, London, Chatham House

Southall R. and Melber, H. (2009) 'A new scramble for Africa?', in Southall R. and Melber, H. (eds) *A New Scramble for Africa? Imperialism, Investment and Development*, Durban, University of KwaZulu-Natal Press

United Nations Conference on Trade and Development (UNCTAD) (2007) 'Asian foreign direct investment in Africa: towards a new era of cooperation among developing countries', Geneva, UNCTAD

Vines, A. and Oruitemeka, B. (2008) 'India's engagement with the Africa Indian Ocean rim states', AFP briefing paper P1/08, London, Chatham House

Wendt, A. (1999) *Social Theory of International Politics*, Cambridge and New York, Cambridge University Press

Zambia Consolidated Copper Mines, Industrial Holdings (2005) 'Preparation of Phase 2 of a consolidated environmental management plan, task reports (Task II–VI)'

3

Upping the ante in Africa: India's increasing footprint across the continent

Sanusha Naidu

> The time has come to create a new architecture for our engage-
> ment in the 21st century. We visualise a partnership that is
> anchored in the fundamental principles of equality, mutual
> respect and mutual benefit. Working together, the 2 billion
> people of India and Africa can set the example of fruitful co-
> operation in the developing world.
>
> Prime Minister Manmohan Singh, India–Africa Summit 2008

Introduction

This chapter has its foundation in two recent publications (Naidu 2009, 2010a). In these chapters I argue that India's presence in Africa remains muted. I suggest that New Delhi is choosing to play this role because such a presence does not provoke strong criticism of its behaviour in Africa, something, which is not the case for China. Perhaps this is because New Delhi benefits from the slipstream position it occupies vis-à-vis China and distin-guishes itself as different in behaviour from Beijing.

Yet in recognising this, I caution that in the foreseeable future, as India embarks on a more aggressive political and economic drive across the continent, it will be difficult for the Indian author-ities and the policy mandarins to insulate or distance themselves from the uneven architecture of political, economic and social power present in Africa's landscape. And as much as India will want to distinguish itself as a more hands-on development part-ner, it must be seen as part of the footprint of emerging powers on the continent. Despite New Delhi's claim to share a common historical platform with Africa, it is hard to ignore that India is a sovereign state guided by parochial national interests and domestic considerations aligned to its global ambitions. African leaders must come to realise that New Delhi alone cannot be a panacea for the continental challenges, especially where India's narrow development interests are a primary factor and inadvertently override the interests of others.

To this end, I note that India's African safari must be judged prudently, particularly because New Delhi is on the hunt to satisfy its resource needs, which are vital to its 21st century industrialisation and modernisation programme. And wherein such interests might become threatened or compromised the underlying question will be whether the South Asian elephant will dispense with the platitudes of South–South cooperation and mutual benefits to exploit Africa's resources for its own gain, even where this might conflict with those of African actors. Such actions might also be motivated by New Delhi's tacit competition with its East Asian neighbour, China, and, in particular, its attempts to gain comparative advantage in response to Beijing's use of political kudos to gain leverage across continental markets.

In this chapter, I expand on these possibilities in light of recent events and developments. India's footprint in Africa appears to be widening and Indo-African relations gaining in momentum. Africa appears to have become a critical feature in India's current foreign policy outreach and thus New Delhi's acknowledgment of its need to put its engagement with the continent on more of a strategic footing. At a recent conference hosted in New Delhi by the Institute of Defence Studies and Analyses (IDSA) it was noted that:

> there is a lack of coherence in India's Africa policy [and] that [although] most African countries give India high regard … and appreciate it for its non-intrusive policy … India has not capitalised on the goodwill it enjoys in Africa because of a lack of vision in its foreign policy. India's Africa policy had been 'request-based' instead of 'initiative-based'. The 'request-based' approach is more rewarding as it increases bargaining power. Now it is high time India looked at Africa from a strategic point

of view and planned accordingly; otherwise it will miss the opportunity. (IDSA 2010)

Such an admission by Indian policymakers, representatives from the diplomatic community and scholars, suggests that India is no longer 'sleepwalking in Africa' as *The Indian Express*, a New Delhi-based newspaper claimed in a 2006 editorial (*The Indian Express* 2006). Yet, upon deeper reflection, the statement seems to suggest that India is beginning to realise that the historical engagement based on images of common struggles of anti-colonialism, non-alignment and an ideological cold war identity, while relevant, must be contextualised given the increasing current economic dimensions of a globalised world and the corresponding footprint of other southern actors, most notably China, who are making their presence felt in Africa. Based on this refocused orientation in India's Africa policy, this chapter will analyse the extent to which India is a resurgent actor in Africa, and to what extent New Delhi is strategically positioning itself as an alternative partner for African countries.

Understanding India's deepening involvement with different African countries and regional associations must start with the government's definition of these relationships, and the extent to which they are managed on a mutual basis. As much as India's engagements in Africa must reflect historical ties (Sharma 2007; Singh 2007; Naidu 2009)[1] we must consider the contemporary geostrategic interests of New Delhi, which are being recalibrated in terms of the global spaces India now occupies in settings like the India–Brazil–South Africa (IBSA) Forum, the BRIC consortium, and its bilateral relations with Washington and the EU, which have brought the South Asian giant into their circle of 'like-minded' states.

Moreover, India's own identity in South Asia vis-à-vis China's encroaching presence and its burgeoning influence among its regional neighbours and within the Indian Ocean rim where relationships with the littoral states are being strengthened, provides the impetus to assess whether India fits into the debate that underpins the current discourse of Africa's rise and what some analysts have identified as the 21st century scramble for Africa (Lee 2006; Southall and Melber 2009).

So what are the factors that motivate India's deepening relations with Africa? Are these born out of political expediency or are they based on economic pragmatism? Where do the lines of complementarity lie and what are the divisions? How much does Africa feature in India's global ambitions? Is there consensus regarding issues of the South and the pursuit of multilateral reform, or is it a case of differing agendas?

Rediscovering Africa after the cold war

In the initial period after independence, and in keeping with then Prime Minister Nehru's expanding engagement with the global South, relations with Africa burgeoned with support for the liberation and independence of African colonies from the yoke of imperialism. Under the banners of the Afro-Asian solidarity platform, the Non-Aligned Movement (NAM) and the promotion of South–South cooperation, the charismatic Nehru advocated 'greater democratisation in international relations and free access to available economic opportunities for the politically weak and economically poor countries of the Third World' (Muni 1991, p. 862). And these Nehruvian principles were gauged by the prime minister's determination to play a significant role in creating a just international setting.

Yet, as much as Nehru must be lauded for the principles and vision encapsulated in an ambitious foreign policy that sought to eschew the polemics of the cold war, India's international status became more marginal and it could no longer shy away from the domino effects of the cold war, which played themselves out on its doorstep with the US-Pakistan military alliance (Naidu 2009). Therefore, despite the efforts by New Delhi to pursue 'an alternative [global] order responsive to the aspirations of the weak and underprivileged, [it itself was] weak and too disorganised to make [its] impact felt' (Muni 1991, p. 862).

Under the leadership of Indira Gandhi, who eventually succeeded Nehru (her father) as prime minister in 1964, New Delhi took less of a homogenous view of Africa. Outwardly it could be perceived that New Delhi's closer ties with Moscow influenced Gandhi's relations with African states. This outlook was broadly aligned to the Soviet Union's growing support for the major

51

continental liberation movements, such as the anti-apartheid struggle of the African National Congress (ANC) in South Africa and the independence movement led by the South West African People's Organisation (SWAPO) in Namibia.

The United Nations, the Organisation for African Unity (OAU), NAM and the Commonwealth became the most significant multilateral institutions through which India exerted its robust support for the anticolonial resistance and the liberation movements. Throughout this period India provided financial and material assistance through mechanisms such as the UN Fund for Namibia, the UN Educational and Training Programme for South Africa and the Action for Resisting Invasion, Colonialism and Apartheid.

Yet for the better part of the cold war, India focused on its own regional and domestic pressures. By the time the divides of the cold war had begun to dissipate, the quasi-socialist system adopted by India after independence, which was intended to concretise equal opportunities for the country's politically underprivileged and economically indigent, had not produced the desired results. Having become associated with relatively slow economic growth and introverted commercial engagement, leading to a 'loss of influence in the years after independence' (Raja 2006, p. 17) and with the international system undergoing an ideological and economic reordering, New Delhi was compelled to reassess its domestic economic conditions. This was essential if India was to improve the material circumstances of the population, increase the country's global leverage and become an economic powerhouse with geostrategic political clout.

The Indian government sought to reconcile its ideological commitments with its emerging strategic economic interests. This became evident in the early 1990s, when annual reports of the ministry of external affairs emphasised that 'in the future, new relationships based on concrete economic, technological and educational cooperation [would] assume enhanced significance' (Singh 2007, p. 10). Underpinning this new trajectory was a strategy of economic liberalisation that facilitated the opening up of the Indian market to foreign direct investment and an aggressive commitment to gaining access to overseas markets. Yet India did not wholly replace its political ideology with geo-economics. Understanding that engagement in the newly multilateralised international system would require a sophisticated blend of geopolitics and geo-economics, New Delhi used its historical platform to consolidate relations with Africa and other regions of the South.

India's orientation toward Africa after the cold war was about reinventing and rejuvenating the previous relationship. In principle, India's relationship with different African countries is premised on the moral high ground that it shared Africa's history of subjection to colonisation. So, officially, India's contemporary Africa policy is aligned to a confluence of interests around justice in the global order aimed at increasing the leverage of their respective global positions to promote a new international order. To this end, commitment to peace, stability, justice, mutual development and the vision of a fairer multilateral global system became the new genre for India's emerging engagement with Africa.

The economic impetus

Alongside other external actors, India 'has discovered that Africa is where the resources and future markets that will fuel its economic growth' (Sorbara 2007) are to be found. India's 'quest for resources, business opportunities, diplomatic initiatives and strategic partnerships' (Pham 2007) is seen in the emerging trade, investment and developmental assistance relations that New Delhi is crafting with African countries. Projections are that by 2030 India is expected to become the world's third-largest consumer of energy, bypassing Japan and Russia and with an economy expected to grow by an average rate of 5 per cent per annum over the next 25 years. Its consequent appetite for energy can be expected to be massive and this is compounded by the projection that it will run out of coal, the primary source of its current energy needs, during the next 40 years.

Therefore new and reliable sources of energy are critical to India's domestic growth trajectories, as well as to position it as a global economic power. Unfortunately with only 0.4 per cent of the world's proven oil reserves, New Delhi has to finance its oil needs elsewhere. As much as Iran is a major oil partner for India, the government is also seeking to diversify its sources of oil so that dependency on a single producer is reduced.

With this in mind, Indian National Oil Corporations (NOCS) have been making some significant investments into Africa's energy sector. The state-owned Oil and Natural Gas Company (ONGC) appears to be making a major footprint. In recent years ONGC has secured exploration contracts and other related energy projects on the continent through its international division ONGC-Videsh (OVL). At present Africa supplies almost 15 per cent of India's oil imports (Chand 2010, p. 16). The biggest supplier is Nigeria with around 10 per cent of India's total oil imports.

In addition to energy and gas, Indian companies have been expanding their involvement to include uranium exploration. This must be seen in the context of the recently signed controversial nuclear civilian deal between Washington and New Delhi. Initiated under the presidency of George W. Bush, the deal allows India to procure materials for its nuclear programme to address demand for more efficient and cleaner domestic energy supply and to have its nuclear programme be recognised despite the fact that it is not a signatory of the nuclear proliferation treaty (NPT). Washington's motivation was to satisfy domestic US corporate interests eager to corner the Indian market and become the primary suppliers of these types of nuclear materials. Granted the opportunity to purchase nuclear materials including fuel and technology, India's corporates are actively looking for possible contracts and uranium exploration projects and Africa provides a backdrop for such deal making.

The trade and investment footprint

Although Indian trade with Africa is still relatively limited, New Delhi is awakening to the reality that Africa is a priority for its intended global commercial expansion. India–Africa trade jumped from $967 million in 1991 to more than $9.5 billion in 2005 (Sorbara 2007). From 2000 to 2005, Indian exports to the continent increased from $2 billion to more than $6 billion. During the same period, Indian imports from Africa increased from $3 billion to more than $4 billion. During the period 2006–09 there was a spike in imports from the continent, which were partly as a result of rising commodities and the peaking of the oil price in July 2008. During the period 2006–07 Indian exports totalled $10.268 billion and imports amounted to \$14.716 billion. For the following year 2007–08 exports were calculated at \$14.192 billion and imports at \$20.471 billion. For the last trading period 2008–09 Indian exports stood at \$14.813 billion and the import bill was \$24.728 billion (Indian Ministry of Commerce and Industry 2010).

According to official Indian statistics total two-way trade with Africa increased very slightly from \$24.986 billion in 2006–07 to \$34.663 billion in 2007–08 and \$39.542 billion in 2008–09. Evidently, India's trade with the continent is not as significant as China's, which reached \$73 billion in 2007, and \$106.84 billion in 2008 before dipping to \$91 billion in 2009 (see Figure 3.2). Yet the pattern seems to indicate that oil forms the bulk of the trade with very little product diversification.

Figure 3.1 India's export and import trade with Africa (in US\$ millions)

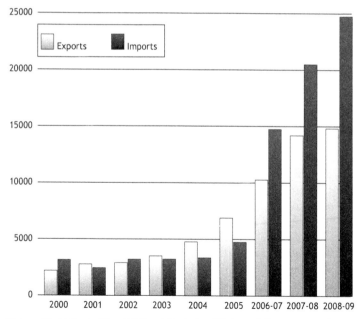

Source: World Trade Atlas 2007 and the Indian Ministry of Commerce and Industry

55

Figure 3.2 China and India's total trade with Africa
(US$ millions)

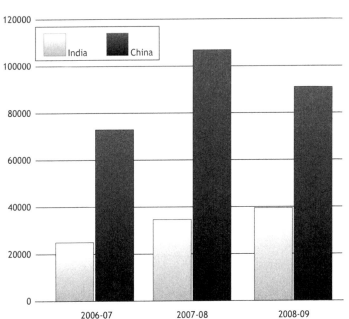

Source: World Trade Atlas 2007 and the Indian Ministry of Commerce and Industry

Beyond oil, Indian companies are also beginning to make significant strides in numerous other sectors. India's official investment in Africa in 2008 was about $2 billion. In the private sector the footprints of the Tata Group, Ranbaxy Laboratories and Kirloskar Brothers, among others, are most significant. These companies have focused mainly on markets in South Africa, Nigeria, Egypt and Kenya (Srivastava 2008). In Zambia, Vedanta Resources has a $750 million copper mining investment and ArcelorMittal has a $900 million management project for iron ore reserves in Liberia and an investment of $30 million (inclusive of an 80 per cent stake by the Delta Steel Company) in a Nigerian steel refinery. Perhaps the biggest deal announced was in 2010 with the purchase of the Kuwaiti telecoms giant Zain's African operations by Bharati Airtel Telecommunications. The deal estimated to be worth $10.7 billion is considered to be one of largest investments by an Indian company in Africa. The acquisition will give the Indian company access to Zain's 42 million subscribers across 15 African nations. Most industry commentators see this as indicative of corporate India's strident foray into Africa.

Furthermore, India has identified Mauritius as an offshore investment enclave. By setting up investment hubs on the island, the government has enabled Indian companies to make significant inroads into the east coast African economies. South Africa is also considered as a strategic investment gateway into the rest of Africa. During a recent trip, South Africa's President Jacob Zuma, accompanied by 300 business executives and captains of industry, highlighted that with almost 200 million people in southern Africa and almost 1 billion people across the continent, massive business opportunities for both India and South Africa existed (see Naidu 2010). With the intention of cementing economic ties and consolidating commercial partnerships, 'SA Inc' is positioning itself as a major partner for India's economic interests on the continent.

Driven by a combination of state sponsored investment and private sector conclaves organised by the Confederation of Indian Industries (CII)[2] these meetings have served as strategic platforms for India Inc to identify potential sectors for business and investment transactions. At the same time it strengthens ties with African governments and corporate linkages with the African private sector for possible joint ventures (Naidu 2010). A meeting held in New Delhi in March 2010 was aimed at expanding the India–Africa Project partnership. Entitled 'Developing Synergies: Creating a Vision', the conclave was a significant gathering of almost 1,000 delegates, (with about 380 participants representing 34 African countries) to discuss business transactions and about 150 project investments to the value of close to $10 billion. This made it one of the largest meetings between political leaders and captains of industry from India and Africa yet to be held. This meeting was significant in that it was hosted as a precursor and intended roadmap to New Delhi's second India–Africa Forum Summit (IAFS), which is scheduled to be hosted in 2011. And it follows closely on the joint action plan between Africa and India, which was launched earlier to follow-up and assist in the implementation of the 2008 India–Africa Summit outcomes (Naidu and Herman 2008). Several undertakings were pledged during the meeting. These included to:

- Increase trade to $70 billion by 2012, in keeping with the IAFS commitment to double trade to $50 billion by 2011
- Establish 19 institutions to develop human resources and capacities in Africa as part of the joint action to implement the decisions of the IAFS. These will include the Africa–India Institute of Foreign Trade, Africa–India Diamond Institute, Africa–India Institute of Information Technology and Africa–India Institute of Education Planning and Administration
- Create 10 vocational training institutions and five human settlement institutes.

Clearly, then, India is beginning to realise that with the second India–Africa Forum Summit not far off, there must be concrete evidence provided to its African partners that New Delhi is serious about its Africa policy. As one official described the 2008 IAFS: 'The Summit will showcase the brand image of an economically resurgent India in Africa' (*Africa–Asia Confidential* 2008).

Other financial instruments of India's Africa policy

Focus Africa was launched as part of the Exim Bank of India 2002–07 strategy. Through this programme the Indian government provides market development financial assistance to various trade promotion organisations and export promotion councils. By early 2007, the total operative lines of credit (LOC) extended to sub-Saharan Africa by the bank amounted to more than $550 million and targeted regional blocs such as the Economic Community of West African States (ECOWAS) and the Common Market for East and Southern Africa (COMESA). Furthermore, in May 2006 the Exim Bank extended a $250 million LOC to the ECOWAS Bank for Investment and Development, to finance Indian exports to ECOWAS member states (Sorbara 2007). In terms of the COMESA region, operative LOCs included $5 million each to the Eastern and Southern African Trade and Development Bank (PTA Bank), the Industrial Development Bank of Kenya and the East African Development Bank. These LOCs are in support of strengthening and expanding export trade between the respective regions and India through deferred payment terms.

More recently the Exim Bank of India gave Ethiopia a $640 million LOC (the largest loan ever given by India to one country) for a package of contracts that include a railway construction project and two sugar factories. It would appear that Ethiopia has been identified as a strategic investment destination with Exim Bank also announcing recently that it is going to open an office in that country.

The Indian government has also embarked on a set of initiatives. These include:

- A $200 million LOC to the New Partnership for African Development (NEPAD) under the India–Africa Fund and designed to promote African economic integration
- A $500 million LOC for the TEAM-9, an initiative with eight Francophone countries[3]
- A $1 billion investment in a joint venture with the African Union (AU) to build the Pan-African e-Network, to provide tele-medicine and tele-education through integrated satellite, fibre and wireless connectivity (Pambazuka News 2009).[4]

Ethiopia, South Africa, Mauritius and Ghana have been identified as the first participating countries for the e-Network. The pilot project was set up in Ethiopia in 2007 and saw 26 students from Addis Ababa University and Harmaya University complete in the MBA programme of the Indira Gandhi National Open University (IGNOU) in New Delhi. Based on the success of the pilot project, memoranda of understanding have been signed with several interested countries, including Benin, Botswana, Malawi, Niger, Rwanda, Somalia, Ethiopia, Egypt, Mauritius and Senegal.

Not everything is economics

India's strength and value best lie in its technical assistance and capacity building prowess. Under the ITEC programme, India has provided more than $1 billion worth of technical assistance and training of personnel has been undertaken. Moreover, in 2005 India became the first Asian country to become a full member of the African Capacity Building Foundation (ACBF) and pledged $1 million towards the foundation's sustainable development and poverty alleviation capacity building initiatives. In line with this it was agreed at the summit that India would establish an India–Africa peace corps aimed at development, especially in the area of public health and increase numbers of educational scholarships and technical training programmes for African students.

Discussion

Returning to the questions posed at the beginning of this chapter, the significant issue is whether India is shaping a new development consensus or discourse in Africa. Until now much of the discourse has been preoccupied by China's increasing engagements across the continent, with some analysts suggesting that a 'Beijing Consensus' could replace the Washington Consensus, on which the western model for third world development is based. Of course New Delhi would definitely like to see its engagements in Africa follow an independent trajectory and not that of China.

This is perhaps what Prime Minister Manmohan Singh was refering to in his remark to the India–Africa Summit in 2008. But it is not entirely clear from India's foreign policy instruments nor its policy on Africa how its engagement with the African states will be different. Despite the recognition that African countries should be treated as equal partners, it appears that India is reading from the same gospel as other emerging actors, albeit shaped by its specific historical relationships.

What is required, therefore, is an understanding of the intersections between India's domestic priorities and its current foreign policy ambitions and how these correspond to the common interests around Africa's sustainable development project. Thus far it it appears that India is on a global offensive to encourage its private sector to invest in Africa and elsewhere. This is revitalising the domestic economy through the private sector's pursuit of market opportunities and pushing India up the global value chain. But it also means that the country's labour force is becoming an integral part of the international division of labour. So how does Africa fit into this paradigm?

It is apparent that India is pursuing a policy of trade, training and technology in respect of Africa. This is infused with a development-centric approach that is aimed at enhancing trade, transferring technology, capacity building and human resource development. The government believes that this gives India a comparative advantage over other actors in Africa. India boasts strong scientific research and development capacity, which has produced cost-effective technology, and its growing presence on the continent means that Africans can potentially access such technology. Moreover the production in India of cheap generic drugs to combat preventable diseases, such as malaria, TB, cholera and yellow fever, and antiretrovirals to treat HIV/AIDS, is also seen as a way to support improvements to Africa's public health systems.

At the same time India believes that it can share with Africa its experience in renewable energy techniques, such as the solar power engineering project in Gabon, and in Ethiopia, Namibia and Nigeria, where small medium and microenterprise development and microfinance prospects are being discussed in respect of rural development projects. India is also increasing the level of scientific cooperation by creating post-doctoral scholarships for African students to study at its prestigious science and engineering colleges and universities. Finally the setting up of vocational training centres to train African artisans and create opportunities for African skills to be developed in sectors like diamond cutting centres, call centre programmes and agricultural development is ongoing.

Although all these developments point to an India that is increasingly aware of the need to improve the material standards of African people in order that the continent's global economic leverage can increase, India–Africa engagement is not without its challenges. In previous articles (Naidu 2009, 2010b) I have argued that India is an aggressive voice championing the rights of the developing and least developed countries at the WTO (World Trade Organisation) Doha Development Round Negotiations.

But recently it has emerged that India is very keen to pursue a free trade agreement (FTA) with the European Union. As much as such an agreement would enable Indian corporates to penetrate European markets and create a reciprocal set of corresponding investments in the Indian economy, one of the complicated issues in the negotiations is that the EU is demanding that India comply with an intellectual property concession, which affects access to generic medicines, data exclusivity, extended patent terms and border measures for other developing countries.

The EU is proposing that generic drugs exported to developing countries via the EU can be confiscated at its border posts. Second, they are pushing for data exclusivity to be enforced for new drugs. This means that generic drugs, which do not normally undergo expensive clinical trials because this has been done with the original, will have to undergo new clinical testing before they are approved. This will protect the EU pharmaceutical companies against any competition while at the same time block the registration of the generic drugs because it is unethical and expensive to repeat the clinical trial. Third the EU is insisting on longer patent periods. This has caused concerns among African NGOs, especially those working in the public health sector. If India accepts these terms it means that generic drugs, which are an integral part of HIV/AIDS and other treatment could become severely compromised and roll back gains made in the public health sector in terms of accessibility to affordable medicine for the poor in Africa and elsewhere.

The question remains whether India will accede to these demands. In 2005 India signed a patent law for its generic drug production in accordance with its WTO membership. Whatever the situation it should not be overlooked that New Delhi is very keen to move ahead with this FTA. And thus the issue at hand is whether India will gravitate towards the EU because it sees the political and economic dividends of forging such a partnership as greater than its moral justifications for a fair and just world.

The implications of the EU–India FTA also hold several implications for India's membership of IBSA, BRIC and BASIC, where it advocates the policy of multilateralism and reforming the international order to strengthen South–South cooperation. And there are other considerations that must also be understood.

Among them is India's constant referral to the Indian diaspora in Africa, which it sees as an important link to the continent and a natural justification for developing closer political and economic ties. But India has in fact neglected the diaspora in Africa, particularly when racial tensions played themselves out in Uganda. In South Africa, support for the ANC was considered to be in line with the political identity of the South African Indian community. The African Indian diaspora, at least in southern Africa, is not a homogenous bloc as New Delhi assumes.

What underpins the connection to the diaspora is a class-driven project in which the economic elites with political connections are those with whom the government engages. This is abundantly clear in the South African case, where the Indian community is celebrating the 150th anniversary of its arrival on South African soil. As much as the South African Indian community recognises its ancestral roots, it does not express a strong political and economic affinity with India. It is primarily the economic elites who enjoy a prosperous relationship with India. And for the majority of the Indians in South Africa it is the anguish of poverty and economic and social inequality that remains a feature of their daily life.

More controversial are Indian farmers (Vashisht 2010) leasing agricultural land in Namibia, Nigeria and the Democratic Republic of Congo. Indian firms invested almost $3 billion in farm acquisitions for commercial food crops and biofuels production between 2007 and 2010. African and Indian authorities claim that such acquisitions are part of the transfer of skills and expertise in technology, but some consternation has been expressed by those who see these investments as mainly aimed at ensuring India's food security by tapping into Africa's bread baskets. For instance, in Ethiopia, there are incentives that allow for food products to be exported almost duty-free to the Indian market. This, indeed, raises concern about Africa's food sovereignty, about the protection of land rights of African subsistence farmers and about the displacement of farmers from their land. Given the sensitive nature of this commercial agricultural investment, India has faced criticism of engaging in a 21st century land grab. Though India's development-centric approach was welcomed by African participants at the 2008 summit, African delegates emphasised that India should be a stakeholder and not a shareholder in the continent's development.

Ultimately, it is how African countries themselves define their relationships with India that will determine whether New Delhi is a scrambler or a development partner. Currently, India's political and economic engagement reflects both its development objectives and its clearly corporate interest in the continent. African states do not have to allow this relationship to mirror the 19th century scramble for resources, and India will have to leverage the international milieu to ensure that it benefits. This will require bold leadership and pragmatic decision making: something that Indian diplomats seem to be taking seriously by making themselves more visible and accessible to their African counterparts.

This was evident as recently as January 2010: at the same time that the Chinese foreign and commerce ministers were making their respective high-profile tours of Africa, there were three other diplomatic missions on the move across the continent. They were India's vice-president, Mohammad Hamid Ansari, who was on a seven-day official visit to Zambia, Malawi and Botswana; India's commerce minister, Anand Sharma, who was visiting Nigeria with oil minister Murli Deora; and the former minister of state for external affairs, Shashi Tharoor, who was in Mozambique. Tharoor's visit was preceded by that of his successor, S.M. Krishna, who visited Mozambique in July 2010.

During his tour, Vice-President Hamid's comments to the media made clear the state's intent:

> The direction in which the Indian economy is going, the major role will be played by the private sector, especially in industrial development. Local employment will be generated. It doesn't make economic sense to take work force from India because it comes with liabilities. When we go for an investment venture, we don't go with the idea of imposing our work force or employment of Indians per se. We seek to limit ourselves to management and financial control of enterprises having an Indian element. (IANS 2010)

If this is the case, then African commentators, activists and social movements need to be tracking the Indian footprint in Africa. We should be asking whether India, indeed, offers something different vis-à-vis Africa's engagement with other external players, or is it more of the same? Moreover, it should not be assumed that because India's involvement in Africa is not in the same league as that of emerging powers or other actors from the global North we can afford to become blindsided by the platitudes that they do business differently.

India's ambitions and vested self-interest in Africa might not arouse the same suspicions as those of China, but in the end we need to ask how they affect elite class formations in African societies and capitalist accumulation. It is important that we are aware of whatever impact such patterns have on people's livelihoods, long-term skilled employment, land rights and environmental justice. Therefore the Indian government would do well to learn the lessons experienced by other actors in the African market and landscape: the type of sensitivities, threats and backlashes that are present and can arise; and how to diffuse these situations before they become the victims of their own self-confidence. The political and economic elites in the Indian diaspora and among Africa's ruling class are only two sets of stakeholders. The ordinary people, civil society groups and others that fall outside this ambit must be consulted if India truly wants to be a different development partner to Africa.

Notes

1. These publications provide in-depth analysis of Prime Minister Nehru's guiding foreign policy principles and India's historical ties with Africa, including support for African independence and liberation movements, the anti-apartheid and racism policies and support for the Non-Aligned Movement.
2. Supported by the Ministry of Commerce and Industry, the Ministry of External Affairs, and the Exim Bank of India.
3. The TEAM-9 initiative was launched in March 2004. It is reported that $280 million worth of projects have already been approved against concessional lines of credit. Some of these include: $970,000 for the construction of the national Post Office in Burkina Faso; $30 million for rural electrification in Ghana; $4 million for a bicycle plant in Chad; a $12 million tractor assembly plant in Mali; and $15 million for potable drinking water projects in Equatorial Guinea. Currently, six more countries from the region are interested in joining the initiative.
4. State-owned Telecommunications Consultants India Limited (TCIL) will implement the network, which India will manage for five years before turning it over to the AU.

References

Africa–Asia Confidential (2008) 'Delhi reaches out', vol. 1, no. 1, p. 2

Chand, Manish (2010) 'Comparing India with China in Africa', *Africa Quarterly*, vol. 50, no. 1, pp. 14–21

Cheru, Fantu and Obi, Cyril (eds) (2010) *The Rise of China and India in Africa*, London and Uppsala, Zed Books and The Nordic Africa Institute

IANS (2010) 'India's private sector will power Africa thrust: Vice President', 12 January, http://www.thaindian.com/newsportal/business/indias-private-sector-will-power-africa-thrust-vice-president-lead_100302698.html accessed on 15 February 2011

India–Africa Summit (2008) 'Address by Prime Minister Manmohan Singh to the first India–Africa Summit', April, http://pib.nic.in/release/release.asp?relid=37177, accessed 24 February 2011

Institute of Defence Studies and Analyses (IDSA) 2010 'Conference Report: India–Africa Partnership: What the future holds?', 28 April, http://www.idsa.in/event/IndiaAfricaPartnershipWhattheFutureHolds_2010, accessed 24 February 2011

Lee, Margaret (2006) 'The 21st century scramble for Africa', *Journal of Contemporary African Studies*, vol. 24, no. 3, pp. 303–30

Muni, S. (1991) 'India and the post-Cold War world: opportunities and challenges', *Asian Survey*, vol.31, no. 9, 862–74

Massalatchi, Aboulaye (2007) 'Uranium exploration firms from India, UK make tracks for Niger', Livemint, 14 May, http://www.livemint.com/2007/05/14235528/Uranium-exploration-firms-from.html, accessed 24 February 2011

Naidu, Sanusha (2009) 'India's engagements in Africa: self-interest or mutual gain?', in Southall, R. and Melber, H. (eds) *A New Scramble for Africa? Imperialism, Investment and Development*, Durban, University of KwaZulu-Natal Press

—— (2010a) 'India's Africa relations: in the shadow of China?' in Cheru, F. and Obi, C. (eds) *The Rise of China and India in Africa*, London and Uppsala, Zed Books and The Nordic Africa Institute

—— (2010b) 'President Zuma's Indian safari', Pambazuka News, 10 April, http://www.pambazuka.org/en/category/africa_china/65083, accessed 24 February 2011

Naidu, S. and Herman, H. (2008) 'No sleeping walking in Africa', *Global Dialogue*, vol.13, August

Pambazuka News (2009) 'Africa: Pan African e-Network: a model of "South-South cooperation"', 24 April, http://www.pambazuka.org/en/category/internet/55920, accessed 24 February 2011

Pham, J.P. (2007) 'India's expanding relations with Africa and their implications for US interests', *American Foreign Policy Interests*, vol. 29, pp. 341–52

Pistilli, Melissa (2009) 'India gains access to Namibia's uranium', *Uranium Investing News*, vol. 3, September, http://uraniuminvestingnews.com/2136/india-gains-access-to-namibian-uranium.html, accessed 24 February 2011

Raja, Mohan (2006) 'India and the balance of power', *Foreign Affairs*, vol. 85, no. 4, pp.17–32

Sharma, A. (2007) 'India and Africa: partnership in the 21st century', *South African Journal of International Affairs*, vol. 14, no. 2, pp. 13–20

Singh, S. (2007) India and West Africa: a Burgeoning Relationship, London, Chatham House

Seth, Shivom (2010) 'India's growing appetite for uranium', Mineweb, 13 July, http://www.mineweb.co.za/mineweb/view/mineweb/en/page7210 3?oid=107883&sn=Detail&pid=102055, accessed 24 February 2011

Sorbara, Michael (2007) 'India and Africa: it's old friends, new games and rules', *The Nation*, 8 February, http://allafrica.com/stories/200702081111. html, accessed 24 February 2011

Southall, Roger and Melber, Henning (eds) (2009) *A New Scramble for Africa?: Imperialism, Investment and Development*, Durban, University of KwaZulu-Natal Press

Srivastava, S. (2008) 'India loads up presents for African safari', Asian Times Online, 12 April, http://www.atimes.com/atimes/South_Asia/JD12Df01. html, accessed 24 February 2011

The Indian Express (2006) 'Losing Africa to China', 16 January

Vashisht, Dinker (2010) 'India's Punjabi farmers investigate farming in Africa', *African Agriculture*, 26 July, http://www.africanagricultureblog. com/2010/07/indias-punjabi-farmers-investigate.htm, accessed 24 February 2011

Part 2
Contemporary India–East Africa engagements

4

The impact of India–Kenya trade relations on the Kenya garment industry

Paul Kamau and Dorothy McCormick

Introduction

The rapid growth and increased openness of the Indian economy, which accelerated sharply at the beginning of the 1990s, leaves no doubt about the country's increasing importance on the global stage. Yet India's trade with Africa and Africa's trading partners is often lost in discussions of the Asian driver economies, which tend to focus on its larger and even more rapidly growing neighbour, China. Indian trade, however, has directly competitive effects in African domestic markets and indirectly competitive effects in third countries (Asian Drivers Team 2006; Kaplinsky and Morris 2008). This paper examines these effects in one country, Kenya, with which India has been closely linked for centuries through trade, investment, migration and social ties. The rapid economic performance of India has influenced global markets especially those of developing countries (Goldstein et al 2006; Li and Zhang 2008), and Kenya is one of the African countries that have been affected by India's ascendancy.

The trade between Kenya and India has grown tremendously since the 1990s and its links are clearly visible in the garment value chain. Not only is there two-way trade in garments themselves, but also there is significant trade in the textile inputs into the industry and trade by both countries with the US. This chapter examines these three aspects of the Kenya–India textile trade, concluding that overall India is the main beneficiary. It then uses the results of that examination to explore whether Kenyan garment producers might be benefiting in ways that are not obvious in the initial analysis. Specifically, the paper assesses two ways in which Kenyan garment firms might benefit from trade with India. The first is through importing inputs used in production of clothing destined for the US under the African Growth and Opportunity Act (AGOA) programme, and the second is through exports of clothing into the Indian market. Both represent feasible strategies that might be used by Kenyan producers, but neither has been examined empirically until now.

This chapter is based mainly on ten case studies of Kenyan garment manufacturing firms conducted in 2008. These case studies are supplemented by secondary literature and published data on Kenyan and Indian trade in textiles and clothing. Lastly, expert opinions on the developmental impact of India on the Kenyan garment industry were obtained through interviews with staff from government ministries, state agencies, diplomatic missions, private agencies and industry representative bodies.

The chapter is divided into six sections. Following this introduction, section 2 presents the conceptual and theoretical underpinnings of the study by briefly discussing the literature on value chains and then outlining a framework for analysing the trade impacts of one country on another. Section 3 provides background for the study by offering an overview of the textile and clothing industries in Kenya and India. Section 4 analyses the direct and indirect competition of India with Kenya in the garment trade. Section 5 presents and discusses two potential industry strategies that Kenyan garment producers could use to mitigate the effects of one-sided trade. Section 6 draws conclusions and makes some tentative recommendations.

Complementary and competitive effects of India's growth on Kenyan textile and clothing sectors

India's potential impact on Kenya is best conceptualised within the larger framework of the Asian drivers (Schmitz 2005; Asian Drivers Team 2006). The realisation that the countries of Asia have been playing an increasingly important role in the global economy is not new, but it has been crystallised only in the past decade. The main channels through which these impacts occur are trade, foreign direct investment, aid and human resource flows. The impacts can be categorised as either complementary and/or competitive depending on their effects on the country (or sectors/interests within it) under consideration. There might also be direct or indirect impacts. Complementary effects occur when, for example, a country (Kenya) imports textile fabric from India to enhance capability of domestic clothing firms to produce for both local and export markets. Another possibility arises if India's growth results in increased demand for clothing – a market that Kenya can tap. Competitive effects occur when, for example, India's clothing products compete with Kenya's either at home or in a third market. Competition in the home market is direct while that in third markets is indirect.

Textile and clothing industries in Kenya and India

The textile and clothing industry is of significant importance to both India and Kenya in terms of spearheading industrialisation, employment creation and foreign exchange earnings. Available evidence suggests that Kenya's trade with India has grown tremendously in the past decade and has been driven by trade in textiles and clothing (McCormick et al 2006; Republic of Kenya 2009). To both countries, the clothing industry is believed to offer excellent 'starter' opportunities for industrial development (Gereffi 1999; McCormick and Rogerson 2004; Tewari 2006; World Bank 2007; Phelps et al 2009). In addition, this industry makes a major contribution towards poverty reduction through its capacity to create both direct and indirect employment opportunities (McCormick et al 2006; Omolo 2006; Adhikari and Weeratunge 2007). There are also distributional effects, especially with regard to gender. Unlike other industries in which male workers predominate, in the clothing industry three-quarters of workers are women (McCormick and Rogerson 2004).

Although Kenya's participation in the global textile and clothing trade can only be traced to the past two decades, production for domestic and African regional markets pre-dates independence. This industry grew rapidly in the post-independence period as a result of the import substitution policies pursued by the Kenyan government, whose main objective was to protect local manufacturers against competition. Furthermore, the government was heavily involved in textile manufacturing activities that fed the clothing industry, at the time dominated by the private sector (Kamau 2009). The import substitution policies worked well for the industry in the early years of independence but ran into difficulties as the heavily protected textile industry grew complacent and settled into inefficiency characterised by low productivity growth in 1970s and 1980s.

Other scholars argue, however, that Kenya's textile firms, even at actual 1980 levels of productivity, would have been able to export if their inputs had been available at international prices and were not subject to tariffs, quotas and the uncertain availability of specific qualities (Pack 1987, pp. 80–1). The introduction of the structural adjustment programmes (SAP) in the mid-1980s exposed previously protected clothing and textile firms to international competition through trade liberalisation. The establishment of export processing zones (EPZs) in 1990 was meant to attract foreign direct investments (FDI) with a view to reviving the industry. But this did not yield much for the industry because its productivity and export capacities were still low (Kinyanjui et al 2004; Omolo 2006). It was not until 2000, when the AGOA gave Kenya duty- and quota-free access to the US market, that the industry was revitalised. This growth was mainly inclined toward garment manufacturing and not textile manufacturing (Phelps et al 2009). This has resulted in the industry being heavily reliant on imported raw materials, much of which are sourced from India.

Turning to India, we note that its textile and clothing industry is the world's second largest after China. The industry consists of several sub-sectors: spinning, weaving, knitting and garmenting, and it uses different raw materials – cotton, jute, wool, silk, artificial and synthetic fibres (Italian Trade Commission (ITC) 2009, p. 33). The textile and clothing supply chains comprise diverse raw material sectors, ginning facilities, spinning and extraction processes, processing sector, weaving and knitting factories and garment manufacturing. The Indian textile industry exhibits varying levels of technology, ranging from traditional handlooms to some of the most advanced industries of the world (ITC 2009).

Textile and clothing is one of the largest industries in India, employing more than 38 million people (18 per cent of industrial employment), contributing more than 7 per cent of the India's manufacturing value added (MVA), about 14 per cent to industrial output and 21 per cent of India's export earnings (Tewari 2006; WTO 2008; ITC 2009). Between the 1960s and early 1980s, the government of India used a variety of regulatory mechanisms to orient the textile and clothing industry towards the domestic market and to shape its structure (Landes et al 2005). By using a strict licensing regime that required firms to seek government permission before establishing new operations or expanding capacity, the government controlled the size, location, scale and growth of the textile and apparel industry (OECD 2004, Vijayabaskar 2002).

The textile industry in India is vertically integrated with large-scale operations, while the clothing industry is characterised by mostly small-scale non-integrated operations. Currently, India is the second-largest producer of raw cotton in the world next to China. Production of both cotton and artificial fibre-based fabrics have increased at a high rate in recent years because of increased cotton production and availability, higher prices, and healthy growth in demand and government incentives (Qureshi and Guanghua, 2006). The spinning sector is the most globally competitive in terms of variety, unit prices, production quantity and technology. In 2008, there were 176 composite mills (integrated large-scale mills) that combine spinning, weaving and sometime fabric finishing with an installed capacity of 5.63 million spindles. Spinning mills that convert cotton or man-made fibre into yarn to be used for weaving and knitting were 2,816 units. The weaving sector is predominantly small-scale and has an average 4.5 power looms per unit, but suffers from outdated technology. Knits have been successful especially in export channels, while the handloom sector serves mainly the low-end rural population (ITC 2009).

The clothing sub-sector is founded on a system of decentralised production, referred to as 'reservation of garment manufacture for small-scale industry' (SSI), which provides certain economic advantages to small-scale labour-intensive firms (OECD 2004). The Indian clothing industry is highly labour-intensive with about 77,000 units spread over the entire country (ITC 2009).

The average size of a manufacturing unit does not exceed 20 machines. The representation of large-scale units in the industry is as yet not significant, though the number of large-scale players is slowly rising in tune with the growth trend of the industry (Landes et al 2005; Tewari 2006; ITC 2009). The industry has two major sectors – knitted and woven cloth. The industry manufactures a wide range of products to cater to the diverse requirements of consumers of varying economic status.

India's main markets for textile and clothing are the US and the EU which on average absorbed nearly 80 per cent of the exports in 2005 and 2008 (ITC 2009). India has a strong presence in all processes of operation and value chain activities. It is one of the largest exporters of yarn in the international market, contributing about 25 per cent of the global trade in cotton yarn. The country has a strong base for artificial fibre of cellulose and non-cellulose origin. Moreover, India is the second largest producer of silk and the only country to produce all varieties.

India commands a significant world market share in textiles and clothing, which was boosted by the MFA (multi-fibre arrangement) termination in 2005; thereafter its world market share has increased steadily. Indian garment manufacturing is conducted mainly in clusters around the country. Textile cluster development in the form of textiles parks is one of the major government policies to boost garment production. Through these clusters the government is able to provide technological and financial assistance to local companies so as to enhance their competitiveness.

Direct and indirect competition between India and Kenya in the garment trade

Trade between Kenya and India in textile and clothing has grown steadily between 2000 and 2008, from $13 million to $36 million (EPC 2009). This trade is, however, skewed in favour of India, which enjoys a surplus trade balance with Kenya. As shown in Table 4.1 almost a quarter of Kenya's textile imports originate from India (26.18 per cent in 2000 and 22.52 per cent in 2008).

Table 4.1 shows the share of textile and clothing trade between Kenya and the two leading trading partners – India and China – during the period 2000–08. In 2000, India absorbed only 0.11 per cent of Kenya's total exports of textile and clothing, while China absorbed 0.8 per cent. During the same period imports of textile and clothing from India and China accounted for 23.18 per cent and 13.5 per cent respectively. In 2008, Kenya's share of textile and clothing exports to India and China was 0.01 per cent and 0.04 per cent respectively, while imports were 21.3 per cent and 49.1 per cent respectively. Of this trade, the import of textile products accounted for the largest share for both India and China, mainly used as raw materials for the industry. On average textile imports from India accounted for 22.5 per cent, while those from China accounted for 26.5 per cent. On the other hand, clothing imports from India and China accounted for 10.8 per cent and 21.2 per

Table 4.1 Share of textile and clothing trade between Kenya and India and China, 2000–08 (%)

	2000	2001	2002	2003	2004	2005	2006	2007	2008	AVR
Exports to India										
Textiles	0.36	0.33	0.52	0.11	0.03	0.02	0.01	0.01	0.01	0.16
Clothing	0.03	0.02	0.03	0.02	0.01	0.01	0.01	0.01	0.01	0.01
T and C	0.11	0.09	0.12	0.04	0.02	0.01	0.01	0.01	0.01	0.05
Exports to China										
Textiles	3.21	2.37	4.56	1.08	0.14	0.17	0.14	0.15	0.12	1.33
Clothing	0.02	0.01	0.02	0.01	0.01	0.01	0.00	0.00	0.00	0.01
T and C	0.82	0.56	0.84	0.22	0.04	0.05	0.05	0.05	0.04	0.30
Imports from India										
Textiles	26.18	22.08	12.58	23.05	21.89	19.80	22.02	22.36	24.10	22.52
Clothing	13.82	11.41	11.60	8.37	11.52	8.34	13.45	n.a.	7.83	10.79
T and C	23.87	20.78	22.83	20.50	20.16	18.82	20.67	19.15	21.33	20.79
Imports from China										
Textiles	12.61	18.31	12.58	12.79	16.69	25.03	52.01	44.29	53.16	27.50
Clothing	17.49	22.48	20.89	12.28	17.60	21.67	23.74	25.28	29.03	21.16
T and C	13.52	18.82	13.74	12.70	16.84	24.45	47.59	41.56	49.05	26.47

Source: Authors' computation from Export Promotion Council Trade Data (2009)

cent respectively. During the period 2000–08, a mere 0.16 per cent and 0.01 per cent of Kenya's total exports of textiles and clothing respectively went to India.

The increased importation of textile products from India has played an important role in enabling Kenya to export to the US market under AGOA. This is particularly important in the short term, while Kenya enjoys the derogation of the rules of origin (Kaplinsky and Morris 2008). Similarly, production for the domestic market has benefited from this trade because producers are able to access relatively higher quality raw materials at lower prices. Therefore, the use of Indian fabrics complements Kenya's performance in the clothing industry.

The US market is Kenya's prime destination for clothing exports, accounting for nearly 90 per cent of its total. But recent figures indicate that Kenya's export to this market has been under threat and is on the decline. Two factors are responsible for this trend – the termination of the MFA in 2005 and the recent global economic recession, especially in the US. The termination of the MFA made illegal the system of import quotas, which had previously favoured small clothing exporters such as Kenya, and allowed larger, more efficient clothing producing countries unlimited access to the US market. The global economic recession, which hit most of the developed world in 2008, reduced overall demand for many consumer goods, including clothing and made remaining customers more price conscious (Kaplinsky and Morris 2008). The result was tough competition between African and Asian producers, including India, in northern markets.

India seems to be coming out ahead in the competition for northern clothing markets. Table 4.2 shows that in both HS 61 and HS 62 categories, Indian exports to the US rose steadily between 2001 and 2008, but dropped slightly in 2009. Kenya's export to the US also rose during the same period, but remained at a very low level. Furthermore, both India and Kenya export a combination of knitted and woven garments, which suggests that India might pose a threat to Kenya in both categories.

Table 4.2 Value of export to the US clothing market, 2001–09 ($ million)

Clothing	2001	2002	2003	2004	2005	2006	2007	2008	2009
India									
HS 61 – knitted or crocheted	505	572	578	680	937	1,163	1,318	1,331	1,237
HS 62 – woven	1,276	1,385	1,479	1,598	2,121	2,079	1,904	1,791	1,649
Total HS 61–62	1,781	1,956	2,056	2,277	3,059	3,243	3,222	3,122	2,886
Kenya									
HS 61 – knitted or crocheted	0.15	23	51	80	75	67	81	95	95
HS 62 – woven	64	103	137	198	196	196	167	151	100
Total HS 61–62	64.57	125.49	187.73	277.17	270.54	262.89	248.16	246.58	195.11

Source: Authors' calculations from Strategis.ic.ca

In 2001, India's export of clothing to the US market totalled $1,781 million. This increased steadily and peaked at $3,243 million in 2006, only to decline marginally to $2,886 in 2009. During the same period, woven clothing comprised a large but declining share of India's US exports. Woven clothing represented 7 per cent of the total in 2001, but by 2009, this had dropped to 5.7 per cent.

Kenyan exports show similar trends. Clothing exports to the US were $64.57 million in 2001, increasing steadily to peak at $277 million in 2004. From 2005, when the MFA termination began to affect Kenyan exports, woven garment exports dropped by almost 50 per cent to just $195 million in 2009. In 2001, woven clothing accounted for 99 per cent of total clothing exports to the US, but by 2009, wovens accounted for only 54 per cent of the total.

Based on these data, we argue that India poses a great threat to the survival and growth of Kenyan clothing exports to the US. Moreover, the fact that Kenya's market share of clothing in the US is driven by the AGOA trade preferences puts it in a precarious situation compared to India. A measure of the Export Similarity Index by Rhys Jenkins and Chris Edwards (2006, p. 27) indicated that approximately 27.7 per cent of Kenyan exports had the same structure as those originating from India in third markets. This corroborates our arguments that India is posing a threat to Kenya in third markets for clothing.

The end of MFA has worsened the situation for Kenya's garment industry because some of the foreign firms established with a view to targeting the US market are gradually closing down their operations. Most of them are relocating back to their home countries where their business environment is much easier. In fact, Kenya's unfavourable business environment, characterised by the high costs of production and stiff competition from Asian countries, has been responsible for the poor performance of the manufacturing sector (Republic of Kenya, 2010). Not only does India pose a threat in the US market, but because of its own growing domestic production following the termination of MFA, it also presents challenges to Kenya's sourcing of raw materials. In addition, the derogation of the AGOA rules of origin allowing Kenya to source raw materials from anywhere in the world and still access the US market duty free is set to come to an end in 2012 (Kamau 2009; Pinaud 2007).

Potential industry strategies for Kenyan producers

Kenyan clothing manufacturing firms – both large and medium-scale – source fabrics and other raw materials from India. Interestingly, firms with Indian connections appear more likely to import raw materials from India than others (see Box 4.1). Several reasons were given by respondents as to why they sourced raw materials from India, notably communication and family ties, but also requirements of buyers in the case of large exporting firms and the availability of high-quality fabrics. Finally, the distance between India and Kenya influenced the decision to import from India because it takes less than one month to get goods shipped from India to Mombasa. Owners of medium-scale firms reported that they sometimes combined visits to friends and relatives in

Box 4.1 The case of firm A in Kenya

Firm A was established in 1992 as an EPZ. Its workforce grew from about 1,000 at its start to 2,200 workers by 2008. This firm specialises in manufacturing trousers — jeans, casual wear, uniforms — and gowns. The owner of this firm is a Kenyan of Indian origin who lives in the US. His base in the US assists the firm in Kenya to get direct orders from US buyers instead of relying on sourcing houses and agents. The owner has established other garment manufacturing entities in Nepal and Bangladesh and distributes orders among these three factories.

Raw materials are obtained mainly from India where the director has good connections. It is only when firms in India do not have enough supply that the firm sources from Hong Kong and China. In most cases, the buyers would recommend different suppliers located in various countries but if the producer can give an assurance of quality and timely delivery they (buyers) can go with the vendor's choice. Being in the US, the director is able to convince buyers to source raw materials from Indian suppliers. It is easier for this firm to source inputs from India than elsewhere because the owner maintains close networks with relatives in India. The firm is able to arrange for trade credit in India, which makes it easier to supply orders on time.

Although many EPZ firms have closed shop in Kenya following the MFA termination, this firm has changed its production strategies to remain afloat. Instead of relying on general merchandisers in the US, more orders are now being sought from corporate customers. The firm has also shifted from making standard trousers to producing jeans that involve additional value-adding activities such as stone-washing, sand-blasting and embroidery. This firm now sources most of its imports from Indian and sometimes Chinese suppliers.

Interview with the Finance Manager, 4 February 2008

India with business to source reliable suppliers of raw materials. Sourcing raw materials from Kenya and/or from the region was not popular among medium- and large-scale firms. They argued that the quality was not good and adequate supply was not guaranteed.

India's rising demand for clothing can be attributed to its growing population, an increasing middle class and industrial development. A unique feature of the middle class in India is their acceptance of western clothing styles, which Kenya's firms can easily export to this market (ITC 2009). The penetration of Kenya's products into this market is facilitated by the close connection of

Table 4.3: Kenya's export of apparel 2001–09 ($,000)

	2001	2002	2003	2004	2005	2006	2007	2008	2009
USA	64,437	125,880	187,749	277,172	270,015	262,074	248,049	246,100	195,104
EU	1,694	1,098	1,383	3,225	3,024	1,726	1,440	1,389	1,067
Canada	33	327	1,911	2,647	2,759	1,701	1,606	1,261	1,631
Others	3,413	3,111	3,478	4,056	4,362	7,664	12,410	n.a	n.a
Total	69,564	130,121	194,521	287,169	281,158	276,158	266,039	274,546	159,245

Source: Calculated from USITC, US Department of Commerce, Otexa Eurostat, Strategies, EPC

Kenya's producers with India as shown in Box 4.1. It is worth noting that Kenyan goods compete not only with local production in India but also with other imports, including those from Italy, for example (ITC 2009). Therefore, penetration into this market requires the strategic positioning of Kenyan manufacturing firms.

Available evidence shows that the US market is the dominant market for Kenya's clothing products, absorbing more than 80 per cent of total clothing exports. This is an indication of low market diversification of Kenya's clothing exports (EPZA 2008, Kamau 2009, Phelps et al 2009, McCormick et al 2006). Table 4.3 demonstrates the dominance of the US market for Kenya's clothing exports.

Although the US market offers an opportunity for industrial growth in the short term, long-term growth is uncertain. First, penetration into this market is mainly based on non-reciprocal AGOA preferences by the US government, something that can be withdrawn without any recourse. Kaplinsky et al (2006) observe that factories established to meet specific requirements of the US market might be unable to switch to other markets.

Furthermore, evidence shows that Kenya's ability to penetrate the Indian market has been limited despite the growing demand for clothing in India. While on the surface, this market appears viable for Kenyan producers, two barriers seem to be blocking its take-off. First, the tariff rates charged by the Indian government on imported clothing products are not only high but also complicated (WTO 2008; ITC 2009). Second, there are other well-established companies and brands known to Indian manufacturers, retailers and consumers. Therefore, accessing the Indian market

81

might require some specialised manufacturing and marketing skills on the part of Kenyan companies, which are lacking at the moment. Finally, lack of competitiveness in the price of Kenyan clothing products seriously hampers efforts to penetrate other markets. Kenya is characterised by high costs of production associated with energy, transport and labour. There is therefore a need to devise mechanisms that would enable local firms to access the Indian market.

Conclusion and recommendations

Our analysis in this chapter shows that India's growth has both complementary and competitive impacts on the Kenyan textile and clothing industry. Two complementary impacts were identified, one actual and largely positive, and the other theoretically possible but, to date, difficult to achieve. The most important and successful complementary impact has been in sourcing fabric from India for production of garments for both the domestic and export markets. The export market, particularly the US under AGOA, has been facilitated by the derogation of the rules of origin allowing low-income SSA exporters under AGOA to source raw materials from any country. Clothing exporters in Kenya have been able to utilise fabrics sourced from India and other Asian countries and still access the US market duty-free. This has a direct complementary impact on the Kenyan textile sector.

A serious concern, however, is the sustainability of Kenya's clothing industry with its heavy reliance on external sources of raw materials. In McCormick et al (2006), it was reported that Kenyan manufacturers were facing shortages of fabric inputs because of increased demand in the supplying countries. Therefore, reliance on India or any other country to supply fabric for Kenyan clothing producers can be at best a short-term measure. Equally important is the fact that the derogation of the rules of origin will come to an end in September 2012 (although AGOA preferences continue to 2015), after which Kenya must have alternative sources of fabric within the Africa region or it will lose its duty-free access to the US market. India also has a complementary impact on the production for the domestic market, which also relies on imported fabrics.

The analysis has shown that the Kenya–India relationship is not only complementary, but also competitive. The two countries' products compete in the US market as well as in the Kenyan and Indian domestic markets. India's surge in the export of woven garments to the US appears to be eroding Kenya's already small US market share. In addition, a competitive effect exists in the domestic market where imports of finished garments compete with locally manufactured products. This has no doubt helped to undermine efforts to revive the clothing industry in Kenya. Furthermore, although there is potential for Kenyan garment producers to export to the growing clothing market in India, export data suggest that this is not happening to any large extent.

Based on this analysis, we make policy recommendations on how India–Kenya trade relations can be better harnessed for the benefit of the Kenyan garment industry. We make our recommendations to three stakeholders: the Kenyan clothing and textiles industry, the US government and the Kenyan government.

First, Kenya's clothing firms need to diversify beyond the US market, which at the moment accounts for more than 90 per cent of the exports. Our analysis of data shows that although India's large population and growing middle-income groups offer potential for Kenyan clothing exports, penetration by Kenya's firms has been limited. Whereas the Indian middle class is a small proportion of the entire population, in absolute terms it is still very large. The approach should be to establish links with buyers and retailers in India whose market segment is the middle-income group in order to understand market requirements for this group. A market survey to better understand the Indian clothing market in terms of manufacturers, retailers and consumer behaviour is necessary. Kenyan firms should also address production inefficiencies to be able to establish price competitiveness.

Although it is possible to have a clothing industry without a textile sector, AGOA requires that benefiting countries develop backward linkages by establishing strong textile manufacturing. However, this seems not to have taken place, arguably because of capital intensity in the textile industry. Countries with notable textile industries capable of supplying fabrics to other countries (South Africa, Mauritius and Lesotho) are hardly able to fulfil their domestic demand for fabrics. Ancharaz (2009) observes that

'Mauritius imports huge volumes of fabrics due to fluctuations in local production as well as a significant volume of fabrics being exported to Madagascar as part of intra-firm trade'.

Currently, Kenya's ability to export to the US is facilitated by the derogation of the rule of origin, allowing the use of raw materials from non-AGOA qualifying countries. Efforts to revitalise the textile industry should start with collaboration between Kenya's and India's investors to establish capital-intensive textile manufacturing firms. Although this approach sounds plausible, it is important to stress that textile ventures – spinning and weaving – require capital-intensive investments which must be supported by domestic resources. Therefore, expecting private FDI to purely finance such ventures might not be easy and involvement of the state is necessary. To attract Indian investors to such ventures, Indian technical support for Africa should be channelled to this industry. Furthermore, the expanded market in the East African and COMESA markets should be used to guarantee investors.

Second, the US government needs to extend AGOA trade preferences beyond 2015 and the derogation of the rule of origin beyond 2012. The US government's stated desire to promote backward linkages in the industry could be furthered by adding some incentives for US firms to invest in textile production in Africa. Third, the Kenya government needs to improve competitiveness by upgrading infrastructure, lobbying the US government for extension of AGOA and making investment in textile manufacturing a priority.

It is argued that India's competitiveness in the textile and clothing industry is anchored on an efficient infrastructure, including roads, water, power and port clearance. But Nicholas Phelps et al (2008) identify infrastructure as one of the key supply constraints inhibiting competitiveness of Kenya's textile and clothing industry. A closer look, however, casts doubt on this argument because India and Kenya are almost at par with regard to this indicator, ranked 89 and 90, respectively (World Economic Forum 2010). Although it is agreed that infrastructural support is critical, there is need for further research to establish factors behind India's competitiveness. As noted earlier, the cluster approach to boosting garment manufacturing is the most important in tackling supply-related constraints in India's clothing industry, something that Kenya should emulate. We recommend that the Kenyan government works to strengthen clusters in the industry to enable provision of much needed supply-related infrastructural support.

The current research has highlighted the need for a more detailed analysis of Kenyan and Indian exports to the US market to determine the extent of competition between specific products, rather than broad product groupings. A second type of research would gather primary data from the Indian side in order to find out exactly what in the Indian market inhibits imports from Kenya. Ideally this would involve close collaboration between Kenyan and Indian research institutions. A third type of research would explore what type of fabric is imported into Kenya and why, despite the shrinking export market for Kenyan garment products, the value of textile imports from India continues to rise. This would disaggregate the types of fabric imported into Kenya from India. Such research would allow an exploration of the possibility of joint ventures in textile manufacturing between investors in both countries.

References

Adhikari, Ratnakar and Weeratunge, Chatrini (2007) 'Textiles and clothing in South Asia: current status and future potential', South Asia Economic Journal, vol. 8, p. 171–203

Ancharaz, Vinaye (2009) 'David v. Goliath: Mauritius facing up to China', European Journal of Development Research, vol. 21, pp. 622–43

Asian Drivers Team (2006) 'The impact of Asian drivers on the developing world', IDS Bulletin, vol. 37, no.1, pp. 3–11

Export Processing Zones Authority (EPZA) (2008) Annual Report, Nairobi, EPZA

Export Promotion Council (EPC) 2009 Kenya's External Trade Statistics, Nairobi, Centre for Business Information in Kenya

Gereffi, Garry (1999) 'International trade and industrial upgrading in apparel commodity chain', Journal of International Economics, vol. 48, no. 1, p. 37–70

Goldstein, A., Pinaud, N., Reisen, H. and Xiaobao Chen (2006) China and India: What is in it for Africa?, Paris, OECD

Italian Trade Commission (ITC) (2009) Market Research on Textile, Apparel and Clothing Industry in India, Mumbai, ITC

Jenkins, Rhys and Edwards, Chris (2006) 'The Asian drivers and sub-Saharan Africa', IDS Bulletin, vol. 37, no. 1, pp. 23–32

Kamau, Paul (2009) 'Upgrading and technical efficiency in the Kenyan garment firms: does insertion in global value chains matter?', unpublished Ph.D thesis, Nairobi, Institute for Development Studies, University of Nairobi

Kamau, Paul, McCormick, Dorothy and Pinaud, Nicholas (2009) 'The developmental impact of Asian drivers on Kenya, with particular emphasis on clothing and textile manufacturing', *The World Economy*, vol. 10, no. 11, pp. 1586–612

Kaplinsky, Raphael (2007) 'The impact of Asian drivers on innovation and development strategies: lesson from sub-Saharan Africa experience', *International Journal of Technological Learning, Innovation and Development*, vol. 1, no. 1, pp. 65–82

—— (2008) 'What does the rise of China do for industrialisation in sub-Saharan Africa?', *Review of African Political Economy*, vol. 35, no. 115, pp. 7–22

Kaplinsky, Raphael and Morris, Mike (2008) 'Do the Asian drivers undermine export-oriented industrialisation in SSA?' World Development, vol. 36, no. 2, pp. 254–73

Kaplinsky, Raphael, McCormick, Dorothy and Morris, Mike (2006) 'The impact of China on sub-Saharan Africa', agenda-setting paper prepared for DFID China office, Brighton, Institute of Development Studies

Kinyanjui, Mary Njeri, McCormick, Dorothy and Ligulu, Peter (2004) 'Clothing and footwear in Kenya: policy and research concerns', in McCormick, D. and Rogerson, C. (eds) *Clothing and Footwear in African Industrialisation*, Pretoria, Africa Institute of South Africa

Landes, Maurice, MacDonald, Stephen, Singh, Santosh K. and Vollrath, Thomas (2005) 'Growth prospects for India's cotton and textile industries', United States Department of Agriculture, CWS-05d-01

Li, Yuefen June and Zhang, Bin (2008) 'Development path of China and India and the challenges for their sustainable growth', working paper no. 2008/67, Helsinki, Unu-Wider

McCormick, Dorothy (2007) 'Impact of China and India on Ethiopia and Kenya with particular emphasis on textiles and footwear', final report prepared for OECD Development Centre, Paris

McCormick, Dorothy and Rogerson, Christian M. (2004) 'Introduction: researching clothing and footwear in African industrialisation', in McCormick, Dorothy and Rogerson, Christian M. (eds) *Clothing and Footwear in African Industrialisation*, Pretoria, Africa Institute of South Africa

McCormick, Dorothy, Kamau, Paul and Ligulu, Peter (2006) 'Post-multifibre arrangement analysis of the textile and garment sectors in Kenya', IDS Bulletin, vol. 37, no.1, pp. 81–9

Morris, Mike and Sedowski, Leanne (2009) 'The competitive dynamics of the clothing industry in Madagascar in the post-MFA environment', in McCormick, Dorothy, Kuzilwa, Joseph and Gebre-Egeziabher, Tegegne (eds) *Industrialising Africa in the Era of Globalisation: Challenges to Clothing and Footwear*, Nairobi, University of Nairobi Press

Omolo, Jacob O. (2006) 'The textiles and clothing industry in Kenya', in Jauch, Hebert and Traub-Merz, Rudolf (eds) *The Future of the Textile and Clothing Industry in Sub-Saharan Africa*, Bonn, Friedrich-Ebert-Stiftung

Organisation for Economic Cooperation and Development (OECD) (2004) *A New World Map in Textile and Clothing: Adjusting to Change*, Paris, OECD

Pack, Howard (1987) *Productivity, Technology and Industrial Development: A Case Study in Textiles*, Washington DC, The World Bank

Phelps, Nicholas A., Stilwell, John C.H. and Wanjiru, Roseline (2008) 'Missing the GO in AGOA? Growth and constraints of foreign direct investment in the Kenyan clothing industry', *Transnational Corporations*, vol. 17, no. 2, pp 66–106

—— (2009) 'Broken chain? AGOA and foreign direct investment in the Kenyan clothing industry', *World Development*, vol. 37, no. 2, pp. 314–25

Pinaud, Nicolas (2007) 'Nipping African clothing in a post-MFA bud?', paper presented to the Africa and China: Economic and Business Perspectives Workshop, Shanghai, 14–16 May

Qureshi, Mahvash Saeed and Guanghua, Wan (2006) 'Trade potential of China and India: threat or opportunity?', mimeo, Helsinki, UNU-WIDER

Republic of Kenya (2009) *Economic Survey*, Nairobi, Government Printer

—— (2010) *Economic Survey*, Nairobi, Government Printer

Schmitz, Hubert (2005) 'Asian drivers of change in the real economy', paper presented to the Asian Driver Workshop, Institute of Development Studies, University of Sussex, 9–10 May

Tewari, Meenu (2006) 'Adjustment in India's textile and apparel industry: reworking historical legacies in a post-MFA world', *Environment and Planning*, vol. 38, pp. 2325–44

Vijayabaskar, V. (2002), 'The garment industry in India', in Joshi, Gopal (ed) *Garment Industry in South Asia: Rags or Riches?* New Delhi, International Labour Organisation

World Economic Forum (WEF) (2010) *Global Competitiveness Report 2010-2011*, Geneva, WEF

World Bank (2007) *Vertical and Regional Integration to Promote African Textiles and Clothing Exports. A Close Knit Family?*, Washington DC, World Bank

World Trade Organisation (WTO) (2008) *World Trade Statistics*, Geneva, WTO

5

Chinese and Indian entrepreneurs in the East African economies

Aleksandra W. Gadzala

Introduction

The rapid economic growth and subsequent global rise of China and India in recent years has raised myriad questions about the implications for the world economy and developing countries in particular. The bulk of such questions are posed with particular reference to Africa, which has become a central geopolitical element in the globalisation strategy of China especially and, increasingly, India. Replete in natural resources and boasting the potential for new market opportunities, Africa is witnessing an inpouring of trade and investment from both Asian drivers, as well as others.

In 2008, bilateral trade between China and the continent reached an unprecedented $106.8 billion. Indian-African trade stood at $36 billion in the same year, marking a 12-fold increase from $3 billion seven years ago. Equally, by 2008 China's Exim Bank was funding upwards of 300 projects in 36 countries across the continent and Chinese companies were running mining operations in 13 African countries and were prospecting in more. Between 2002 and 2005, too, Indian firms topped the list of greenfield foreign direct investment (FDI) projects in Africa at 48, compared to 32 from China (UNCTAD 2007).

In view of the strategic importance Africa has come to wield in both Chinese and Indian foreign policies, it is unsurprising that the debate about China and India's respective African engagements concentrates overwhelmingly on the implications of this new-found role for Africa, with especial attention on macro-economic variables pertaining to trade, aid and investment. To date, few studies have examined the implications of China–Africa and India–Africa linkages as they impact upon African small and medium enterprises (SMEs), for instance, or individual entrepreneurs labouring in the continent's informal economies (Gadzala 2009; Mohan 2009). Equally, studies focused on China and India in a comparative perspective have thus far failed to appreciate the ramifications of economic and political competition between both 'drivers' on their respective foreign policies and global economic strategies, arguing instead over the broader geopolitical ramifications of their African exploits.

Accordingly, this chapter seeks to fill a dual void by addressing not only Indian and Chinese economic engagement at the micro-economic level, but also further examining the implications of the entrepreneurial activities of the latter upon the former. Indeed, inasmuch as Chinese and Indian prospecting for resources and the surrounding investments stand to influence Africa's economic growth and development, it is in fact the entrepreneurial activities of the Chinese especially that bear the greatest ramifications for African economies. With a growing number of Chinese-owned and operated firms, particularly in the manufacturing and service sectors – among the continent's key sources of employment – local, African-owned enterprises are increasingly forced to fore-close, in turn heralding heightened unemployment levels and the associated complications. Equally, the influx of Chinese SMEs in similar ways impacts the pre-existing population of Indian-origin entrepreneurs, as well as those seeking entry to the new market.

The objective of this chapter is thus to elucidate the unfolding dynamics between African and Chinese, and Indian and Chinese entrepreneurs in East Africa, and in so doing shift the focus of this seemingly triangular relationship to the micro-economic levels of engagement. As systematic data on the subject is generally dispersed, and in many cases altogether unavailable, much of the analysis contained in this chapter is derived from fieldwork conducted in Kampala, Nairobi and Lusaka in 2007, and supplemented by anecdotal evidence.

The chapter begins by highlighting parallels between business strategies pursued by Chinese entrepreneurs today and Indian-origin entrepreneurs during both the colonial and contemporary periods. It subsequently outlines how, despite such apparent similarities, Indian entrepreneurs are in many cases being driven out by their Chinese counterparts – in the medicine and textile industries in particular – and new market entrants face an uphill battle. The chapter concludes by positing potential explanations for this reality, speaking especially to the strength of the Chinese entrepreneurial and diasporic networks, which the Indians are only now apparently rediscovering, and Africans have in many cases seemingly not yet properly enjoyed.

Chinese entrepreneurs in Africa: the new dukawallas?

Over and above government relations, multi-billion dollar construction projects and foreign aid, the stories of both India and China in Africa are those of individuals and families exploring market opportunities beyond their native homelands. Although much is made of the alleged novelty surrounding such Chinese entrepreneurialism in East Africa today, a cursory overview of not only early Chinese but also early Indian overseas economic ventures in Africa, and indeed elsewhere, suggests that the reverse is in fact true. From the 15th century through the early 19th centuries, for instance, Gujarati merchants – the most prominent of which were Hindus and Jains – dominated Indian entrepreneurial migration to East Africa because, as Jean Aubin remarks, Gujarat was the 'keystone of commercial structure of the Indian Ocean' at the time (Aubin 1971, p. 3).

Early detailed impressions of Gujarati Hindu business practices in East Africa observe: '[t]hese [people] are [like] Italians in their knowledge of and dealings in merchandise…. They are men who understand merchandise; they are so properly steeped in the sound and harmony of it […] There are Gujaratees settled everywhere. They work some for some and some for others. They are diligent, quick men in trade' (Cortesao 1944, pp. 41–2) Toward the end of the 16th century, a less flattering description transpired:

They are most subtil and expert in casting accounts and writing, so that they do not only surpass and go beyond all other Indians and other nations thereabouts, but also the Portingales: and in this respect they have much advantage, for [that] they are very perfect in the trade of merchandise, and very ready to deceive men. (Burnell 1885, pp. 252–3)

As later evinced in this chapter, similarly divergent observations are drawn with respect to Chinese entrepreneurs in East Africa today. Gujarati merchants left significant economic and demographic footprints in East Africa. In the 16th and 17th centuries, for instance, the principal trading goods for East African trade were Gujarati cloths, which, some scholars argue, subsequently facilitated the growth of cotton textile manufacturing industries in the East African city-states (Alpers 2009). Moreover, unlike the Punjabi Indian migrants of the late 19th century, who were recruited to labour on various public works projects and who mostly returned to India upon completion of their contracts, many Gujaratis remained in East Africa or migrated to other parts of the continent. Many South Asians in Africa today are indeed Gujarati descendants.

Contemporary Chinese migration to the African continent (1990s–present) seemingly proceeds as a reverse-image of that of the early Indians. Initially recruited to labour on construction projects in, especially, African oil and mining sectors, many Chinese migrants have subsequently relocated into domestic wholesale and service sectors where they operate small-scale, competitive ventures which are susceptible to business succession. Laundries, grocery stores, shops and restaurants require little skill, cluster on the low end of the wage scale, and function in accordance with Chinese cultural and political norms. Although labour migration continues to inform present-day Sino-African relations, it is rapidly becoming an antiquated tale. The majority of Chinese arriving in East Africa since especially the mid-2000s are rather small-scale entrepreneurs who come through family or kinship-led chain migration in search of business opportunities to gain relief from 'the pressure cooker of domestic competition and surplus production' (Gu 2009, p. 5) that characterises the Chinese economy. Data on Chinese migratory figures is dubious at best, with some estimates positing the number at between 270,000 and 510,000 (Mung 2008) and others (French and Polgreen 2007) estimating there are as many as 750,000 Chinese working or living for extended periods across all of Africa.

Beyond the migration figures, data on Chinese businesses in Africa suggests that private enterprises operated by the Chinese diaspora constitute approximately 80 per cent of all Chinese firms on the continent (Wang 2009). Most prominent among such ventures are Chinese shops, largely tantamount to those found in traditional Chinatowns in Southeast Asia or North America. Indeed, Africa's Chinese entrepreneurs today are in many respects Africa's new shopkeepers or, more specifically, the new *dukawallas*.

Dukawallas, or Indian shopkeepers, together with Gujarati merchants, have played a leading role in the story of Indian entrepreneurs in Africa. During the period of British colonialism, *dukawallas* used their extensive and long-standing family networks to insert themselves into colonial African economies; areas of trade abandoned or never penetrated by the colonial states or by imperial capital. For instance, tending shops in the interior areas, trading in more affordable goods, and processing cotton for export became the preserve of Indian merchants in many British colonies. Small urban commerce in the colonial economies – Uganda and Kenya in particular – later took the form of laundries, butchers, and groceries and gradually came to serve the local economies.

Similar to the Chinese in East Africa today, the Indians occupied a middleman position in the colonial and post-colonial African economies, engendering a direct link between ethnic group members and the receiving societies, and often driving out local competitors. Among such ventures were Indian restaurants, which initially began by catering to the Indian migrant populations in African city-centres, and later expanded to serve the local clientele. Nairobi today is dotted with Indian restaurants; in Kampala, too, Indian restaurants have assumed a distinct position in the local market, such that of the top five rated restaurants in the city, three are Indian.

Chinese SMEs in East Africa today occupy a similar role. As of early 2007, for instance, there were 40 Chinese restaurants in Nairobi alone, many of which serve both Chinese and local cuisines. In Kampala, Fang Fang Restaurant – highly rated by the Ugandan government – has gained popularity among local residents for offering both Chinese and local dishes. In Mombasa a Chinese medicine clinic run by Li Changcheng and his wife provides services for the Chinese expatriate, as well as local African and Asian-Kenyan, communities. Li and his wife are among the hundreds of Chinese who came to Kenya seeking riches through their practice of Chinese medicine.

As is true of many Chinese in Kenya, Li's decision to migrate turned on economic desperation: state hospitals in China could no longer afford to pay the Chinese-medicine doctors a living wage, so he and his wife headed to Mombasa where they had heard from relatives that a medical clinic was needed (Beech 2001). Today, they administer acupuncture to squeamish patients, and employ an additional six doctors and administrative employees, all of whom are either immediate family or kinship members.

For the majority of overseas Chinese businesses, the family indeed remains the basis of organisation. In fact, one of the most notorious features is related precisely to the fact that in the Chinese culture, contrary to most western and African cultures, there is no rigid frontier or clear distinction between the network of professional, family or social relations, all of which interlink and intermingle in a creative synthesis (Bongardt and Neves 2007).

A comparable fusion between business and family is likewise discernible amongst both colonial and contemporary overseas Indian ventures, which similarly adhere to the model of the family firm. Enterprises are vertically integrated with concentration of authority in a dominant family leader (usually the family patriarch); family members occupy key managerial positions, and capital expenditures are financed through trusted relatives and moneylenders. For early Indian merchants and shopkeepers, the efficiency of such personal network ties facilitated access to key firm inputs, subsequently enabling them to undercut the prices of local commerce and gain leverage over the largely un-networked and under-sourced Africans.

In much the same vein, the structure of most Chinese shops in East Africa today conforms to the 'entrepreneurial familialism' (Teixeira 1998) historically endemic among overseas Chinese businesses: family members occupy key management and strategic functions and the family engages in economic competition and risk-taking as a unit. Accordingly, employees labouring in African-based Chinese shops are most often family members who have been recruited from the Chinese mainland as a form of cheap labour and a source of key industrial input. Though locals might be employed to undertake menial work, Chinese staff are preferred and are imported through legal and illegal means.

Chinese firms in Africa hire the largest percentage of workers from China, accounting for 17 per cent of total employees (Broadman 2007). When locals are hired, they normally hold low-skill, manual positions which carry little potential for the spillover of technology and skills. In Chinese shops in Nairobi, for instance, local employees are responsible for assisting customers (owing to the language barrier between shop owners and locale clientele) and to guard against shoplifting. There is limited evidence of local workers being entrusted with the handling of money or being elevated to managerial positions in the shops.

For this reason among others, the emergence of small family-run Chinese enterprises is proving increasingly problematic for East African entrepreneurs, as co-ethnic employment policies sustained by Chinese firms hinder the potential for local employment, and both African and Indian-origin industries are finding it difficult to parry Chinese market competition; the competitive advantages enjoyed by Chinese businesses often result in the fore-closure of many local firms.

As discussed in later sections of this chapter, the key advantage concerns the cohesive local and trans-continental network structures sustained by Chinese entrepreneurs, from which in turn flow critical market resources. African merchants frequently complain of Chinese traders who come to East Africa to gauge consumer demand, return to China where the high-demand goods are mass-produced at lower prices, and subsequently return to Africa to sell them cheaply on the local markets. A former Zambian textile factory worker observes:

> The cost of production for a single Zambian-made shirt is four to five times higher than a shirt from China. Even though the quality of locally-made clothes is better, a customer will still opt for the cheaper products, because of low wages that the majority of people in Zambia earn. (Mpundu 2005)

Although on the one hand the entry of cheap Chinese goods into African markets serves to increase African purchasing power, it simultaneously bears damaging consequences for local African and Indian industries.

Sino-Indian and African economic competition

Among the sectors negatively affected by the entry of Chinese enterprises into East African economies is the hitherto Indian-dominated medical industry, in which the Indian population had enjoyed particular predominance since the colonial era. Concomitant with their role as traders and merchants, Indian entrepreneurs in East Africa also fulfilled professional roles, with many pursuing careers as doctors and lawyers. As early as 1892, for example, an Indian merchant by the name of Sewa Haji established a hospital for Africans, Indians and Arabs in the Tanzanian capital, Dar es Salaam.

Located on the foreshore close to the docks, the hospital opened in 1893 and served the capital for nearly 70 years (Illiffe 1998). In 1905, hospital staff included five Tanzanians out of approximately 20 employees in total (the remainder were Indian) (Illiffe 1998). During the same period, Indian-origin doctors frequently laboured as sub-assistant surgeons, supplying government medical services, tending to rural communities and in many cases heading small rural hospitals.

In recent years, the Indian medical presence in East Africa has evolved to assume an increasingly impersonal role, with the export of Indian-manufactured pharmaceuticals as the foremost business model pursued. In 2007–08, for instance, Kenya imported Rs.342.4 crore ($75.3 million) worth of Indian medicines and Africa as a whole accounted for 14 percent of India's $8 billion medicine exports in the same time period (Mathew 2009). Despite its removed character, the continued market presence of Indian-origin medicine in East Africa underscores Harry Broadman's (2007) assertion that unlike the Chinese, who are relative newcomers to the region and have therefore not as yet integrated into African business communities in any meaningful way, East African Indians enjoy a much longer tradition of diasporic ties to the continent, with many in fact identifying not as Indians but, rather, Africans.

History, however, seemingly fails to translate into marked economic gain. Time-honoured diasporic ties notwithstanding, East Africa's Indian-dominated medical sector is being gradually eclipsed by its Chinese counterpart – this, owing partly to the unaffordability of generic Indian drugs (despite their already low costs) on the one hand, and controversy in 2009 over exports of allegedly counterfeit Indian medicines on the other. An increasing number of consumers in places such as Kenya and Uganda are turning to Chinese medicines and medicine clinics, which, unlike their African and Indian-origin equivalents, operate generally in the informal economies and subsequently charge minimal fees. In Kampala, for instance, the most prominent Indian-origin clinic, Ayurhome Ltd, targets primarily the city's up-market clientele; the largest variety of mid-range and low-cost clinics in the city are today mainly Chinese.[1]

In Tanzania, Chinese clinics have integrated traditional local and modern urban Tanzanian elements into their practices, and offer both combined biomedical and traditional Chinese products and procedures. Clinics provide medicines with explanations in Swahili, have lower prices and shorter waiting periods (10–20 minutes) as compared to locally-run clinics in which patients are often left waiting for hours (Hsu 2008). In Kampala, too, Chinese-operated massage parlours and herbal clinics are full of patients on a daily basis, many of whom state that they appreciate the lower prices and personalised services. Though the quality of the services might be subject to scepticism, locals increasingly frequent Chinese clinics for the very reason which likewise informs their procurement of poorer-quality Chinese goods: affordability.

The medical sector is but one example of growing market competition between Chinese and Indian entrepreneurs in the East African economies. In a 2007 interview, Shalendra Kundra, the director of Tata Uganda, noted that until recently he supplied 1,500 vehicles every year or so to the Ugandan army. Today, the army places all of its orders with Chinese suppliers. And, while Kundra struggles to sell Tata's Safari multi-utility vehicles to Ugandan consumers, the Chinese automobile manufacturer Geely International has successfully established and is profiting from its Ugandan-based vehicle and motorcycle assembly plant. In Kampala business circles, it is believed that the Chinese will outnumber the Indians within the next few years in both the macro- and microeconomic sectors (Bhandari 2007).

In Kampala's Garden City Mall, shoppers in 2007 observed a marked decline in the number of small-scale Indian shops and restaurants – and a subsequent burgeoning of their Chinese counterparts (personal communication with Indian storeowner, Kampala, September 2007). Employees at Amarson's Collections, a fabric shop in Nairobi that specialises in Indian silks, expressed concern over the growing influx of Chinese garment wholesalers, whose colourful and cheaply priced goods attract local buyers away from the slightly higher-priced Indian merchandise.

Similar worries abound among Nairobi's African-origin street vendors, who rely especially on pedestrians for their market base and lack both the economic and technical resources that would allow for the manufacture of elaborate and distinctive products. Conversely, Chinese roadside stalls and shops abound in colourful handbags, attractively packaged and finished handicrafts, garments and jewelery, which attract local buyers away from the 'unimaginative designs' (McCormick 1997, p. 111) of local manufacturers.

The East African textile industry is indeed being squeezed by exports of Chinese cloths, fabrics and related goods. Unlike the Gujarati cloth trade of the 16th and 17th centuries, which some scholars argue helped to spawn the East African textile markets, the Chinese equivalent bears an altogether different effect. The burden falls most heavily on African-origin informal sector employees, who are in many contexts those most prominently engaged in textile manufacture and trade.

In Kenya, for instance, textile work, including tailoring, dressmaking, knitting and sewing of textile products comprises the largest percentage of informal sector workers. The textile industry employs about 30 percent of the labour force and supports the livelihoods of upwards of 200,000 small-scale farmers through its provision of cotton markets (Chen et al 1999). In Zambia, too, the textile trade is among the most dominant activities in the country's informal sector, contributing to 79 percent of total informal sector employment (Haan 2002).

With a growing influx of Chinese textile manufacturers and traders into the East African markets, however, these figures are rapidly declining. In 2004, for instance, the Chinese-operated firm Chipata Cotton Company in Zambia began a registration programme targeting 20,000 small-scale cotton farmers to work with the company, a move aimed at positively affecting a size-able portion of Zambia's labour force (*The Times of Zambia* 2004). Although the repercussions of this scheme for Zambia's farmers are not yet publicly known, since 2006 Zambian textile producers and traders have been experiencing significantly reduced sales volumes and employment levels (Civil Society Trade Network of Zambia, Malawi Economic Justice Network and Economic Justice Coalition of Mozambique 2007). In personal interviews conducted with Zambian entrepreneurs in Lusaka's Kamwala Market in 2007, several textile producers confessed that they were contemplating either manufacturing cheap, low-quality products to compete with 'underhanded' Chinese retailers, or ceasing production entirely.

Such complications, created as they are by the entrance of new foreign competitors into the East African markets, are certainly not the first of their kind – nor are the associated criticisms. Recall, for instance, the denunciatory comments articulated vis-à-vis Gujarati merchants in the 16th century. Indian merchants in Kenya during the colonial period were also frequently stereo-typed as 'unscrupulous [...] trader[s] who [made] profit by cheat-ing [their] customers and society at large' (Hart and Padayachee 2000, pp. 683–712).

Albeit in many cases exaggerated by the racist policies of Afri-can governments, particularly at the time of Kenya and Uganda's Africanisation policies in the 1960s and 1970s, such accusations suggest the selfsame concerns as those expressed about the Chi-nese commercial presence in East Africa today. The current trouble stems partly from the fact that Chinese entrepreneurs vend items, provide services, and pursue strategies largely analogous to those offered by their local African- and Indian-origin counterparts – only at lower costs, on grander scales and with greater efficiency. In Kamwala Market, for instance, Chinese shops sell a range of items including kitchenware, wall clocks, watches, electric-powered torches, shaving equipment handbags and garments.

Though diverging little from merchandise sold in neighbour-ing Zambian stores, the items are offered at one-fifth the price of locally produced goods. Chinese, Indian and African-origin shops in Kampala and Mombasa furthermore occupy comparable spaces insofar as they are located in malls and plazas, which allow for cheap, small rooms and counters. Moreover, SMEs operated by Indian and Chinese entrepreneurs in particular adhere to the family firm structure of enterprise: vertically integrated with family members occupying key strategic and management roles, and ties between employers and employees predicated as much on moral obligations as on formal contractual ties.

Such parallels suggest that the market competitiveness of Chinese entrepreneurs in East Africa's economies is predicated less upon the medium of their ventures, but more upon the particular mode by which they are organised and pursued. And, so long as the Chinese are able to retain such a competitive edge, existing and potential African- and Indian-origin producers and retailers will continue to be displaced by their Chinese counterparts.

Chinese *guanxi* and Indian diaspora networks

In addressing the advantages Chinese businessmen currently enjoy over their Indian-origin and African counterparts in many East African contexts, we must speak above all else to the highly networked Chinese business structure, predicated as it is upon *guanxi* ties. *Guanxi* is generally understood as a special kind of personal relationship in which long-term mutual benefit is more important than short-term individual gain (Alston 1989) and as the status and intensity of an ongoing relationship between two parties (Kirkbride et al 1991). The emphasis on close personal relations in *guanxi* renders such networks highly circumscribed, with significant importance placed on reputation (the Chinese notion of 'face') and the abiding nature of obligations.

Accordingly, Chinese garment textile wholesalers in Nairobi, for instance, are often linked to producers, shop owners, bankers, other garment producers, and sewing machine vendors. *Guanxi* ties sustained between them facilitate access to credit and other inputs, help to overcome problems of incomplete information, and provide a ready-made consumer and labour base. The distinct nature of network obligations implicit in *guanxi* further guarantees the kind of employer relations and work ethnic fundamental to SME productivity.

Much like the Chinese, however, African and newly arrived Indian entrepreneurs in East Africa are likewise dependent upon personal networks for the growth and efficacy of their enterprises. In Kenya, for instance, weakened incentives for long-term cooperative business relations created by economic instability have resulted in tight, ethnically predicated networks in which ethnic considerations remain foremost in affecting SME market entry, credit access and productivity.

The majority of Kenyan mini-manufacturers, for instance, are likely to be Kikuyu (Akoten and Otsuka 2007), who participate in various economic sectors including garment production and sale. As with the overseas Chinese, ethnic solidarities among Kikuyus facilitate access to key firm inputs. In some trades, too – most notably food and garments – Kenyan customers seemingly prefer to patronise businesses run by people of their own ethnic group, which in turn supplies key consumer bases to indigenous enterprises.

In a similar vein the ethnic fraternity of Indian immigrants, who arrive in East Africa and subsequently establish small-scale ventures akin to the shops and clinics of the Chinese, likewise facilitates the market entry and inclusion of co-ethnic enterprises. Entrepreneurial migrants from the Indian subcontinent arrive most often through kinship-based chain migration, which inculcates similar moral obligations vis-à-vis their employers as do *guanxi* networks. Omkara Maharaj, aged 47, for instance, came to Kampala from Jaipur to manage staff at Masala Chaat House, a popular informal Indian restaurant. He was sponsored by colleagues and family who were operating the restaurant and required further assistance.

Similarly, Prashant Choudhary – who had been working for Pepsi Co. in Calcutta – was informed of better job prospects in East Africa and was recruited by a friend to work in a start-up mobile company in the city. Today, he and his wife reside in a housing complex opposite Kampala's Nakasero market. Their apartment building houses about 20 other families – all from India – which, according to Mrs Choudhary, renders the transition to Ugandan life easier because it provides a ready-made support network for the newly arrived migrants (Reddy 2007). As with overseas Chinese and indigenous Africans, ethnic solidarities among Indian entrepreneurs facilitate not only social networks, but also provide access to key resources such as raw materials and credit and provide a consumer base in which to sell their goods.

Lacking the strength and cohesiveness of the Chinese, however, both African and Indian networks often fail to facilitate access to key firm inputs to the same degree as their Chinese equivalents. Kenya's decades-old ethnic tensions, for instance, frequently exacerbate the exclusionary effects of tight networks – restricted entry, ethnic status and sunk transaction costs – in turn producing a kind of 'lock-in': rather stable business networks and rather static patterns of business exchange. As Deborah Brautigam (2003) aptly observes, business networks in sub-Saharan Africa have not generally produced the strong links characteristic of Chinese networks, and are subsequently less likely than Chinese networks to provide the credit, information and examples necessary to foster innovative activity and yield a competitive advantage.

Despite the historically predicated ties and sustained high levels of migration between the Indian subcontinent and East African states[2] both the composition of the contemporary diaspora as well as the nature of its relations with pre-existing Indian communities and the Indian government likewise preclude access to positive network externalities, which could gain them leverage over other market competitors.

Unlike the Chinese diaspora in East Africa, which currently consists primarily of small-scale entrepreneurs, merchants, traders and, peripherally, contracted labourers, the Indian equivalent is fundamentally composed of professionals, with small-scale entrepreneurs of the kind discussed in this chapter factoring only marginally in the overall make-up of 'India-in-Africa'. Such a diasporic composition in turn disadvantages Indian entrepreneurs in especially the manufacturing, retail and service sectors. Some lack the economic inputs necessary to pursue start-up ventures on even as modest a scale as single-room shops, and are subsequently unable to access them from among the Indian migrant communities in the fashion analogous to that of the Chinese.

Moreover, because the population of East African Asians – Indians who have long been resident in East Africa – consists primarily of high-skilled professionals and industrialists working in sectors that require distinctive skill-sets and expertise, unskilled Indian migrants who arrive in East Africa in search of market opportunities are unable to insert themselves into the well-established Indian-origin business communities. Although the presence of educated and professional Indian-origin business communities in East African economies has, on a few occasions, benefited especially large Indian conglomerates such as Essar, Vedanta and Kirloskar Brothers, which have tapped into such circles to increase their labour force and enhance their market presence, such linkages are the exception rather than the norm (see McCann, Chapter 6 in this volume).

Conversely, for Chinese entrepreneurs, the pervasiveness of *guanxi* ties endows them with not only key firm inputs and market resources, but also creates enabling environments within which migrants obtain information pertaining to low-skill employment opportunities or, moreover, skills training necessary to advance into other economic sectors. Through reliance on the far-reaching diaspora networks, Chinese traders are able to capitalise upon cheap communal labour in especially the coastal provinces of Fujian, Zhejiang and Guangdong.

Many Chinese shop owners with ventures in Kenya and Uganda travel to China at least once a year to import goods to sell in their shops. Nicknamed 'astronauts', these migrants are mostly male household heads who are unwilling to forego life at home and resort to commuting between work and family, in so doing further gaining insights into general consumer demands, technologies, and production and marketing strategies.

Chinese entrepreneurs in East Africa are furthermore increasingly organised around business associations as, for instance, the Association of Chinese Corporations in Zambia (ACCZ) and the Chinese Centre for Investment Promotion and Trade (CCIPT). Established under the economic and commercial counsellor's office of the Chinese Embassy, the ACCZ serves as the de facto Chinese chamber of commerce in Lusaka, catering to the interests of Chinese companies, communicating and promoting the cause of Chinese investors, and educating its members on the rules and regulation of Zambia (Kragelund 2008). The CCIPT similarly identifies suitable investment projects and provides practical support to newly established Chinese companies and entrepreneurs – this is quite unlike the Indian High Commission in Zambia, and elsewhere in East Africa, which generally fails to supply newly established and emergent Indian enterprises with information pertaining to local business climates and potential investment opportunities.

Recently arrived Indian entrepreneurs throughout much of East Africa indeed complain that the Indian government has hitherto not paid sufficient heed to the new cohort of Indian businesses in the region, choosing instead to focus on European and American markets. As suggested in the introductory remarks to this chapter, however, the growing importance of Africa in India's foreign policy has led to gradually shifting tactics, marked perhaps most prominently by the African Union–India Forum Summit hosted in April 2008 and the Indian government's Africa Policy (Africa–India Forum Summit 2008; Beri 2003). The latter elucidates specific measures pertaining to strengthening ties with both the established and fledgling Indian diasporas, which together account for nearly two million people in the anglophone countries of eastern and southern Africa alone (Dubey 2008) and through their remittances contribute significantly to India's economic growth and development.

At the time of publication, however, India's Africa policy is not nearly as evolved as its Chinese counterpart and it remains to be seen whether Indian entrepreneurs will in the long term be able to again become strong market competitors in the East African economies such as the Chinese are today.

Conclusion

The foregoing does not, of course, imply that Indian businesses in the East African economies are being entirely sidelined by their Chinese competitors. Indeed, the realities portrayed in this chapter are but component pieces of an ever-evolving and complex puzzle, and must be appreciated as such. On the macroeconomic level, for instance, an increasing number of Indian conglomerates are making significant forays into the continent.

Data collected in 2008 indicates that the Indian company Fouress International now manages a power plant in Uganda; KEC International has undertaken a $40 million project to construct a 132 Kv power transmission plant in Ethiopia; Mashuli

Gashmani Ltd is operating an $18 million commercial prawn fishery plant in Uganda; and Kamai Engineering Corporation is constructing a transmission line between Zambia and Namibia.

Such diversity of Indian investments again signals the burgeoning importance of East Africa, and Africa in general, in the overseas strategies of India's political and business communities, as well as a desire on the part of leaders within both communities for India to again assume a prominent role in African markets in a way that pays tribute to the long-standing historical ties between the regions.

Although the bulk of such ambitions are currently manifest most prominently on the macroeconomic level, the story of India-in-Africa, like that of China-in-Africa, is articulated on many fronts, among them that of small-scale entrepreneurs. For the newly arrived Indians, however, the superiorly networked Chinese entrepreneurs currently hamper and indeed undermine the successful establishment and expansion of their business ventures, as well as those of local Africans and long-standing Indians.

Current dynamics between Indian and Chinese entrepreneurs in East Africa indeed suggest that the latter have today assumed a role historically held by the former – that of the *dukawallas*. Yet we must at the same time bear in mind the fluidity of both Chinese and Indian engagement in the region: the continuous reshaping of strategies, the escalation of investments on the part of both Asian drivers, the persistent migration of Indian and Chinese entrepreneurs and, most importantly, increasing African agency vis-à-vis both international actors.

Though unexplored in this chapter, it is ultimately how African countries manage their relationships with India and China that will influence the economic pursuits and strategies undertaken by both and will, as a result, determine the future course of relations between not only African and Chinese entrepreneurs, but also between the Africans, Chinese and, indeed, the Indians.

Notes

1. Key examples are Chinese Body and Beauty Care, Chinese Clinic, Chinese Medical Centre and Bangi Medical Centre, a Malaysian-operated facility, as noted in the February 2010 edition of *The Uganda Record*.
2. Of about 20,000 Ugandan Asians today, for example, only about 10 per cent are 'returnees' (those expelled in 1972 during the country's

Africanisation programme) and the remainder are new immigrants from the Indian subcontinent. See Reddy (2007)

References

Africa–India Forum Summit (2008), http://www.africa-union.org/root/au/Conferences/2008/april/India-Africa/India-Africa.html, accessed 13 May 2008

Akoten, J.E. and Otsuka, K. (2007) 'From tailors to mini-manufacturers: the role of traders in the performance of garment enterprises in Kenya', *Journal of African Economies*, vol. 16, no. 4, pp. 564–95

Alpers, Edward A. (2009) *East Africa and the Indian Ocean*, Princeton, Markus Wiener Publishers

Alston, J. (1989) 'Wa, Guanxi, and Inhwa: managerial principles in Japan, China and Korea', *Business Horizon*, March/April, pp. 26–31

Aubin, Jean (1971) 'Alburquerque et les negociations de Cambaye' in Aubin, J. (ed) *Mare Luso-Indicum. Etudes et documents sur l'histoire de l'Ocean Indien et des pay riverains a l'epoque de la domination portugaise*, Centre de Recherche d'Histoire et de Philologie de la IVe Section de l'Ecole Pratique des Hautes Etudes, IV, Hautes Etudes Islamiques et Orientales d'Histoire Comparee, 2, Geneva, Droz and Paris, Minard

Beech, H. (2001) 'The ends of the admiral's universe: Zheng He's fleet went to Africa seeking exotic treasures. The Chinese still do', *Time*, August, http://www.time.com/time/asia/features/journey2001/africa.htm, accessed 8 November 2007

Beri, R. (2003) 'India's Africa policy in the post-cold war era: an assessment', *Strategic Analysis*, vol. 27, pp. 216–32

Bhandari, Bhupesh (2007) 'India feels the heat of the dragon in Uganda', *Business Standard*, 26 November

Bongardt, Annette and Neves, Miguel Santos, 'The role of overseas Chinese in Europe in making China global: the case of Portugal', Economics Working Papers, Aveiro, Department of Economics, Management and Industrial Engineering, University of Aveiro

Brautigam, D. (2003) 'Close encounters: Chinese business networks as industrial catalysts in sub-Saharan Africa', *African Affairs*, vol. 102, no. 408, pp. 447–67

Broadman, Harry (2007) *Africa's Silk Road: China and India's New Economic Frontier*, New York, The World Bank

Burnell, A.C. (ed) (1885) 'The voyage of John Iluthn van Linschollt to the East Indies', The Hakluyt Society, LXX, vol. I, no. 60, pp. 252–53

Chen, M., Sebstad, J. and O'Connell. L. (1999) 'Counting the invisible workforce: the case of homebased workers', *World Development*, vol. 27, no. 3, pp. 603–10

Civil Society Trade Network of Zambia, Malawi Economic Justice Network and Economic Justice Coalition of Mozambique (2007) *Chinese Economic Activities in Zambia, Malawi and Mozambique*, Lusaka, Southern African Trust

Cortesao, Armando (tr. and ed) (1944) 'The stinca oriental o' Tome Pires', The Hakluyt Society second series, LXXXIX, vol. I, pp. 41–42

Dubey, Ajay (2008) 'Foreign policy of India with special reference to India's Africa policy', lecture delivered at the Institute of International Politics and Economics, Belgrade, 21 November

French, H. and Polgreen, L. (2007) 'Chinese flocking in numbers to a new frontier: Africa', *International Herald Tribune*, 17 August

Gadzala, Aleksandra W. (2009) 'Survival of the fittest?: Kenya's *jua kali* and Chinese businesses', *Journal of Eastern African Studies*, vol. 3

Gu, Jing (2009) 'China's private enterprises in Africa and the implications for African development', Institute of Development Studies, p. 5

Haan, H.C. (2002) 'Training for work in the informal sector: new evidence from eastern and southern Africa', Turin, International Training Centre of the International Labour Office

Hart, Keith and Padayachee, Vishnu (2000) 'Indian business in South Africa after apartheid: new and old trajectories', *Comparative Studies in Society and History*, vol. 42, pp. 683–712

Hsu, Elisabeth (2008) 'Medicine as business: Chinese medicine in Tanzania', in Alden, C., Large, D. and Soares de Oliveira, Ricardo (eds) *China Returns to Africa: A Rising Power and a Continent Embrace*, London, Hurst and Company

Illiffe, John (1998) *East African Doctors: A History of the Modern Profession*, Cambridge, Cambridge University Press

Kirkbride, P.S., Tany, S. and Westwood, R. (1991) 'Chinese conflict preferences and negotiating behaviour: Chinese and psychological influence', *Organization Studies*, vol. 12, no. 3, pp. 365–86

Kragelund, P., (2008) *Knocking on a Wide-Open Door: Chinese Investments in Africa*, Copenhagen, Danish Institute for International Studies

Mathew, Joe (2009) 'Kenyan cloud over India's pharma exports to Africa', *Business Standard*, 11 January, http://www.business-standard.com/india/news/kenyan-cloud-over-india8217s-pharma-exports-to-africa/345803/, accessed 15 February 2009.

McCormick, Dorothy (1997) 'Industrial district or garment ghetto? Nairobi's mini-manufacturers', in Van Dijk, M.P. and Rabellotii R. (eds) *Enterprise Clusters and Networks in Developing Countries*, London, Frank Cass

Mpundu, Mildred (2005) 'The last Zambian textile factories?', Panos, 14 December, http://www.panos.org.uk/?lid=19757, accessed 8 October 2007

Mohan, Giles (2009) 'Chinese migrants in Africa as new agents of development? An analytical framework', *European Journal of Development Research*, vol. 24

Mung, M.E. (2008) 'Chinese migration and China's foreign policy in Africa', *Journal of Overseas Chinese*, vol. 4, pp. 91–109

Reddy, Mrinalini (2007) 'Indian return to Africa', Immigration Here and There Project, Evanston, Northwestern University Medill School of Journalism

Teixeira, Ana (1998) 'Entrepreneurs of the Chinese community in Portugal', in Benton, G. and Pieke, F.N. (eds) *The Chinese in Europe*, London, Macmillian

The Times of Zambia (2004) 'Chipata Cotton Company woos more growers', 16 June, p. 5

United Nations Conference on Trade and Development (UNCTAD) (2007) *Asian Foreign Direct Investment in Africa: Towards a New Era of Cooperation among Developing Countries*, Geneva, UNCTAD

Wang, Tina (2009) 'China to deploy more capital abroad' 9 June, http://www.forbes.com/2009/06/09/china-foreignlending-markets-economy-investment.html, accessed 11 June 2009

6

Diaspora, political economy and India's relations with Kenya

Gerard McCann

In late March 2010, Bharti Airtel, one of India's corporate tele-communications giants, announced the successful completion of a multi-billion dollar deal that would see it take control of the African operations of Kuwaiti firm Zain in some 13 countries. The deal's very fruition, following repeated failures of both Bharti and Reliance Industries to merge with South Africa's MTN since 2008, seemed to herald a new potency of Indian firms to diversify their various 'safaris' in Africa (*India Today* 2010).

The sheer scale of the deal (reported to be worth $10.7 billion) in one of Africa's most dynamic economic sectors briefly captured the imagination of the media in India and many parts of Africa, as well as the business sections of western newspapers. The agreement marked the second largest foreign buyout by an Indian company after Tata's $13.6-billion acquisition of Anglo-Dutch steel maker Corus in 2007. The Bharti-Zain deal made clear that, as never before, Africa was now very much in India's economic crosshairs.

The headquarters of Bharti's African operations were to be located in Nairobi, a convenient investment hub that would act as a gateway to the eastern African region (*Daily Nation* 2010). Bharti flying its colours in Kenya's capital was not the first such act by an Indian firm. In 2008 Essar, another major Indian conglomerate, inaugurated Kenya's fourth mobile phone network after a $500 million injection the previous year (*International Herald Tribune* 2008). In July 2009, Essar also acquired a 50 per cent share in Kenya Petroleum Refineries, the sole oil refinery in eastern Africa.

As is widely known these recent relations are preceded by much deeper economic, political and cultural connections between India and East Africa; bonds which have existed for decades, if not centuries, through historic South Asian 'diasporic' communities. Not surprisingly then, perceptions of contemporary relations between India and nations of East Africa have been inflected by this heritage of connectivity. This chapter suggests that assumptions made about such linkages are somewhat problematic. Like a number of non-western actors, Indian investors are becoming increasingly prominent in Kenya. Yet few are utilising India's new-found conviviality with its diaspora to lubricate their designs. In fact, East African Asian networks could provide obstacles to India–Africa partnership in the context of Kenya's historically ethnicised political economy and ambivalent diasporic relations with post-colonial India.

India–Africa relations: going 'above the radar'

Despite substantial 21st century transitions in the nature of India–Africa relations (see Mawdsley and McCann 2010, and Part 1 of this book), reporting on this dynamism has been somewhat lethargic, except perhaps in the columns of India's business pages. Only rarely, and then often according to certain well-worn tropes, have these transactions been situated within India's broader endeavours in Africa and the world.

It is often the spectre of China, in the context of India's historical regional competition with Beijing, that has occasioned public writing on the strategic consequences of Sino-Indian competition in Africa, whether in reference to oil concessions or complicity in supposed 'land grabs' in Africa (*Hindustan Times* 2009). In the past few years, a greater quantum of writing has emerged from Indian universities and think-tanks. Nevertheless, like much of the media output, the reflection has tended to align with older discourses about 'third worldist' Indo-African solidarities. The latest volley of investment, trade and diplomacy is often viewed as the most recent avatar of a linear historical friendship under the new moniker of 'South–South cooperation', a discourse that can be repeatedly found in the pages of the re-incarnated *Africa Quarterly*, to name but one notable Indian forum.

The Bharti-Zain deal did, however, seem to reinforce recognition that such historical relations were being conditioned by the commercial imperatives that had transformed India since liberalisation and were now energising extroverted private sector activity and even government policy. The two are indeed linked, with the Indian state coming to act as a kind of steward for Indian businesses with African ambitions, especially through the Confederation of Indian Industry (CII).

Since 2002, the CII has teamed up with India's Export-Import (Exim) Bank to arrange a series of India–Africa business conclaves, events which provided the basis for the more high-profile India–Africa Forum Summit of April 2008. The concerns of market and resource seeking, which were central to these gatherings, marked new directions in the India–Africa partnership. Yet it is the rhetoric of historical continuity that colours the vast majority of analytical examinations.

Naturally, historical relations (from Nehru's support of African nationalism to solidarities within the Non-Aligned Movement) have important impacts in framing and forming contemporary relations. There is a genuine tale of long-standing Indo-African friendship, which is celebrated in the increasingly frequent gatherings of African and Indian diplomats and business delegations on both sides of the Indian Ocean. It is also apparent, though, that such declarations of conviviality are often articulated according to certain standard narratives, relating an arguably teleological progression from Indian Ocean trading cosmopolitanism to today's 'partnership for mutual benefit' through Gandhian struggle against oppression in South Africa and Nehruvian lobbying for African freedom.

It seems that laudatory rhetoric about historical friendship, at times, obscures tensions between various African and Indian actors. India's African policies have undergone an undoubted sea change in the 21st century. We might characterise this as a transition from the anti-colonial and third worldist political solidarities of old, to relations built more assiduously on commercial foundations (although informed by older notions of 'South–South cooperation'). The Bharti-Zain deal strikingly demonstrates the thrust of this evolution, change that needs to be disaggregated in terms of its challenges as well as its opportunities.

However, a more critical stance is required to unpack the various strands of engagement. Criticism has only very tentatively been forthcoming in India's vibrant media, for example in the premier source of public critique, *Economic and Political Weekly*. In December 2009, an editorial entitled 'The government of India's economic relations with Africa are increasingly becoming exploitative' (EPW 2009) went some way to framing more problematic analyses. Other contributors posed similar questions in broader contexts, asking whether India's role as an emerging donor might potentially erode goodwill with developing world partners and potentially open up India to charges of hypocrisy, given its critiques of its own donors (EPW 2003; Chanana 2009; Mawdsley 2010).

Such self-reflection in reference to India's activities in Africa has been rare thus far, with internationalist attention devoted more to India's relations with the US (particularly after the 2008 nuclear deal), the European Union, China and South Asian neighbours, or to India's leadership of developing world collectives within the WTO or G77 for instance.

As it stands, much of the existing literature on India–Africa is characterised by comfortable assumptions about India's inherently progressive or benevolent agendas in Africa, notably in lauding India's own developmental experience. Such emphasis is often worthwhile. The lessons learned during India's 'green revolution' from the 1960s, its ICT adroitness, and cheap pharmaceutical production are frequently cited nodes of potential productive cooperation with Africans. Time will tell whether such endeavours can bear fruit, but there is cause for hope.

With a few notable exceptions, such as Gupta (1970), much output stresses such historical and contemporary nodes of productivity (and their location within older modes of cooperation), but without sufficiently raising issues of potential discord. In Chapter 10 of this volume, by contrast, Emma Mawdsley demonstrates that the rituals and rhetoric of Indian development cooperation 'euphemise' aspects of India's activities in Africa. These are concealed by the rhetoric of 'win-win' and historic partnerships voiced by both Indian and African elites forging commercial deals in the oilfields of Angola, the copper mines of Zambia and the markets of Ethiopia.

As Clapham (2008) argues, foreign powers engaging with African societies face resilience to, and incorporation of, their external influences. Like others before them, Asian powers will necessarily have to broadly conform to long-established patterns of Africa's external engagement rather than fundamentally transform them. Despite unique histories of friendship, the realities of local political risk or ethnicised accumulative structures – whether in oilfields of the Niger Delta or boardrooms of Nairobi – will affect the nature and success of neoliberal relations. African contexts matter. Such realities could stymie rhetoric of India–Africa partnership for mutual benefit in the long term, and it is here that more scrutiny must be placed on India, as it has been so copiously for China.

Indeed, Indian officials and a number of commentators have been at pains to emphasise the inherent disparities between India's relationship with Africa and that of China. Despite obvious historical and contemporary differences in the modes of India's and China's relative African engagements, such loaded 'othering' does not always stand up to scrutiny, for example in Sudan's hydrocarbon sector. India has been 'below the radar' (Mawdsley and McCann 2010) and in China's 'slipstream' (Carmody, Chapter 2 in this volume) in Africa, a low profile that has served it well as its footprint grows and a range of global and local stakeholders debate the human rights and developmental consequences of Asian investment.

More critical treatments of India–Africa relations in the 21st century are thus overdue. Above all, this will emerge from greater African participation in the debates. Some writing has focused on African perspectives on Chinese investment (Manji and Marks 2007; Baah and Jauch 2009), and it's to be hoped that similar works might emerge in reference to a wider range of rising powers, India included.

It is, of course, unsurprising that China has been the initial subject of this reflection as it is enormous and varied Chinese investment that is so obviously transforming a plethora of African landscapes. During fieldwork in Nairobi in 2009, most interviews conducted by the author with Kenyan elites about India in Africa soon turned to China. Yet, this is changing slowly, and a number of African commentators are pointing to the paramount importance of Africans themselves in shaping a wider range of

Africa–Asia interactions in the 21st century (Cheru and Obi 2010). A recent Chatham House report highlighted the impressive abilities of Angolan leaders to shape engagement with Asian state oil firms (Vines et al 2009), while Simona Vittorini and David Harris (Chapter 12 in this volume) signpost the capacity of the administration of Ellen Johnson-Sirleaf in Liberia to renegotiate a disadvantageous iron ore deal with a major Indian-origin company.

Further such studies, below the panoramic analyses that have characterised the India–Africa studies (see Introduction this volume), can highlight the problems (as well as the complementarities) in India–Africa relations, and, most importantly, elevate cognisance of African agency in the so-called 'new scramble for Africa'.

Problematising India–Kenya historical relations

In putting India 'above the radar' in Africa, the remainder of this chapter focuses on India's relations with Kenya – a nation with which India has seemingly had close links because of the historic presence of South Asian communities in the region and Nehruvian support for African liberation. The following sections do not, however, tread the same terrain as vibrant older literatures celebrating Indian support for African freedom (see INC 1976; Reddy 1987; Chhabra 1989) or the better-known body of work describing ancient Indian Ocean cosmopolitanism and the legitimate place of South Asians within African polities (see *AwaaZ* magazine; Patel and Rajan, Chapter 8 in this volume). It aims to present a brief, critical interpretation of India–Kenya relations in the 21st century, based on literature reviews and a number of interviews conducted in early 2009 with 'Kenyan Asian' businesspersons, African political elites and various diplomats.

The chapter is informed by the older histories of solidarities and Indian Ocean connectivity. Nevertheless, it holds that the politics of India's changing post-colonial relations with its diaspora in Africa, as well as tense Afro-Asian race relations within Kenya itself, paint a different picture to intuitive notions that India's historic relations with East Africa provide it with a headstart in its renewed regional ambitions. Moreover, as the chapter shows, the context of Kenya's elite political sphere is seminal in shaping liaisons and not always to India's advantage as a host of cash-rich Asian powers, devoid of acrimonious historical baggage, knock on the door.

India's links to East Africa are centuries old. Generations of western Indian groups, like a wide range of communities on the Indian Ocean littorals, utilised the monsoon winds in their peripatetic trading lives. Many settled in East Africa, initially on the Swahili coast, and later 'up-country' as the economic opportunities of British colonial rule and infrastructure proliferated, and restrictive imperial policies of mobility territorialised the Indian Ocean arena and transformed its economic character.

Linkages between India and Africa were not severed, but rather re-shaped with kin and pilgrimage networks continuing to forge connections within new imperial contexts. This cultural traffic was supplemented by political links, with Indian agitators in eastern and southern Africa appealing, with mixed success, to the Indian National Congress (as well as British rulers in India, Africa and London) for political rights relative to various groups of white settlers.

Such concerns are lauded in the context of renewed contemporary India–Africa relations, yet it is also on the example of Indian independence for aspirant African leaders, and the personality of then Prime Minister Jawaharlal Nehru, that rhetorical emphasis has been particularly laid. Nehru, and his emissary to East Africa in the 1950s, Apa Pant, were vocal in their support for Kenyan nationalism (if not the violence of Mau Mau – a contested part of the Kenyan independence narrative in any case). A more nuanced picture of Nehru and Pant's views (especially on multiracialism in 1950s Kenya) might be unpicked, but there was respect for India's leadership and achievement in many African circles. Nehru even took a principled stand on South Asian diaspora in Africa, instructing non-resident Indians that their loyalties should lie with their African homelands, placing African nationalist concerns above those of ethnic Indians.

This dominant tale of Indo-African anti-colonial solidarity and its repercussions on today's partnership are frequently stressed. Moreover, historical diasporic linkages between the two regions have been somewhat intuitively interpreted as providing India with an established node of linkage, or as a promotional device, in its African relations in general. Such impressions are strengthened as India has re-engaged its diaspora since the late 1990s, when the election of the Bharatiya Janata Party led to a policy shift toward Indians in the diaspora in order to attract capital from overseas (and bolster support for Hindu nationalism). This engagement initially focused on Indian communities in the West and Gulf region, but in recent years its remit has come to extend to Africa. This was a reversal of Nehruvian diasporic dissociation, but to assume this has automatically created or buttressed avenues of liaison in Africa is somewhat ahistorical.

Indeed, the policies of distance toward East Africa's 'Asians' implemented by Nehru and his successors created ambivalence (even feelings of abandonment) towards India in Kenyan, Tanzanian and Ugandan South Asian-origin communities. This has resulted in the transnational gaze of many East African Asians being cast to Britain and North America, rather than back to their ancestral homeland, while others have pledged their loyalty to their African homelands without reserve.

Furthermore, although one strand of the India–East Africa story is of anti-colonial brotherhood, another is linked to the suspicion and hostility that some Africans of Indian origin have confronted – most violently and dramatically expressed by Idi Amin in Uganda in 1972. We might argue that a fractious history of colonial and post-colonial race relations coloured many Kenyan leaders' impressions of India, despite the rhetoric of solidarity emanating from New Delhi, particularly when African freedom had been achieved and India's relevance as a pioneer of liberation diminished.

It is well known that many popular African impressions of local 'Asians' (as Kenyans of South Asian origin were simplistically known) were fundamentally homogenising, with almost no disaggregation of diverse South Asian regional, religious or caste origins for instance. Many, if not most, African impressions dwelt on sentiments of Asian exploitation rather than friendship (Theroux 1967; Furedi 1974). This tension, which exists to some extent today, has deep structural roots based on the position of Asians (especially as traders) within the colonial economy, and the sites of Indo-African contact that this created. African antipathy was not much assuaged by the key organisational roles of a few 'Kenyan Asians' in anti-colonial protest – much to the chagrin of the greater number who celebrated this heritage.

Kenya's relations with India were partially viewed through the lens of this localised 'Asian question', especially as even many elite Kenyans falsely believed local Asians to have closer links to India than existed (despite Nehru's proclamations). Such tensions and conflations were manifested during the 1962 Sino-Indian War, when a bizarre public spat saw a number of Kenya African National Union (KANU) leaders openly supporting China (despite profound suspicion of communism within the party), and prominent Asian party members defending India, but asserting their paramount local identity.

Moreover, at the height of anti-Asianism in 1968, B.R. Bhagat, the then India minister of external affairs, was denied an audience with Kenyatta on the grounds that India was interfering with Kenyan affairs (*Daily Nation* 1968). Such events, contingent on changing political moods in Kenya and India, provide more complicated pictures of historical India–Kenya relations than are often expounded. It is this heritage that is to be explored in light of India's renewed 21st century interest in East Africa.

Contemporary Indian investment and the political economy of Kenya

Kenya provides an important African investment destination for India. As the Bharti and Essar telecommunications examples demonstrate, Kenya's positional and infrastructural advantages provide a gateway to markets in the eastern African region, as well as a sizeable set of markets nationally. Today, India's contemporary activities in Kenya reflect private sector market-seeking, characteristic of Indian forays in a range of non-resource-rich African nations. This prominence of capital at the frontier of India–Kenya relations has some historical continuities, although capital was far more state-directed before India's liberalisation in 1991. A very small amount of investment was aimed at the local diaspora, for example through the Bank of Baroda, but the majority of these meagre flows in the 1960s through to the 1980s aimed to capture local manufacturing markets (consider Birla's famous and controversial formation of Pan-Paper, East Africa's biggest paper manufacturer).

International trade relations and a certain eastern African bias to the Indian Technical and Economic Cooperation (ITEC) programme, also forged certain relations from the 1960s. Despite such activity, however, India's early post-colonial South Asian foreign policy introversion, economic autarky and diasporic dissociation actually dictated weak de facto Indian linkages to East Africa, except in rhetorical, kinship and cultural senses. Kenya's own foreign policy priorities (with a certain focus on western business and western donor development assistance under Kenyatta and Moi respectively), in addition to tense local Afro-Asian relations, compounded India–Kenya aloofness. India's African energies from the 1960s to the 1990s were in fact devoted principally to international lobbying against the injustices of apartheid in the global multilateral arena, rather than manifested in East Africa.

Economic relations today have been rejuvenated, with business actors as the vanguard. Indian corporations have begun to penetrate a range of Kenyan markets from Essar's and Bharti challenges to the Safaricom telecommunications behemoth to Tata's soda ash production in Lake Magadi, Sanghi's cement factory in West Pokot or Karaturi Networks floriculture holdings on Lake Naivasha. Yet, few of these firms are utilising the diasporic linkages ostensibly binding India and East Africa together. Indeed, we see that the heritage of local race relations could in fact provide Indian firms with potential obstacles, hence a disinclination to utilise such connections. This is for several intertwined reasons in the context of Kenya's historically 'ethnicised' political economy and the foreign investment preferences apparent in Kenya's ethnically fragmented political sphere.

The ethnicisation of Kenya's political economy (built on its colonial predecessor and post-war developmentalist foundations) gained momentum immediately after Kenyan independence with Jomo Kenyatta accused of patronising his Kikuyu support base with land and advantage in the industrialising economy. Kenyatta's presidential successor, Daniel arap Moi, despite early rhetoric to the contrary, set about dismantling Kikuyu dominance to shore up his own political base (especially following the 1982 coup attempt) and boost material opportunities. In this transition, Moi skilfully mobilised certain Kenyan Asian (and some Indian) capitalists to his ends within a political economy in which Asians and emergent Kikuyu capitalists sat uneasily together.

For example, Kenyatta had attempted to protect 'indigenous' (largely Kikuyu) business concerns from competitors by forcing Asians out of trade in certain commodities and into manufacturing. Given the relative paucity of non-Kikuyu capital in the same environments as elite Kikuyu business, it seemed that utilisation of an historically unpopular, but economically astute, minority (Asians) provided Moi with a means for personal aggrandisement and ostracised certain competitors, while cleverly diverting blame for economic failure and graft from himself and his cadres.

Detailed research is overdue on the minutiae of these slippery and controversial themes. Given the continued salience of such history to contemporary accumulation and electioneering, as well as the methodological difficulties in identifying evidence on these opaque machinations, such research might prove highly problematic. Nevertheless in general senses, Kenyan Asians certainly became typecast as close to Moi, and were perceived to impede the advance of Kikuyu capital in the 1980s–90s.

The fall of KANU in 2002 altered the situation, with Kikuyu capital resurgent under the National Rainbow Coalition (Narc) and Party of National Unity (PNU) to varying degrees (Wrong 2009). Many Kikuyu elites have not forgotten the enforced competition with Asian entrepreneurs under Moi and it may be that President Mwai Kibaki and his allies have a posture to India conditioned in some ways by the highly competitive position of historical Asian vis-à-vis Kikuyu capital, and given the range of new foreign actors with economic ambitions in Kenya.

The high-profile complicity of a number of Asians such as Kamlesh Pattni and Ajay Shah to Moi's kleptocracy in the 1990s compounded (unfair and essentialised) historical impressions of Asian greed. This is not to say that Asians were exclusively blamed for graft in Kenya, merely that their organisational centrality became unfairly exaggerated in the context of historical antipathy.

Within today's ethnically divisive elite sphere, certain continuities might be identified. Raila Odinga, the prime minister and leader of one branch of the coalition government formed in 2008, is perceived to be close to a number of Kenyan Asians for instance.

This impression was no doubt buttressed by the presence of Odinga and several Orange Democratic Movement (ODM) ministers at the Vibrant Gujarat Global Investors Summit in January 2009. Asians had made contributions to the political ventures of Oginga Odinga, Raila's father, whose relations with Kenyatta became increasingly acrimonious in the mid- to late 1960s. The fact that these older ethnicised issues of competition and collaboration are entering into ODM/PNU rancour (whether accurately or not) could well affect investment from Asian nations.

Given the homogenising imperatives of racial conceptualisation in Kenya, informants indicated that the fallout from this political economy of competition might partially affect perceptions of agents from India too, despite the very localised nature of the acrimony. There is a surprising conflation of older Kenyan Asian business with new Indian concerns even among elite Kenyans, as evidenced in numerous interviews. This negative posture of Kikuyu and other Kenyan capitalists to Asians might transfer to India itself – despite distant de facto links between India and its diaspora in Africa – and impact India's competitive abilities relative to other suitors.

It is clear that ethnic divisions are shaping Kenya's foreign investment climate. Significant streams of capital from China, North Africa and the Middle East have flowed into Kenya (across a range of projects) and allegedly into the coffers of PNU leaders, who have cultivated relations with Libyan, Qatari, Chinese and other capitalists and diplomats.

Prime Minister Odinga even publicly flagged such bias in the avenues of foreign investment. In April 2009, the presidents of Turkey and Iran visited Kenya, during which time economic agreements and memoranda of understanding were passed. Such deals occurred at Kibaki's State House in the absence of Odinga, despite the fact he is leader of one branch of the coalition (*Sunday Nation* 2009). Relations with a range of rising powers in recent years are thus situated within long-standing elite-negotiated and personalised mechanisms of governance and accumulation in Kenya, which will not be fundamentally transformed by Asian investment.

Dynamic Kenyan association with China and certain Middle Eastern countries can be placed against tense historical relations between black Kenyans and Kenyan Asians, their effects on perceptions of India, and the historically aloof relations between Kenya and the Indian state described above. Moreover, India's ambitions in Kenya are being pressed through large firms, whose de facto concern with older diasporic and Afro-Indian solidarities are slight, despite strands of rhetoric (principally articulated by diplomats rather than CEOs) to the contrary.

India's relative positioning within Kenyan investment circuits is informed by historical dynamics, but it is also crucially related to the mechanics of politico-corporate liaison within Kenya's ethnicised contemporary polity. The methods of large deal-making in Kenya (as in a number of African states) are often conducted in markedly opaque, clandestine and extremely elite state-to-state (and face to face) arenas, such as State House. The business elite and political mandarins are closely linked, and often one and the same. India's domestic polity and economic profile render access to these controversial avenues of economic advantage sometimes problematic relative to other powers.

Despite a degree of state stewardship for business relations (through the CII or the High Commission), India's largely private sector-led Africa initiatives (and therefore responsibility to shareholders), as well as its diplomatic abilities, have consequences within African contexts. This is often telling relative to state-led corporate bids from China or Middle Eastern sovereign wealth funds, which frequently enjoy higher capital intensity and links to a partisan Kenyan politico-business elite.

These newer actors have, in short, quickly developed more statist access-led styles to a tranche of influential Kenyan decision makers, which is more effective within the existing contexts of local rentier statehood. The re-ascendance of Kikuyu capital under Kibaki, and the willingness of Libya and China to create convivial relations with PNU leaders particularly, exacerbates India's relative disadvantages in the context of Kenya's historical political economy.

The character of the Indian state, notably its admirably democratic foundations, also render similar liaisons to those forged between some African elites and China or the UAE often impossible or undesirable to create. Yet, there is also a degree of lethargy in India's diplomatic architecture. For one, Kenya is a low priority in India's renewed diasporic re-engagement, certainly relative to

South Africa. Furthermore, it was apparent in several visits to the Indian High Commission in 2009 that India's official mission in Kenya appears to be a poor conduit of state-to-state relations, and an ineffective propagator of the economic imperatives that increasingly characterise India's new African initiatives. This is in marked contrast to the Chinese Embassy.

It is argued that the Indian High Commission has been hitherto driven by personalities articulating concepts of traditional South–South cooperation, rather than institutionally energised by the economic ambitions that preoccupy a younger generation of New Delhi technocrats. This is slowly changing, although Nairobi lags far behind sister missions in Johannesburg, Dakar and even Addis Ababa. These cities each now boast a branch of India's Exim Bank, an increasingly influential institution in moulding India's 21st century African policies.

Conclusions

The arguments outlined above do not imply that Indian businesses cannot compete, or that they are excluded from the boons of Kenyan ventures. Bharti and Essar demonstrate that. Indeed, Essar's bid to win a stake in the Kenyan Petroleum Refineries in 2009 saw them eventually beat off Libya's Tamoil (which had initially enjoyed Kenyan governmental support in the joint venture), because local energy crises and a major oil scandal in Kenya dictated pressure for more transparent and efficient official deal-making.

There are varied African historical and contemporary factors that influence the ability of certain Indian and indeed all actors to win contracts. These issues also influence the inclination to invest in Kenya in the first place, when a range of African states offer lucrative markets and resources. In 2008, for example, India became the largest foreign investor Ethiopia, another regional powerhouse. In any case, contrary to much assumed knowledge, those Indian firms that are courting Kenyan partners, are not utilising Kenyan Asian networks to garner competitive advantage, gather local intelligence or lubricate the wheels of their economic activities. For one, there are often few cultural links between Gujarati or Punjabi-origin Kenyans and new Indian capital from other parts of the subcontinent, an aloofness compounded by post-colonial diasporic estrangement.

More importantly, the aforementioned statist biases of much corporate liaison in Kenya dictate that many local Kenyan Asians (other than one or two exceptional individuals) are poor conduits to local power-brokers, because Asians have been conspicuously distanced from the post-colonial Kenyan state. It is perhaps for this reason, above all, that few Indian firms have utilised such an apparently intuitive instrumental asset as the diaspora in Africa.

Following Indian liberalisation in the 1990s and the belated excursions of Indian companies into the West and other parts of Asia, Africa is now also very much a new horizon of opportunity. This short chapter has raised complications to intuitive narratives of the continuities of historic and contemporary India–Africa engagement. A fractious history of race relations in Kenya, and the cynosure of African homogenisation of Asians within an ethnicised post-colonial political economy, might well affect certain Indian endeavours, certainly as a range of capital-rich foreign suitors devoid of such historical baggage forge their place within Kenya's particular political economy.

This optic contradicts much official rhetoric and a broader literature arguing that diasporic networks facilitate entrepreneurship in creating avenues of local liaison and thereby establishing globally competitive transnational production networks.

South Asian diasporic communities, long-resident in East African polities, estranged from post-colonial India and asserting paramount local allegiances, actually appear to be remaining aloof from incoming Indian capital. Such realities might frustrate, rather than facilitate, what one report has speculated might be a 'Tatafication of Africa' as a result of Indian corporate engagement (Centre for Knowledge Societies 2008). That said, an international capitalist class, Indians included, has been adept at adapting to various opportunities in Africa. It is a story that will fascinate for decades to come in terms of geopolitical transition, but, more crucially, for equitable development.

Above all, this chapter aims to show that African contexts matter. Asia-African relations in the 21st century depend on ambition and ability on the part of various Asian actors, but also the particulars of African locales. Patey has shown how Sudanese political will to diversify its investment base away from China was crucial in opening the door to Indian oil firms (Patey, Chapter 9 in this volume). Kenya's historical political economy and the fissures of its elites are also conditioning capital inflows (and their consequences, for better or worse). President Kibaki has been openly charged with 'selling' Kenya to China, India, Libya, and even Iran, by ODM opponents. The competitive interest of a range of new suitors has allowed African leaders, not least in Kenya as this paper implies, unprecedented choice in international negotiations. The danger, however, is that these new liaisons can reify divisive socio-political conflicts in which many African nations are mired. This appears to be pertinent to Kenya where strains within the elite political sphere are being somewhat exacerbated by foreign investment, particularly from China and the Arab world.

References

Baah, A.Y. and Jauch, H. (2009) *Chinese Investments in Africa: A Labour Perspective*, Windhoek, African Labour Research Network

Carmody, P. (2011) 'India and the "Asian Drivers" in Africa', in Mawdsely, E. and McCann, G. (eds) *India in Africa; Changing Geographies of Power*, Oxford, Pambazuka Press

Centre for Knowledge Societies (CKS) (2008) *Emerging Economy Report*, New Delhi, CKS

Chanana, D. (2009) 'India as an emerging donor', *Economic and Political Weekly*, vol. 44, no. 12

Chhabra, H.S. (1989) *Nehru and Resurgent Africa*, New Delhi, Kalinga Publications

Cheru, F. and Obi, C. (eds) (2010) *The Rise of India and China in Africa*, London and Uppsala, Zed Books and The Nordic Africa Institute

Clapham, C. (2008) 'Fitting China in' in Alden, C., Large, D. & Soares de Oliveira, R. (eds) *China Returns to Africa*, London, Hurst

Daily Nation (1968), 'Indian Minister denied audience', 27 March

—— (2009) 'Foreign affairs ministry to open new diplomatic stations', 28 July

—— (2010) 'Bharti African HQs to be set up in Nairobi', 1 April

Economic and Political Weekly (EPW) (2003) 'Aid: old morality and new realities', 14 June

—— (2009) Editorial: 'India in Africa. The government of India's economic relations with Africa are increasingly becoming exploitative', 19 December

Furedi, F. (1974) 'The development of anti-Asian opinion among Africans in Nakuru District', *African Affairs*, vol. 73, no. 292, pp. 347–58

Harris, D. and Vittorini, S. (2011) 'India goes over to the other side: Indo-West African relations in the 21st century', in Mawdsley, E. and McCann, G. (eds) *India in Africa: Changing Geographies of Power*, Oxford, Pambazuka Press

Hindustan Times (2009) 'India joins race for land in Africa, China way ahead', 4 May

India Today (2010) 'The African safari', 1 April

Indian National Congress (1976) *India and the African Liberation Struggle*, New Delhi, Indian National Congress

International Herald Tribune (IHT) (2008) 'Indian company to invest $500 million in Kenya', 21 August

Gupta, A. (1968) 'Assessing the reality in Africa: an Indian point of view' *Economic and Political Weekly*, vol. 3, no. 18, 4 May

—— (1970) 'A note on Indian attitudes to Africa', African Affairs, vol. 69, no. 275, pp. 170–8

Manji, F. and Marks, S. (eds) (2007) *African Perspectives on China in Africa*, Oxford, Fahamu

Mawdsley, E. (2010) 'The non-DAC donors and the changing landscape of foreign aid: the (in)significance of India's development cooperation with Kenya', *Journal of Eastern African Studies*, vol. 4, no. 2, pp. 361–79

Mawdsley, E. (2011) 'The rhetorics and rituals of 'non-western' development cooperation: notes on India and Africa', in Mawdsley, E. and McCann, G. (eds) *India in Africa: Changing Geographies of Power*, Oxford, Pambazuka Press

Mawdsley, E. and McCann, G. (2010) 'The elephant in the corner? Reviewing India–Africa relations in the new millennium', *Geography Compass*, vol. 4, no. 2, pp. 81–93

Patel, Z. and Rajan, Z. (2011) '*AwaaZ*: A personal and collective journey', in Mawdsley, E. and McCann, G. (eds) *India in Africa: Changing Geographies of Power*, Oxford, Pambazuka Press

Patey, L. (2011). 'Fragile fortunes: India's oil venture into war-torn Sudan', in Mawdsley, E. and McCann, G. (eds) *India in Africa: Changing Geographies of Power*, Oxford, Pambazuka Press

Reddy, E.S. (1987) *Struggle for Freedom in Southern Africa: Its International Significance*, New Delhi, Mainstream

Sunday Nation (2009) 'Raila: I am not willing to take insults and acts of defiance from PNU', 12 April

Theroux, P. (1967) 'Hating the Asians', *Transition*, vol. 7, no. 33, pp. 46–51

Vines, A., Wong, L., Weimer, M. and Campos, I. (2009) *Thirst for African Oil: Asian National Oil Companies in Nigeria and Angola*, London, Chatham House

Wrong, M. (2009) *It's Our Turn to Eat: The Story of a Kenyan Whistle Blower*, London, Fourth Estate

7

Offshore healthcare management: medical tourism between Kenya, Tanzania and India

Renu Modi

Introduction

The term medical tourism is used in common parlance to describe the phenomenon of foreign patients seeking healthcare in another country at better equipped hospitals and/or at rates comparatively cheaper than in their home countries. India has been a destination country for some time. For example, the Chennai-based Apollo group of hospitals was one of the first to receive international patients, mainly people from the United Kingdom seeking cataract surgery in the early 1990s at a time when the British healthcare sector was under pressure because of funding and staff constraints. The inflow from the UK was followed by individuals from other European countries, the United States, Middle East, South East Asia, and later from the African continent. A particularly strong demand comes from the 20 million strong Indian diaspora scattered across the globe.

This chapter deals with medical tourism from Africa, specifically from Kenya and Tanzania, to Indian hospitals particularly in the city of Mumbai. It also comments on the growing relationship emerging between private healthcare providers in India and East Africa, as well as Indian government support for health initiatives. We can understand this evolving industry in the current context of globalisation and liberalisation, which has impacted on all the sectors of the Indian economy.

India is emerging as a global healthcare provider because of its ability to offer world-class expertise at developing world costs. There has been a proliferation of new healthcare facilities at private centres of medical excellence in Mumbai specifically. High-class medical infrastructure facilities, coupled with improved and cheaper air connections and easy access to visa facilities, are some of the factors that have contributed to the emerging scenario.

Methodology

This chapter is based on primary and secondary sources. The primary data are derived from interviews conducted with 52 African patients admitted to various hospitals in Mumbai between March and June 2008. Of these only four patients were of Asian origin, while 48 were black Africans – 41 from the East African countries of Kenya and Tanzania. The rest were from Ghana, Burundi and Democratic Republic of Congo (DRC). In this sample, 35 were men, seven were children below the age of 18 and 10 were women.

This research focused on black Africans because they were easily identified as Africans by the hospital staff. The researcher was informed that several Asian Africans, mainly Gujaratis, went for treatment to the hospitals in Ahmadabad and other cities in Gujarat because they had family members there.

Interviews were conducted among African patients in four leading hospitals in the city, namely the Hinduja Medical Research Centre, Wockhardt Hospital, Prince Aly Khan Hospital, and the Asian Heart Research Institute. African medical tourists also visit other hospitals in the city such as Jaslok, Tata Memorial, Saifee and Breach Candy Hospitals in addition to smaller private clinics and diagnostic centres. The author also made enquiries at several leading dental clinics, cosmetologists and spas, Ayurvedic centres and yoga institutes in the city and was informed that most of the clientele for dental treatment, body contouring, liposuction and stress management were from Europe, North America and the Middle East.

It became clear that the majority of the African patients (including patients of Indian origin) seek treatment in India for mainly medical ailments that have not been diagnosed accurately in their country of origin or for severe medical conditions, for which locally there is inadequate expertise and lack of high technology facilities.

Information was gathered through semi-structured interviews to explore the pattern of flows of African patients to Indian hospitals, namely their countries of origin, reason for seeking medical treatment, the system of referrals, the success rate/satisfaction of treatment, the costs involved, how they raised funds for treatment and the system insurance cover. Interviews were also conducted in Africa with 12 patients from Kenya and Tanzania who had returned and were willing to share information about the follow-up mechanism of check ups and investigations once back in their home countries.

I faced several constraints in the course of the interviews as would be expected when dealing with patients who are seriously ill. These included ethical concerns about interviewing vulnerable people, the busy and erratic schedules of doctors and caregivers, or their unwillingness to talk about this issue. I also tried to get access to data on the number of African patients disembarking at Mumbai international airport with a medical visa. However, the customs officials were reluctant to provide this information and also stated that there was an absence of country-wide disaggregated data on Africans as such or for those coming in for medical treatment.

Another problematic issue was the term medical tourism, which was not familiar to a number of respondents. They tended to interpret it literally and were initially puzzled by (and disapproving of) its use. 'Tourism in the conventional sense conveys fun, sightseeing and holiday. Chemotherapy in India is certainly not my idea of tourism', stated a senior oncologist at a hospital in Mumbai. For this reason, the author stopped using the term in interviews, and referred instead to 'offshore health management'. Since there is relatively little published secondary literature available on this specific subject, the author relied on other sources, such as newspaper articles in leading Tanzanian and Kenyan dailies, and online resources such as Pambazuka News, World Bank development reports and websites of the ministries of health in Kenya and Tanzania or the African Union.

The paper is divided into three main parts. The first deals with the health contexts of Kenya and Tanzania. The second analyses the Indian context and the reasons why it is a preferred destination for many African patients. The third, concluding section highlights the efforts taken on the continent to improve the state of public health delivery and augment existing medical facilities.

Private and public health provision in Tanzania and Kenya

The two East African countries of Kenya and Tanzania have a population of 37.5 million and 40.4 million respectively (World Bank 2008a, 2008b). Healthcare is organised in a pyramid structure in both countries, with government-run dispensaries forming the broad base of the medical system and comprising the first point of contact, principally for simple ailments. At the higher levels of public provision there are health centres, sub-district hospitals and provincial hospitals, which are referral points for district hospitals. The more complicated cases are sent to the national referral hospitals. Alongside this formal system is a substantial system of 'traditional' healthcare.

Healthcare in these two neighbouring countries has in theory laid emphasis on primary healthcare at affordable rates, making them pioneers in sub-Saharan Africa. The distribution of health facilities has a heavy rural emphasis because more than 70 per cent of the population lives in rural areas. Plans for the establishment of health facilities have in the past taken into consideration the facility/population ratio, but with time this has in some areas been seriously overtaken by the high population growth rate. Moreover, good medical care is not within the reach of the majority of the least developed countries such as Kenya and Tanzania where governments with considerable budgetary constraints have been the principal providers of both preventive and curative treatment.

Public health delivery in Africa in general is lacking in affordability, accessibility and quality. It is marred by limited human resource capacity and is understaffed in the face of many pressing health issues, including the HIV/AIDS epidemic. In many places the personnel shortage is worsened by the flow of health professionals to richer countries in search of better salaries and working conditions. Public provision is also beset with problems of poor management and corruption. The underfinanced medical health delivery system, in which there is a wide chasm between needs and the resource pool, has worsened in the wake of the current credit crunch.

The healthcare system in most African countries, including Kenya and Tanzania, was hit hard by the 'structural adjustment' policies introduced and imposed by the International Monetary Fund and the World Bank in the 1980s. Their insistence on low inflation rates and cuts in wage and budgetary expenditure in borrowing countries have proved detrimental to social sectors like health, with particularly damaging impacts for the poor. Hospitals often work under highly unfavourable conditions, especially the public hospitals which lack the basic infrastructure for healthcare. There is little access to healthcare because the poor, who form a sizeable section of the population, are unable to pay either the user fees or the transport costs.

The problem is compounded by the fact that the continent is heavily dependent on imported pharmaceutical products that lead to the high cost of medicine. The vagaries of transportation at times result in the withdrawal of medicines, including life-saving drugs, from the market. Traditional healers and birth attendants continue to be important providers of health services, especially in rural areas and poorer urban areas, such as Kibera in Nairobi.

According to the World Bank sources and based on household budget surveys, 36 per cent of the population of Tanzania lives below the national poverty line, and life expectancy at birth in Tanzania is only 52 years (World Bank 2008b). Total government expenditure on health as a percentage of gross domestic product in 2006 was 6.4 per cent whereas private expenditure on health as percentage of total expenditure on health in the same year was 42.2 per cent. External resources as a percentage of total expenditure on health comprised 27.8 per cent in 2006. In the following year the total government expenditure on health as a percentage of gross domestic product fell to 5.3 per cent while the corresponding data for external resources as a percentage of total expenditure on health rose to 49.9 per cent (World Health Organisation 2010, p. 136).

The Kenyan Household Budget Survey indicates that absolute poverty declined from 52.3 per cent in 1997 to 46.1 per cent in

2005/06, which is still very high compared to Tanzania and neighbouring Uganda (about 31 per cent). The average life expectancy is about 54 years. In 2005/06, of the total population of 36 million, 16.7 million were below the poverty line. The central government expenditure on health as a percentage of gross domestic product in 2005 was only 4.6 per cent (World Bank 2009). We discuss now in more detail healthcare in both Tanzania and Kenya.

Tanzania

During the colonial era, the private providers of health services included non-government organisations – mainly religious organisations and the voluntary agencies – as well as various state health institutions, often explicitly or tacitly defining clientele according to racial demarcations. The religious organisations were and are categorised as 'private not for profit' providers of health services.

Following independence, healthcare was considered to be more definitively a domain of the state, yet a limited number of private facilities were provided in major towns of the country. But in 1975 the government of Tanzania nationalised all the hospitals including those run by the Christian Missions and in 1977 'private health service for profit' was banned under the Private Hospital (Regulation) Act. The practice of medicine and dentistry as a commercial service was also prohibited. Julius Nyerere believed that human health should not be a commodity to be exploited. However, this act had a negative impact on the delivery of health services because it led to the roll back of the private sector and resulted in the shrinking of the supply of medical services (Government of Tanzania 2002/03). About a decade and a half later the government again recognised the role of the private sector in healthcare. The law was amended with the Private Hospitals (Regulation) Amendment Act 1991, whereby qualified medical practitioners and dentists could run private hospitals with the permission of the Ministry of Health.

The phenomenon of medical tourism from Tanzania is not new. More affluent patients have been going abroad for treatment or have been treated by foreign doctors since the early 1980s. A doctor at a hospital in Dar es Salaam drew an analogy of African medical tourists to India as 'unhealthy refugees' who had to flee their own borders to seek medical treatment in other parts of the world. I was informed that in 1983, Dr Rajani Kanabar, a medical practitioner and director of Regency Medical Centre, a leading private hospital in Tanzania, had facilitated a private team of heart surgeons to come to Dar es Salaam and conduct 50 heart surgeries with the support of the Round Table Association, an international philanthropic organisation. He also organised surgeries for Tanzanian children with congenital heart disease at the Metropolitan Medical Centre at Minneapolis in the USA in the 1980s through the Lions International and the Tanzania Heart Foundation. Dr Kanabar made efforts to get treatment for Tanzanians in India as well. Since 1986, 50 children have been sent to Mumbai through the sponsorship of the Lions Club, Dar es Salaam and the Ministry of Health in Tanzania.

Over the past few years about 1,000 Tanzanian patients have sought treatment at the Apollo Hospital in Hyderabad, the Madras Medical Mission in Chennai, and the Narayan Hrudalayalaya Heart Institute in Bangalore, under the guidance of internationally reputed heart surgeons, such as Dr Devi Shetty and Dr K.M. Cherian, and at a discounted price of rupees 1,650 (a fee that includes boarding and lodging).

The former president of India, Dr Abdul Kalam, in his capacity as patron of the Care Hospital in Hyderabad, donated ten free heart surgeries for Tanzanian patients. He also offered cardiac surgery training for government doctors, who were to be identified through the Tanzania Ministry of Health at the same hospital. Over the past three decades about 2,000 heart surgeries have been facilitated in Indian hospitals because of the international quality medical standards and near 100 per cent success rate (about 99 per cent) at one-third the cost of similar surgery in developed nations. Tanzanians have also been sent to Manipal hospital in the state of Karnataka, for treatment of kidney ailments and dialysis, given the lack of a kidney treatment centre in their country.

Although India is able to provide relatively affordable medical treatment, this is still something only affluent Africans can afford, leaving the vast majority of the population under-served. In Tanzania every year more than 7,000 children with congenital heart disease and adolescents with rheumatic heart diseases await open-heart surgery treatment. In an interview, Dr Kanabar described the financial assistance he had sought through various international communities and charities to import state-of-the-art medical and surgical facilities that are currently unavailable in Tanzania. Even so, these would still be within the private sector and thus inaccessible to the poor, except through occasional charitable cases.

Through Dr Kanabar's efforts, Dr Kiran and Dr Pallavi Patel of Global Understanding Foundation, a US charity, visited Tanzania in July 2005 and pledged their support and equipment of up to $2 million. The government of Tanzania has promised a land grant, the Lions Club International has agreed to bear the cost of infrastructure and Narayan Hrudalaya, Bangalore, will send in a core team.

So it seems likely that Tanzania will soon have a medical centre for heart patients. A Tanzanian newspaper reported that heart examinations would be done free of cost in Dar es Salaam and Zanzibar under the auspices of the Lions Club and their chairperson, Dr Kanabar. It also reported that Narayan Hrudalaya would conduct 50 heart surgeries at reduced rates through 2007 and 2008 (Mwendapole 2007).

Treatment in private Tanzanian hospitals such as Regency Medical or Aga Khan Hospital is expensive. But patients often have no alternative as these are the better equipped hospitals. The other hospitals, such as the Hindu Mandal (founded in 1918 as part of a local sociocultural association thanks to donations from Indian trusts and individuals) are only relatively cheaper, hence the costs of treatment are still unaffordable for many patients.

The Indian doctors who visit Tanzania establish their initial point of contact between the patient and the doctor through their local consultants. The patients get information about the visits of the Indian doctors ahead of time and the dates and venues of their consultations are advertised on the Indian television channels in Dar es Salaam and in local newspapers. Those diagnosed with complicated aliments that need advanced treatment are advised by the visiting Indian doctor to travel to India for treatment.

Kenya

In Kenya too, the medical situation is critical, with insufficient doctors, nurses and other trained providers available to run basic health services, compounding problems of severely constrained funding. Following the doctor's strike of 1994, many medical personnel in the country left for better pay packages in South Africa, Botswana, Lesotho and Swaziland. Nurses also emigrated to the United Kingdom. An October 2005 communication from an NGO coalition to the November 2005 High Level Forum on Health Millennium Development Goals noted that between 1991 and 2003, the Kenyan government reduced its work force by 30 per cent – cuts that hit the health sector particularly hard. For the period between 2000 and 2002 alone, the government was scheduled to lay off 5,300 health staff. Those conditionalities were externally imposed by the International Monetary Fund (IMF) and World Bank in the 1980s as a part of their structural adjustment programme. As a consequence, local health clinics and dispensaries had fewer supplies and medicines and user fees became more common.

The public hospitals saw their standard of care deteriorate, increasing pressure on the largest public facility, the Kenyatta National Hospital in Nairobi. The hospital, once the leading health facility in East Africa, withdrew subsidies and requested patients' families provide food, medicine and medical supplies. Professional staff members have taken jobs (some part time, some full time) at private healthcare facilities, or have migrated to Europe or North America in search of better pay (Ambrose 2006). The costs of treatments are high in private hospitals. Those who are critically ill and can mobilise resources opt to travel abroad to countries like India for treatment.

India as a destination for medical tourism

African patients of Indian origin have been coming to India for several years, but black Africans from Burundi, Côte d'Ivoire, DRC, Ethiopia, Kenya, Mozambique, Nigeria, Rwanda, South Africa, Tanzania and Zambia have been accessing treatment since the late 1990s. African patients can access quality treatment at internationally accredited Indian hospitals. The 20-million strong

Indian diaspora in general, and especially the Gujarati clientele of Indian origin in East Africa, who have roots and established connections on both sides of the Indian Ocean, have come to India for treatment, as stated, but have also helped in the building of 'brand India' through good publicity for potential patients from Africa.

There is no organised manner of referrals for potential patients who seek treatment in India. Patients come mainly through word of mouth, for example through their relatives who have had a satisfactory experience in Indian hospitals. The initial contact with Indian doctors is established through referrals by their local consultants (African doctors meet Indian doctors at medical conferences in various parts of the world) or through initial contact with Indian medical practitioners who visit Africa through local religious, philanthropic organisations such as the Lions or Rotary International or through private hospitals.

Doctors in India also approach prospective patients in Africa through associations of general practitioners in various African countries. Some hospitals, such as Prince Aly Khan Hospital in Mumbai, one of the Aga Khan group of hospitals, regularly send their teams to Tanzania and Kenya to set up initial contact with patients through medical centres such as Regency Hospital in Dar es Salaam and the Aga Khan hospitals in Tanzania and Kenya. Promotional tours are also conducted by Indian hospitals. In order to promote Apollo as a destination for healthcare, representatives were sent to the ITB Exhibition of travel and tourism held in Berlin in 2003, where it showcased its facilities.

The response was overwhelming and Apollo started an international marketing division soon after. The hospital has now teamed with more than 10 international insurance companies and has its own health insurance company – Apollo DVK – and third party administrators abroad (Medindia 2008). The CEO of Apollo pointed out the attraction of India in that 'a heart surgery works out to rupees two lakhs [about $ 4,350 at current exchange rates] here and it is not a small amount. It is the rupee value that makes healthcare cheaper here' (quoted in Medindia 2008). More recently, in August 2008, a delegation of the Confederation of Indian Industries – a national forum for promoting Indian business – met the Tanzanian president and other high-ranking officials in Tanzania and Madagascar.

Hospital groups are engaged in setting up promotional and relationship-building exercises through established hospitals and individual doctors who are currently travelling to African countries on a personal basis. Some of the Indian hospitals, such as Apollo, Fortis and Wockhardt are now geared to receive international patients and details about the services offered can be accessed through the internet and teleconferences. The appointments with doctors, the dates of surgery, and so on, are fixed prior to their arrival. In Mumbai, the Asian Heart Research Institute and Wockhardt hospitals have oriented toward an international patient clientele with a separate marketing division that facilitates in providing airport pick-ups, accommodation for relatives in nearby hotels, blood collection facilities and lodges where the patients stay during the post-discharge recovery period.

Furthermore, a new category of service providers are the medical tourism facilitators, such as AAREX India, Fire Runner Health Care Consultants, Infotrex Services Private Limited and MedicaltourisminGujarat.com, who contact patients in African countries through the internet and link them to Indian hospitals according to the nature of treatment required, the budget and other preferences. However, some of these brokerage agencies are open to accusations of corruption. The author found that one such facilitator company in Mumbai was owned by the nephew of the leading doctor in Tanzania and it was alleged by other doctors that this nephew-uncle team routed patients to a particular hospital in Mumbai for 'good commissions'.

Response of informants (patients and doctors)

One of the patients the author met in Tanzania had undergone a knee replacement at the Shelby hospital in Gujarat. She stated that doctors from hospitals that include Shelby, Prince Aly Khan in Mumbai, Apollo Hospital in Hyderabad and several others visited Dar es Salaam at regular intervals to establish contact with the patients. Her son then did some background research to reconfirm the costs involved by phone and the internet. He stated that the treatment at Shelby hospital was very expensive but the facilities offered were five-star and allowed him to do his office work through wifi connectivity provided in the hospital room and also attend to his elderly mother undergoing treatment.

Most of the patients were extremely satisfied with the outcome of treatment/surgery in India. Two of them stated that they had suffered so long because of wrong diagnosis in their home countries because the doctors were not so skilled and that they did not have the 'big machines' that they saw in Indian hospitals. They were surprised that every Indian hospital had an MRI machine, which is not the case in Africa. They also stated that they were happy with the extra care and treatment provided by doctors and the attendant staff.

However, three of the patients interviewed stated that they were not happy with the nurses, who they thought were 'not sincere'. Some of them complained about the vegetarian food being served in Indian hospitals as it was too spicy. With regard to the expenses involved, most of them thought that hospitals in India were quite expensive but they were definitely cheaper than hospitals in the West, which in most cases were unaffordable for most of the patients from middle or lower-middle-class backgrounds. For example, knee replacement surgery in the US would cost about $41,000, while in India the costs are about $9,000; a heart bypass would cost $122,000 in the US, but in India it would cost about $10,000 (Medical Tourism Gujarat 2009). On an average the costs in Indian specialty hospitals are about a quarter the cost of comparable services in the US.

Several patients raised their medical expenses and airfare costs by pooling small contributions from family members. A spouse or an elder child would usually be the caregiver. In the case of some patients, relatives and children working in United States or Britain assisted in efforts to fund treatments. In other cases, friends and members at the local church made small contributions. Very few patients had insurance cover. A doctor in the Aga Khan Hospital in Nairobi, estimated that only between 2 and 3 per cent of the population in Kenya and Tanzania have private health insurance. He said that only the younger, educated, and the middle and upper-middle classes and those with salaried jobs in corporate sector can afford such insurance.

Insurance companies, such as Medex, AAR, the Bank of Tanzania and Bupa are recent entrants into African markets. Four of the 41 East African patients interviewed were covered by their corporate/government/international agency employers and the remainder paid out of their own pockets.

A doctor in Tanzania noted certain issues with the phenomenon of 'medical tourism' in general, and in India specifically. He stated that patients on medical visas were expected to register at the foreigners' registration office, which was time consuming and problematic for the physically infirm. Another doctor stated that the system of referrals abroad was an 'organised racket' but a necessary evil at times because hospitals in Tanzania did not have the required equipment. It is 'pure business', 'a profit making joint venture', with local doctors who referred to Indian hospitals receiving 'high cuts' for the referral to their Indian counterparts. He stated candidly that, at times, the patients go through too many tests, some of which are not essential for the treatment, but were 'good for business'.

Post-recovery follow-up was done through email, by phone or through the local consultant in the patient's home country. This worked well for diseases for which one-off treatment is required and there is no chance of relapse. But for patients who had come for cancer treatment, for example, this system certainly had its limitations. One Kenyan patient, who had been treated at Hinduja Hospital in Mumbai, was admitted to the Aga Khan Hospital in Nairobi soon after his return, and succumbed to the disease about 10 months thereafter.

The patients and doctors admitted that treatment abroad has its limitations, not least because some ailments require repeated treatment, careful monitoring and a prolonged recovery period, which is not possible with offshore healthcare, given expenses and time demands.

Government support for health cooperation

Beyond 'medical tourism', more recent developments in healthcare relations between India and Africa are noteworthy, particularly the Pan African e-Network, launched on 26 February 2009. The system of telemedicine, based on the use of electronic information communication and technology, shares India's quality healthcare with African counterparts.

Currently the network offers online medical services through teleconsultation, by linking the 12 specialty hospitals in India to practitioners on the African continent. Ethiopia was selected for the e-network pilot project in 2007. Tele-education programmes between Addis Ababa University, Haramaya learning centres, and the Black Lion and Nekempte hospitals in Ethiopia with Care Hospital in Hyderabad were established.

The AU has short-listed three leading regional universities and two regional hospitals for participation in the e-network. These include Makerere University in Uganda, Kwame Nkrumah University of Science and Technology in Ghana, the University of Yaounde in Cameroon, Ibadan Hospital in Nigeria, and the Brazzaville Hospital in the Republic of Congo.

As a part of the telemedicine project, live consultation is being offered for one hour every day to each of the 53 member states of the AU in 18 medical disciplines, ranging from cardiology, neurology and urology to gynaecology, infectious diseases, ophthalmology and paediatrics. Furthermore, offline consultation for five patients per day from selected hospitals has been provided. The project also offers skill upgrading through the sharing of information with medical personnel in African countries through its continuing medical education (CME) programme. It is however at a nascent stage and the care offered through telemedicine can be limited for surgical treatment and complicated cases that require state-of-the-art technology. There remains an urgent need to build sustainable heath delivery systems on the continent.

Conclusion

The thriving medical tourism industry and the various business ties and investment opportunities emerging between India and Africa provide the possibility of affordable, high-quality healthcare for those who can afford to pay for treatment abroad. In the years to come, the expanding footprints of the Indian hospitals in various parts of Africa might result in the reversal of the phenomenon of medical tourism to India. The provision of quality healthcare on home ground would certainly be advantageous for the African patients as they can be in a familiar environment and have access to follow-up treatment as well an extended network of caregivers. But the critical issue is whether African govern-ments negotiate terms of contract such that medical facilities can be accessed by both the rich and the poor.

However, with the highly uneven and donor-driven healthcare policies currently in place, African countries need to develop healthcare solutions for the tens of millions of their inhabitants who cannot afford to travel abroad for healthcare. They need to look at financing the health sector in innovative ways, such as social insurance and affordable local user fees.

References

Ambrose, S. (2006) 'Preserving disorder: IMF policies and Kenya's health care crisis', 1 June, http://www.pambazuka.org/en/category/features/34800, accessed 9 April 2010.

Economic Times (2008) 'Medical tourism can make healthcare affordable for poor', 2 February

Government of Tanzania (2002/03) 'Hotuba ya Waziri wa Afya Mheshimiwa Anna Margareth Abdallah, Mbunge, kuhusu Makadirio ya Matumizi ya Fedha kwa Mwaka', http://www.tanzania.go.tz/health.html, accessed 12 April 2010.

Medical Tourism Gujarat (2009), 'Medical tourism: cost difference', http://www.medicaltourismgujarat.com/medical_tourism.html, accessed 12 October 2010.

Medindia (2008) 'India emerging as international medical tourism hub', http://www.medindia.net/news/healthwatch/India- Emerging-as-International-Medical-Tour, 22 September, accessed 11 November 2009

Mwendapole, J.N. (2007), 'Daktari wa moyo kutoka India kuwasili wiki hii', http://www.ippmedia.com/ipp/nipashe, 28–9 June, accessed 10 November 2008

Pan-African e-Network Project (2009) http://www.panafricanenetwork.com/portal/AboutProject.jsp, accessed 12 April 2010

World Bank (2008a) 'Kenya at a glance', 24 September, http://devdata.worldbank.org/AAG/ken_aag.pdf, accessed 16 March 2009

World Bank (2008b) 'Tanzania at a glance', 24 September, http://devdata.worldbank.org/AAG/tza_aag.pdf, accessed 16 March 2009

World Bank (2009) 'Country brief, Kenya', January, http://www.who.int/countries/ken/en/, accessed 16 March 2009

World Health Organisation (2010) 'Health expenditure', in *World Health Statistics*, http://www.who.int/whosis/whostat/EN_WHS10_Part2.pdf, accessed 10 October 2010

8

AwaaZ: a personal and collective journey

Zarina Patel and Zahid Rajan

AwaaZ is a magazine that has been published from Nairobi since 2002. '*AwaaZ*' means 'voices' in several northern Indian languages and was founded in light of the concern for a greater exposure and understanding of the legitimacy of the South Asian community in Kenya. Its editors are the authors of this chapter. Herein, we will give a very brief macro-view of the history of colonial and independent Kenya and the situation of the South Asian peoples within it. We will then look at the genesis of *AwaaZ*, its development, history and current status. We set out a personal account of the challenges and issues we faced, the motivations and beliefs that shaped our approaches over time, and the ways in which the magazine has grown and developed.

History

Trading links between the peoples of the Indian subcontinent and the East African coast date back at least 2,000 years, and perhaps even further. However, major settlement and the thrust into the interior really accelerated with the building of the Uganda Railway between 1896 and 1901. A total of 37,747 indentured labourers were imported from India; of these 2,493 died and 28,254 returned home. The remaining 7,000 were joined by families and relatives responding to the push/pull influence of the empire – colonial restrictions on the one hand and the lure of opportunity on the other.

In 1911, South Asians numbered 11,787 or 0.66 per cent of the total population of Kenya; at independence this number had risen to 176,613 (2.05 per cent) and by 1989 had dropped to 89,185 (0.42 per cent). It is estimated that the contemporary proportion sits at around 0.2 per cent.

In spite of their small numbers, Indians, motivated and inspired by the movement for independence in their motherland, played a significant and dynamic role in the anti-colonial struggle in Kenya – from founding the first nationwide political organisation in Kenya, the East Africa Indian National Congress, to the demands and agitation that forced the British government to declare 'African paramountcy' in Kenya in 1923, which put paid to the settlers' dream of dominion status.

Major landmarks in Kenya's march to independence from colonial rule included the organising of Kenya's workers into a formidable trade union movement, the publication of newspapers (especially the *Daily Chronicle*), which gave voice to the anti-colonial struggle, and the work of lawyers who defended the victims of colonial injustice. All this was achieved against a backdrop of persistent efforts by the colonialists to undermine Asian/African unity.

The ousting of colonialism was replaced only by 'flag' independence, as neo-colonialism had entrenched itself. White faces were substituted with black faces, but the colonial structures remained the same. The cold war, ideological differences and vested interests took their toll. The patriotism and involvement of South Asians in Kenyan society were seriously undermined: South Asian civil servants were unfairly retrenched and hounded out of the sector; Pio Gama Pinto was assassinated; Pranlal Sheth was deported; Makhan Singh, Jaramogi Oginga Odinga and others were marginalised; Africanisation compelled South Asian traders to close shop; and Idi Amin's expulsion of the South Asians in Uganda received popular support. Moreover, the single party dictatorship formulated by Jomo Kenyatta and later refined by Daniel arap Moi further suppressed democratic participation by Africans and South Asians. Multipartyism was achieved in 1992, and the Moi-KANU regime was defeated in 2002. It is this opening up of the democratic space that facilitated the birth of the forerunner of *AwaaZ* and the subsequent establishment of the magazine in 2002.

Genesis

In the early years of independence Zarina Patel, like many other South Asians, confronted herself with questions of 'Who am I? Kenyan? British? Asian? And what legitimacy do I have in this country of my birth?' In 1972 she set up and headed the Community and Race Relations project in the National Christian Council of Kenya. She began a journey of discovering her community's role and participation in Kenya's history and was joined in the 'hunt' by fellow traveller, Zahid Rajan. There was a paucity of written material to refer to, so research and oral interviews had to be undertaken. A special mention must be made here of Robert Gregory's *India and East Africa: A History of Race Relations within the British Empire 1890–1939* – a bible for Kenya's South Asians, published in 1971. Another source of information was J.S. Mangat's *A History of Asians in East Africa, c.1886 to 1945*, published in 1969. Gradually, and with the participation of like-minded comrades, the picture began to take shape and a wealth of information was harnessed.

The voyage of 'self-discovery' was amply rewarded and gave impetus to this group of Kenyans to share their 'discoveries' with other Kenyans with the aim of changing society and building the nation. The very repressive political climate made it virtually impossible to write or speak publicly about the discoveries. The despots were not about to entertain narratives about patriotic comrades who gave their all for the people. Zarina Patel, who had studied art at school, then launched into executing a series of large oil paintings depicting the heroic struggles of the Kenyan people against colonialism and later, dictatorship.

A group of like-minded Kenyans contributed their ideas and organised to exhibit the paintings clandestinely in church and school halls. Given that a majority of Kenyans were at the time illiterate, this activity was seen as an ideal way to communicate Kenya's patriotic history. The first painting depicted women's liberation. The others commemorated the struggle waged by the Giriama heroine, Me Katilili; Makhan Singh and his trade union movement; the tensions in the current education system; the evils of unbridled tourism; the killing of Njeri, a sex worker, by a US marine; and the grabbing of land in Kongowea. The paintings had anti-imperialism as their underlying theme.

As the tempo for multipartyism accelerated, Zarina and Zahid were caught up in the national fervour. But just months before the goal was reached, an event was to affect Zarina personally. In 1906, her maternal grandfather, Alibhai Mulla Jeevanjee, had donated to citizens a public park in the centre of Nairobi. Because of his struggle for equal rights and justice, the authorities both in colonial and independent Kenya paid scant attention to the upkeep of this park. Nevertheless, Jeevanjee Gardens continued to be a very popular resting place for workers, the adjacent university fraternity, lovers and preachers.

In 1991, the city commission, which had replaced the municipal council, began to implement a plan mooted in the 1980s to 'develop' Jeevanjee Gardens into an underground shopping mall and parking space. It was a land grab concocted by some of the highest powers in the land. Zarina and her mother, Shirin Najmudean, Professor Wangari Maathai (now Nobel Laureate), *The Nation* newspaper, and *wananchi* (the people), rose up in protest and the Gardens were saved. 'Who was Jeevanjee? Why did he give this garden to us?' Zarina was often asked. She started to research the history of this man who had been cast as a 'hustler' by both colonial and independent governments of Kenya. The end product was a 283-page biography revealing the role not only of Jeevanjee but also those other early Indians in Kenya's freedom struggle.

In 1992, Section 2A of the constitution was amended and Kenya once again became a democracy. It was far from perfect, but some democratic space had opened up. Zarina and Zahid joined George Anyona's Kenya Social Congress and also became involved in the constitution review process. South Asian businessmen, together with some of their African sympathisers, formed the Eastern Action Club of Africa (EACA) to voice their concerns and organise around them. But generally the South Asians remained reluctant to show their hand and participate in the politics of the country.

At the dawn of the new millennium, EACA requested Zahid to take on the regular publication of a newsletter for the organisation. It was a pro bono appeal and Zahid was given total charge of content, design and layout. Being a printer and graphic designer by profession he willingly accepted and agreed with his partner,

Zarina, to take charge of the content. EACA formed a newsletter committee comprising convenor Madhukant Shah, editor Zahid Rajan and member Zarina Patel. Together they published five issues of the *Voice of EACA*.

The first issue, a slim volume, was published in August 2000. The cover in blue, white and red had a dancing figure of Mr Kilowatt. The inside story was titled 'The Power Vacuum' and written by Tom Maliti. Other articles focused on the economy (including taxation and land tenure), EACA activities, the Asian African heritage exhibition in the national museum and Jeevanjee Gardens. There were also sections dealing with philanthropy, community issues, health, book reviews, anecdotes, cartoons and profiles of prominent persons in South Asian-Kenyan history.

The next issue came out in December with the same 'imperial' colours. The main feature was about building civil society in Kenya and included contributions from the Kenya Alliance of Resident Associations, an article on the Ufangamano constitutional review process and another on leadership. The focus on the economy was continued with articles about the insurance industry. The Equality Bill 2000 was discussed by Alamin Mazrui, while Issa Shivji wrote a piece on the Zanzibar election. The historical piece was about K.P. Shah, a pioneer Kenyan freedom fighter.

The January/March 2001 issue featured a new look. With environmental colours, the *Voice of EACA* proclaimed 'Save our forests' and explained it all in a lead article titled 'Trees and life'. The economic angle was captured in a piece on Bretton Woods and another on the pitfalls of shrewd business. The constitutional crisis in Zanzibar was again discussed and the role of modernity and change in the lives of Muslims came under the spotlight. Another pioneer freedom fighter, Haroon Ahmed, made the history pages.

Joseph Murumbi, the Asian African, embellished the cover of the second edition of 2001, now expanded to 32 pages, with the Kenyan flag, Maasai shield and all. And inside, the leader article, 'M.K. Gandhi – A reflection from the Transvaal', affirmed that history had indeed moved to the fore. Letters to the editor were in evidence, one from as far as Canada, proving that readers were responding and generally welcomed the project. Correspondent Tom Maliti wondered if, with the appointments of Professor Yash Pal Ghai, Shakeel Ahmed and Raj Binde to prominent roles within the public sphere, Kenyan South Asians were not just talking politics but were getting involved. Also included in this issue were posters from a campaign, which had been formulated under Zahid's direction and had won an award from the Association of Practitioners in Advertising (APA).

The first edition of 2002 featured a lead article on constitutional reform and other articles on ethnicity, minorities and politics, a land rights campaign in Nairobi, peace efforts in Kashmir, efforts to save the coral reefs on the Kenya coast and the role of art in preserving culture. Short stories and the now regular historical profile were also featured.

The contributors wrote for us pro bono, as they so kindly do to this day. Several were based in Kenya, but we also had contributors from Canada, India and the US. A qualitative change occurred around this time. The sections on history aroused great public interest and the demand for more could no longer be contained within the format of a newsletter. Also, 2002 was election year and change was in the air. There was a need for South Asians to move out of the wings and get back onto the national stage. It was thought that a literary journal could help to expedite the process. *Challenge to Colonialism – The Struggle of Alibhai Mulla Jeevanjee for Equal Rights in Kenya* had been published and Zarina was working on her second biography *Unquiet – The Life and Times of Makhan Singh*. We were discovering a wealth of historical material concerning Kenya's South Asians.

With the blessings of EACA, Zahid and Zarina appointed themselves executive and managing editors respectively and went ahead to convert the newsletter into a magazine, which would focus on Kenyan South Asian history and culture in the national context. It was envisioned that three issues would be published annually and the two editors undertook to source the content, write, edit, market, sell and distribute. They appointed Lakhvir Singh as designer and Colourprint Ltd. as the printer.

The magazine now needed a distinctly South Asian feel and Lakhvir Singh suggested the name *AwaaZ*. And so *AwaaZ* it was, and is. Financing the magazine was of course a major challenge. To keep costs to a minimum, the editors worked from home using their personal equipment and resources. *The Voice of EACA* newsletter had been paid for by supportive advertisers; now the costs would be much higher and the editors were dependent on their goodwill.

A further change was the choice of nomenclature to describe Kenyan Asians. The Kiswahili reference was *wahindi* – people from India or Hind. The terms 'Indians' or 'Asians' were used in English. But in 1947 when the subcontinent got its independence and Pakistan was created as an Islamic state, Asian Muslims objected to being called Indians because they identified with Pakistan. To overcome this hurdle, the term 'Asian' was adopted and for the rest of the century the community was known as 'Kenyan Asian'.

In 2000 a well crafted historico-cultural exhibition of Kenya's Asian community was mounted at the National Museum in Nairobi, from which a new term came into being: 'Asian African'. It derived from the community's roots in Asia and confirmed its identity as African. The term has been in use for almost 10 years, but apart from being adopted in a few academic papers, it remained relatively unknown and not widely used. More importantly, the rank-and-file Kenyan Asian did not identify with it, especially as 'African' was generally seen as a racial and not a geographic category.

We at *AwaaZ* were concerned not to lose our Kenyan identity at this particular historical juncture, but we did sense a need to redefine ourselves more accurately. The term 'Asian' was too broad because it included the Chinese, Vietnamese and Malaysians. The subcontinent, comprised of India, Pakistan, Bangladesh and Sri Lanka, was being increasingly referred to internationally as 'South Asia' and so, prioritising our national identity and affirming our roots, we chose to call ourselves Kenyan South Asians. We find this term is gradually becoming the lingua franca and is particularly useful currently, because of the sharp increase in the Chinese population in Kenya.

The first issue of *AwaaZ* was published in 2002. The cover was a dual tone of olive green and black. Emblazoned on it was a head and shoulders portrait of Girdhari Lal Vidyarthi. With his round-rimmed spectacles, stubbly beard, and plebian shirt and coat he looked every bit the pioneer for Kenyan press freedom. The year 2002 was an election year and the KANU government was introducing legislation to muzzle the press in a bid to prevent exposition of its failures. Vidyarthi was the first Kenyan journalist to be charged with sedition, as the editor of the 'free, frank and fearless' *Colonial Times*.

A major objective of the *AwaaZ* editors has been to encourage South Asians to write about their family histories and to provide a platform for publication. For example, Shravan Vidyarthi, a grandson of Girdhai, was studying in the US, and visited Zarina Patel to learn about her grandfather, A.M. Jeevanjee. Zarina encouraged him to write about his grandfather and so he penned the cover story for the first issue of *AwaaZ*. Later he was to go on to research the life of his uncle, Priya Ramrakha, the well-known photojournalist who was killed covering the Biafran war. Shravan eventually made a documentary film about Ramrakha with the cooperation of *Life Magazine*. The film won critical acclaim and three awards at the Zanzibar Film Festival in 2009.

The early editions of *AwaaZ* included book and film reviews, as well as leisure features. New additions were the obituary page, quotes and articles ranging from the media to democracy, racism, brain drain and the constitutional review. Letters to the editor were published and Zahid continued to write the editorial or 'Last Word'.

The general election was held at the end of the year of 2002 and 39 years of an increasingly repressive and authoritarian KANU government was ended. There was great joy, hope and optimism in the land and much to write about. The sentiments of several South Asian writers were captured in the pages of the first issue of 2003. Eddie Pereira, the fierce nationalist, graced the cover and was the subject of the main story.

But although the interest of both readers and contributors was burgeoning, finances became more constrained. We had launched *AwaaZ* with the intention of publishing it tri-annually, but this had not been possible. And so early in 2003, we took the rather precarious step of relinquishing the job, hoping to earn our living through exploring avenues compatible with our individual and collective talents.

AwaaZ was not, and is unlikely to be, an income-earning project. *AwaaZ* is a labour of love we value highly and strive to keep afloat, occasionally even at personal expense. And so we continue. We chose Manilal Ambalal Desai, a great, but relatively unknown leader and nationalist in the first quarter of the 20th century, as our main story for the second issue of 2003. Owing to the paucity of information about this bachelor who had no descendants that we could consult, considerable research was involved in the writing of the 6,000 word story.

The article on African Sufis was the start of a trend of collecting information on the movement of people from the African continent to South Asia. Kenya was still riding on the euphoria of the newly installed Narc government and *AwaaZ* celebrated the recognition of several South Asians, such as Dr Manu Chandaria, Salim Lone, Davinder Lamba and others. But we were also saddened by the very untimely death of our beloved writer and humorist, Wahome Mutahi or 'Whispers' as he was affectionately known. Pranlal Sheth, a renowned Kenyan and close associate of Jaramogi Oginga Odinga, also passed away in exile at about the same time.

Sheth – the 'rebel with a cause' – became the focus of the main story of the first issue of *AwaaZ* in 2004. We were able to include a tribute to Indumati Sheth, his widow, who passed away in February of the same year. A photo collage from the collection of the late Mohammed Amin, Kenya's world-renowned photographer, formed the centre spread. We also inserted a fictional photographical story called 'A Love brewed in the Parklands lot'. It was first published in *Kwani?* an anthology of African, largely Kenyan, writing. We reproduced the story in *AwaaZ* because very few South Asians are readers of *Kwani?* The story was about an 18-year-old South Asian woman, Sangeeta, who falls in love with Ogot, an ice-cream seller. The editors got some quite monstrous reactions, basically admonishing them for publishing the piece. 'We had to staple the pages, because our children read *AwaaZ*,' we were told.

This was a forerunner of a large section of the South Asian community's unease at exposure of its 'underbelly' and the magazine's interest in the current socio-political issues. Advertisers were reluctant to support *AwaaZ*, partly because of the content and also because of its low circulation. This was a chicken-and-egg story, because we needed the advertisements to be able to invest in increasing the sales. We soon began to identify and contact potential donors for the magazine.

For the year 2004, we were determined to fulfil their earlier plan to publish tri-annually, and we did. The late Achhroo Ram Kapila, the brilliant lawyer who assisted in the defence of the Kapenguria Six (nationalists who had been arrested and imprisoned by the colonial authorities in 1952), was the subject of the second issue. Pheroze Nowrojee's rare postcards of the 1895–1920 period made the centre spread and we bid farewell to Edward Said and Ray Charles. A new writer, John Sibi Okumu, joined *AwaaZ* at this time and he has become a permanent fixture and a loyal friend.

For the third issue of 2004 we featured Sugra Visram, Uganda's reluctant hero. A member of parliament during Milton Obote's reign, she later became President Museveni's economic adviser in the UK. On our cover, she appeared with President Museveni and some of her fellow MPs. This was a departure from the solo figure on the cover – the style that *AwaaZ* had adopted thus far. And there was a reason. *AwaaZ* was now being read by Kenyans of varying backgrounds and in the diaspora. The editors felt the need for a wider consultation and so set about identifying potential members to form an editorial board. One of the observations made in the preliminary talks was that whereas our cover stories invariably highlighted the close cooperation between South Asians and Africans, this was not reflected in our cover designs.

The editorial board was formed early 2005. It comprised of John Sibi Okumu, writer, teacher and media personality; Sunny Bindra, management consultant, writer and lecturer; the now late Wanjohi Makokha, lecturer; and ourselves. The board's composition has, of course, changed over the years with members moving on and new members coming in, but we do have one member who is still with us from those early days and that is John Sibi Okumu. John attends unfailingly, not just board meetings, but also *AwaaZ* functions and is always there for us. The journalist Rasna Warah also joined the board for a short period.

The first issue of 2005 marked the 40th anniversary of the assassination of Kenya's first independence martyr – Pio Gama Pinto. In keeping with the new thinking in *AwaaZ*, the front cover had a picture of Pinto with comrades Bildad Kaggia and Joseph Murumbi. The main story was constructed by the editors and included extracts from the Pan-African press and contributions from several writers. The story, with photographs, ran for 40 pages – the longest in the magazine to date.

149

A very welcome addition to our galaxy of writers was Sunny Bindra, who became, like John Sibi Okumu, a regular columnist in *AwaaZ*, in addition to his work on the board. In May of 2005, we organised the SAMOSA festival I. The name was chosen because the triangular shape of the 'samosa' encapsulates Asian-African fusion and symbolises the cultural identity common to both communities. The highlights were a photographic exhibition of exemplary South Asian leaders and their African counterparts, singers Eric Wainaina and Gupz, Indian classical dance by Suki Mwendwa and her troupe, as well as films and panel discussions.

'The photographer that Kenya forgot' was the cover feature of the second issue of 2005. Shravan Vidyarthi in 'Life through his lens' put together the story and a collection of rarely seen photographs taken by his uncle, Priya Ramrakha, before he was gunned down in the Biafran civil war in 1968. This issue also saw the entry of Dipesh Pabari who crafted a cartoon strip together with artist, Kevin Amenya. Another extraordinary woman, Sophia Mustafa – who entered the Legislative Council in 1958 as a TANU candidate and was in the forefront of Tanganyika's freedom struggle – graced our next cover, this time together with Mwalimu Nyerere.

In early 2006, Zarina launched her second biography, this time documenting the life story of Makhan Singh, the founder of the trade union movement in Kenya. The cover of *AwaaZ* showed a garlanded Makhan Singh being carried shouder-high by his fellow workers on his return home after 11 years in detention. Ramnik Shah wrote the story and later graduated to being a regular columnist for *AwaaZ*. In July, the editors were invited to the 9th Zanzibar International Film Festival, where they presented their documentary on Makhan Singh and introduced *AwaaZ*.

The next two issues benefitted from funds donated by the Heinrich Böll Foundation, hence the donor's interest in the topics of women and the environment were emphasised. This change kicked off a transition to shifting the focus to more contemporary issues, a move that had been considered by the board for some time. We also began printing the magazine in full colour throughout, a trend that continues. November 2006 was the month of SAMOSA festival II and the highlight was Kachumbari – a multiracial, traditional instrumental band that we put together. It took many months of rehearsing to get the sounds to blend, but the end result was fabulous and the band provided a night of soul-stirring music. Kachumbari has now made a mark on the national music scene, has launched a CD and plays regularly in public.

Around this time we held a board workshop to strategise about revisioning *AwaaZ*. One of our main concerns was to learn more about our readership: who were we writing for and why? After four years we were still reaching a very small section of the South Asian community. Two new members came on board: Tom Maliti – a journalist with Associated Press and Dipesh Pabari – an environmental activist and writer. Only two issues of *AwaaZ* were published this year, the main stories being 'Africa – A *chotara* [mixed race] future?' and 'Ghosts of Mabira – a rain forest resurrects racism in Uganda'. The absence of a third issue was due to financial constraints.

The next year, 2007, was another election year in Kenya and the political climate became increasingly ethnicised and tense. The elections, held on 27 December, were allegedly rigged and the largely unpopular result was forced upon the people. The year 2008 began with an unimaginable orgy of violence, hatred and brutality. The fighting ended but real peace remains elusive. By 2008 Zarina had started writing her third biography – that of Manilal A. Desai – and the research took us to the UK. There we were able to organise a public meeting to launch *AwaaZ*, as well as meet with students of a secondary school in the east end of London.

Issue 1 of *AwaaZ* in 2008 featured Sri Appa Pant, India's first high commissioner to Kenya. Issues 2 and 3 looked at 'Minorities within us' and 'The old photographic studios: reliving an era' respectively. The third SAMOSA festival was staged in November, this time organised by a team as opposed to the editors alone. The theme was 'Celebrating daily life', which a photographic exhibition and fashion show portrayed. Ex-East African 'slam' poets from the UK kept audiences enthralled and a youth forum at the University of Nairobi tackled the unmentionable 'Jungu, Miro and Choot' – racially charged epithets! Children's activities, film screenings, an entrepreuneurs' cocktail and a Kachumbari night were all part of the festival.

Kenyan society continued to be plagued with human rights violations and grand corruption. Addressing these concerns, the

2009 *AwaaZ* topics featured stories of the struggles waged by Indian activists in South Africa and those employing non-violent methods. In April, Emma Mawdsley and Gerard McCann of Cambridge University, in association with the British Institute in Eastern Africa and British Association for South Asian Studies, organised a major conference with the theme 'Contemporary India–East Africa relations: shifting terrains of engagement'. *AwaaZ* presented a paper titled 'Race relations between Kenya's Africans and South Asians'.

An appeal for funds elicited the support of the renowned Ghai brothers. Professor Yash Pal Ghai offered to finance property rental and so *AwaaZ* was able to open an office at the Godown Arts Centre in Nairobi. This year also saw the addition of Akiba Uhaki, a social justice and human rights organisation, as a funder for *AwaaZ*. The year ended with a strategy workshop which guided *AwaaZ* into a new direction with revised structures geared to reach a wider audience. Many more non-South Asians, both in Kenya and in the diaspora, were reading, and writing for, the magazine, therefore it was evident that there was a need to widen the focus to include minority and diversity issues. 'Non-violence for change' in the third issue of 2008 was already a step in that direction; 'Land grabbing and the rise of social movements' was the feature of the first issue of 2010.

AwaaZ is now recognised as a premier magazine on minority and diaspora issues, both in the region and overseas. It champions issues which are central to good governance and nation-building and provides a platform for activities to promote national cohesion and integration.

9

Fragile fortunes: India's oil venture into war-torn Sudan

Luke Patey

The decision by India's national oil company, OVL, to invest in Sudan was not such a straightforward venture to carry out, despite the 2003 exodus of western companies from the country. This chapter aims to disentangle some of the dynamics and motivations behind India's oil engagement in Sudan that have often gone neglected in broad treatments of New Delhi's expanding African energy interests. It does not seek to carry out an in-depth analysis of the impact of India's oil investments in Sudan, but rather provides some background to how the commercial ambitions of ONGC-Videsh – OVL for short – were realised in parallel with India's heightened political relations with the Khartoum government.

It begins by exploring how the risks of entering Sudan were considered in Indian political circles during a period in 2002–03, when one civil war between northern and southern Sudan was coming to an end and another in the western region of Darfur was just beginning. Second, it analyses the diplomatic shuffle in New Delhi and Khartoum to push through the deal in the face of Chinese and Malaysian opposition. Finally, it explores how the potential 2011 secession of southern Sudan might present future risk to India's oil interests.

Buyer beware

Oil was strongly associated with armed conflict in Sudan when OVL first won approval to invest from the Indian government's cabinet committee on economic affairs in late 2002. The killing and displacement of thousands of civilians by the Sudan Armed Forces (SAF) and pro-government militias in and around southern oilfields, where the majority of Sudan's reserves are located, had intensified the North–South civil war between the central government in Khartoum and the rebel Sudan People's Liberation Army/Movement (SPLA/M) in the late 1990s and early 2000s. In an effort to drain the sea of rebel support, Khartoum was also keen to lay waste to local communities in the south in order to ensure there would be nothing to threaten the flow of oil revenues.

The first crude exports were shipped out in August 1999 offering it a strategic, financial advantage in the war. Along with its support for local armed militias, the SAFs had terrorised civilian populations with Antonov bombers and helicopter gunships that became more readily available as oil revenues grew. However, despite Khartoum's manipulation of divisions in the Nuer and Dinka ethnic ranks of the SPLA, the rebels would continue to resist. Knowing very well the implications of oil development, the SPLA targeted oil installations, disrupting the exploration and production activities of companies active in the region.

During the North–South civil war, and under the leadership of the late Dr John Garang, the SPLA stated that oil companies in Sudan were legitimate military targets given the wealth they extracted for Khartoum from the depths of southern soil. The threat became very real on numerous occasions for the Chinese, Malaysian, Canadian and European companies active in the sector because military attacks and kidnappings often led to a suspension of activities and a constant preoccupation with security. The scorched-earth military tactics of Khartoum to push back the rebels would also lead western corporations, mainly Canada's Talisman Energy, to face heavy criticism from human rights advocacy groups in North America and Europe, who saw the oil companies as complicit in the violence (Patey 2007).

Activist pressure, coupled with support from the US government, pushed Talisman and other western corporations out of Sudan, paradoxically opening up the way for OVL. In 2002, Talisman began to actively seek buyers in its highly profitable 25 per cent interest in the Greater Nile Petroleum Operating Company (GNPOC), in which China's National Petroleum Corporation held the largest stake, along with Malaysia's Petronas and Sudan's national oil company, Sudapet. In October 2002, the Canadian company announced it had found a buyer in OVL and hoped to finalise the deal with the Indian company by the end of the year.

Farther south of the GNPOC concessions, which straddled the border of northern and southern Sudan, Lundin of Sweden had suspended its operations in early 2002 because of insecurity. In June 2003, it would sell its leading stake in Block 5A to Petronas. Its European partner, OMV of Austria, would also sell its stake in 5A and the adjacent Block 5B, with OVL eagerly buying the shares. The turn of events could not have been better for OVL which, as the foreign arm of India's Oil and Natural Gas Corporation, was keen to capture overseas petroleum assets to bolster the stagnating domestic production of its corporate parent and begin to take on the challenge of responding to New Delhi's rising energy security concerns. However, it would not be a clear path for OVL to enter Sudan.

Western oil companies were exiting Sudan just as the prospect of peace between the Khartoum government and SPLA rebels was on the rise. The Machakos Protocol was signed in late July 2002 as a framework for the Comprehensive Peace Agreement of January 2005. However, at the time of OVL's entry into Sudan, insecurity was still a major concern with oil development under persistent physical threat and human rights activists ramping up pressure on western companies.

In India the debate about the risks of OVL's engagement in Sudan predominantly focused on the company's safety rather than the morality of investing in a country in which heinous human rights abuses had been committed during the civil war. Its request of approval for the $720 million investment from the cabinet committee on economic affairs had multiple domestic opponents. Some members of the Indian parliament and then ruling Bharatiya Janata Party cabinet regarded committing hundreds of millions of dollars of a developing country's budget to a war-torn region as a 'risky venture' (*Outlook* 2002).

They also questioned the rationale of investing in a country ruled by an Islamist government that had once harboured international terrorists, such as Osama bin Laden. India had its own problems with domestic security and did not want to appear to encourage international terrorism. Moreover, contractors in the

Indian oil sector lobbied that the investment would threaten the scope of ONGC's activities at home if such funding was provided to its subsidiary OVL abroad. Although an agreement between Khartoum and the southern rebels appeared to be on the horizon, if peace was to fail in Sudan, and it often did, OVL risked losing its investment. Its corporate parent ONGC would not sit idly by waiting for the fate of its subsidiary to be decided by politicians in New Delhi.

Subir Raha, the former ONGC chairman stepped in to make his case for pushing OVL in Sudan. He reminded politicians that ONGC had experience of mitigating sabotage and conflict. In fact, in the summer of 2002, separatist militants in Assam had killed six ONGC workers (*Calgary Herald* 2002). In his eyes, India was missing a golden opportunity. If CNPC and Petronas could operate in Sudan as state-owned companies surely OVL could too (*Oil and Gas Journal* 2003).

The ministry of external affairs weighed in on the debate. It did not want OVL's Sudan investment to become a political embarrassment for New Delhi, and wanted to make sure that the same events that led to the Canadian company's exit would not befall OVL (interview, former government official, New Delhi, 16 December 2008). After all Talisman was not exactly exiting Sudan, just as windfall profits were rolling in, of its own accord. After some analysis, the ministry pegged Talisman's exit to be the result of civil society pressure in Canada and the United States rather than insecurity from the civil war.

The fact that CNPC and Petronas did not budge as western oil companies rolled out was an encouraging sign. As a majority government-owned company, with New Delhi holding 74 per cent, OVL could avoid the divestment pressures from activists that had plagued Talisman. Because of their high levels of state-ownership, OVL and the other Asian national oil companies simply cannot be influenced in the same manner as western companies, which are typically prone to divestment pressures through their capital positions and consumer reputations in home markets (Patey 2009). In the end, a compromise between critics and proponents of the deal was struck after OVL agreed to acquire the appropriate political risk insurance for the Sudan investment. However, the company's troubles were not quite over. While the Indian government was internally bickering about misgivings concerning the Sudan deal, a familiar opponent was swooping in to claim the prize. The Chinese oil company CNPC already dominated the oil sector in Sudan and was hungry for more.

Facing down the Chinese dragon

In its bid to enter Sudan in 2003 OVL would face staunch competition from its Asian counterparts CNPC and Petronas. At first glance the presence of the Chinese and Malaysian oil companies provided a guiding light for India. Clearly the international oil industry was not the sole domain of powerful western oil majors and menacing Middle Eastern and Russian state-owned companies.

However, although the Indian oil company pictured its involvement in Sudan as strengthening the international relationship with its Asian counterparts (*Financial Times* 2003), CNPC and Petronas had other ideas. Holding a contractual right of first refusal in the consortium the two companies could technically have initial access to Talisman's abandoned shares. They were more interested in increasing their share of the lucrative oil venture than building a noble union between Asian oil companies abroad. The CNPC and Petronas already held a 40 per cent and 30 per cent share respectively in the GNPOC venture. The quarter stake offered in Talisman's departure, however, presented the opportunity to benefit further from a consortium that was producing oil and reaping profits. The sudden outside opposition fuelled the Indian government's desire for OVL to win the bid.

It appeared to be a momentous task for OVL to derail the interests of their Asian rivals. China in particular was considered the Khartoum government's most coveted ally. From the time the National Islamic Front – now the National Congress Party (NCP) – attained power in a 1989 military coup, it had rapidly moved to win Beijing's political backing and Chinese interest in its oil sector. In combination, China's economic investment and permanent seat on the UN Security Council offset the unilateral sanctions of the United States and deterred threats of multilateral sanctions over the Darfur conflict.

The OVL was in a tight position with both CNPC and Petronas

having until the end of December 2002 to initiate their contractual rights of first refusal for Talisman's stake. In the face of opposition, Atul Chandra, the managing director of OVL, pleaded his company's case for political support to the Indian government. He hailed the Sudan investment as 'a great leap forward in terms of national oil security' (*Outlook* 2002). Subir Raha, the ONGC chairman would echo this call, saying that there was 'no alternative but to go overseas for equity oil' and that the rapid expansion of Chinese companies offered a lesson for India (*Oil and Gas Journal* 2003). Raha implored Arun Jaitley, the Indian commerce minister, and Ram Naik, the oil minister, to promote OVL's position to the Khartoum government (International Petroleum Finance 2003).

New Delhi would respond in rapid fashion. The interest shown by the Chinese and Malaysian companies toward increasing their share in the oil concession had largely dispelled the Indian government's previous doubts about insecurity in Sudan. If CNPC and Petronas were keen to expand their shares in the country, then it surely was an opportunity upon which New Delhi had to capitalise. It initiated a diplomatic lobbying mission to convince Sudan to counter rights of first refusal to CNPC and Petronas (Dutta 2003), jumping on any chance to persuade the Sudanese to lean in its company's favour.

In the end, much to the surprise and dismay of CNPC and Petronas, the Khartoum government would strongly back the entry of OVL. Chinese power was important to the Khartoum government, but not exclusively so. At the end of the day, its sovereign rights would trump any contractual obligations. Bringing in the Indians was part of the Khartoum government's larger foreign policy agenda. It was better to diversify corporate and political partners than place all its eggs in one Chinese basket. Moreover, if CNPC and Petronas were to have split Talisman's 25 per cent share in GNPOC, it would result in CNPC gaining majority control of Sudan's most important oil project. The NCP decided to rule out any single company from owning more than 40 per cent in the consortium (*Times of India* 2002; Haggett 2003; Varcoe 2003).

But the Khartoum government still also wanted to appease China and Malaysia. It dispatched Mustafa Osman Ismail, the foreign minister, or as he was known in foreign diplomatic and aid circles in Sudan: 'Mr. Smiley', personally to both Beijing and

Kuala Lumpur to present the government's case. Ismail employed his flair and charm to persuade corporate and bureaucratic officials in both Asian capitals to back down and accept Sudan's political determination. After two months of delay, OVL's bid for the Talisman shares would be passed by Khartoum, a decision reluctantly conceded to by China and Malaysia. The Indian government's diplomatic support fitted well into Khartoum's pragmatic calculations allowing OVL to enter Sudan.

India captured its prize. In March 2003, OVL finalised its purchase of Talisman's share in the GNPOC concession. After such difficulty in winning the oil stake it moved quickly to add other investments to its repertoire as activists were pressuring western oil companies out of Sudan. The OVL gained government approval from the cabinet committee on economic affairs in New Delhi on 23rd August 2003 to buy stakes in Blocks 5A and 5B in southern Sudan (*Financial Express* 2003). The oil company would benefit immensely because its entry was timed perfectly with an exceptional oil boom in Sudan. Total crude output shot up from 305,000 barrels per day (bpd) in 2005 to 480,000 bpd in 2008 as Sudan's crude rose 42 per cent in value on account of enormous spikes in international prices (BP 2009; Government of Sudan 2009).

The visit of Indian President A.P.J. Abdul Kalam to Sudan on 20th October 2003 was the culmination of the political thrust that brought OVL into the African country. Kalam was the first Indian president to visit the country in more than 28 years, but he nonetheless praised 'centuries-old and time-tested relations between the two countries' (Government of India 2003; Vyas 2003).

Yet, rather than the historical and cultural bond that the Indian president spoke of fondly, it was oil that had reacquainted the long-lost friends. Sudan went on to state its support for India's ambitions to attain a permanent seat on the UN Security Council and India returned the favour by advocating Sudan's entry into the World Trade Organisation (WTO). Sudan was also a participant in India's ITEC scheme, which focused on cooperation in information technology, human resource development, and academic and cultural exchanges.

India would continue to support Sudan's 'unity and territorial integrity' as pressure mounted on Khartoum to cease its military activities against civilian populations in Darfur. Later, in June 2005, India made a commitment of almost 3,000 troops to the UN peacekeeping mission in southern Sudan (Government of India 2005). It had also pledged $100 million in concessional bilateral credit and $10 million in grants for economic reconstruction as part of the donors' conference in Oslo for south Sudan, with further foreign investment coming from multiple state-owned and private sector corporations in India (*Hindustan Times* 2005). The sudden strengthening of political ties between Sudan and India had a distinct economic flavour. Although OVL managed to orchestrate its entry into Sudan with a helping hand from New Delhi, there remain plenty of risks on the horizon for India's oil interests in that country.

Danger ahead?

The ministry of external affairs in New Delhi was correct in predicting that OVL would evade the same divestment pressures that led to the withdrawal of the Canadian oil company Talisman from Sudan. The growth of activism in the US around the Darfur civil war would lead to a renewed divestment campaign against oil companies. Along with CNPC and Petronas, OVL was one of the campaign's primary targets, however, as a majority state-owned company, such pressures were regarded as unthreatening. One warning from the California Public Employees' Retirement System (CalPERS) indicating that it would not invest any of its more than $200 billion US portfolio in corporations involved in Sudan's oil sector was brushed aside. R.S. Sharma, the former ONGC director of finance was quoted as saying: 'we do not care if CalPERS will invest with us or not. We have more than 300 FIIs (Foreign Institutional Investors) as our investors. We will continue our operations in Sudan' (*Financial Express* 2006).

Along with Malaysia and Japan, a major buyer of Sudanese crude, India has been able to avoid much of the negative publicity directed toward China by activists and the media in the West. The US-based Save Darfur coalition in particular sought to exploit the 2008 Beijing Olympic Games as a pressure point to push China to use its strong ties with Sudan to alter the Khartoum government's political behaviour in Darfur (*Wall Street Journal* 2007).

Nonetheless, although OVL and India managed to quietly side-step much of the defamation that western companies and China faced through their connection with armed conflict in Sudan, the persistence of insecurity on the ground could not be avoided.

Fears that OVL might lose hundreds of millions of dollars by investing in war-torn Sudan did not come to pass. The oil interests of India, however, have not gone completely unhindered. In May 2008, four Indian subcontractors were kidnapped at gunpoint near the oil town of Heglig, close to the North–South border. The armed men who took the Indians were part of the local Misseriya ethnic group, which had seen little benefit from oil development since the signing of the 2005 Comprehensive Peace Agreement (CPA) and were now directing their grievances toward oil companies in the area. After months of ordeal, two of the Indian oil workers managed to escape, the release of another was negotiated, but the last worker was presumed to have died after he had succeeded in eluding his captors.

The kidnapping was one of several violent events involving oil companies and armed groups from disenfranchised local communities in oil-bearing regions during the interim period of the CPA. Indeed, oil remains at the centre of festering political tensions in Sudan (Patey 2010). The threat that armed conflict might disrupt the activities of OVL and other oil companies stems from the possibility of renewed civil war between the North and South, persistent insecurity in southern Sudan and increasing violent reactions of local communities toward oil development.

The risk of renewed armed conflict between Khartoum and the former rebels of the SPLA has hung over the interim period of the CPA since 2005. Possible future civil war between the two sides would almost certainly be centred on control of the oil fields that lie precariously across the North–South border in Unity State and Upper Nile State. In recent years, the two sides have been militarising the border, with the oil-bearing areas of Abyei and Malakal already having witnessed several violent confrontations.

Khartoum could lose considerable revenues because southern oil production accounts for more than 80 per cent of total crude output in Sudan. However, except for the 1,600km oil pipeline heading north to Port Sudan and export terminals on the Red Sea, Juba will have few immediate options available to sell its oil in large amounts should it secede, although Toyota Tsusho Corporation is considering the construction of a 1,400km, 450,000 bpd capacity pipeline from southern Sudan to the Kenyan port of Lamu at a cost of $1.5 billion (Jopson 2010). Arrangements to share oil revenues at the end of the CPA are under negotiation. But political dynamics around oil remain tense and could transform considerably in the years to come after the South voted for independence in a January 2011 referendum. India's oil investments would be very much on the frontline should hostilities break out. Furthermore, there is no guarantee that even if the North and South maintain a peaceful border that southern Sudan will remain secure.

There is no need to predict future armed conflict in southern Sudan. More than 2,000 people were killed in 2009 from violence between ethnic groups, the consequences of which have stalled the exploration work of oil companies operating deeper in the South, such as France's oil major Total. The former rebels in Juba have struggled to end inter-communal conflicts and rein in militia groups with the manipulation of Khartoum always a background factor (Small Arms Survey 2009).

There is also a lingering lack of political consensus among the SPLM movement elite around the oil sector, with certain individuals remaining engaged with oil companies outside of the agreed terms of the CPA. This is an ongoing state of affairs that brings into question the existing contracts of OVL and other companies signed with Khartoum should the south gain independence.

Finally, there has been growing violent resistance to oil development at the local level in Sudan. A lack of social development and the largely unchecked and spreading environmental degradation linked to oil development in southern Sudan has pitted local communities against negligent oil companies, something that could evolve into a protracted Niger Delta-esque scenario.

Corporate responsibility from OVL and other oil companies has more often than not been poorly thought out and limited in scope, and at times has undermined rather than encouraged positive relations between oil companies and local communities (Moro 2008). Insecurity surrounding the oil sector in Sudan ranges from the theft and commandeering of oil company equipment and vehicles to armed kidnappings and killings. The issue will be one that remains with oil companies even after southern Sudan gains independence in July 2011.

Conclusion

The exit of western companies in 2002–03 might have opened the door for India's national oil company in Sudan, but its fortunes in the African nation have nonetheless been put at risk. In contrast to burgeoning general surveys mapping the expansion of India's oil interests in Africa, this detailed analysis pinpoints the various obstacles OVL faced at home and in Sudan. Political opposition in New Delhi at first regarded OVL's interest in buying the abandoned Talisman stake in Sudan as putting hundreds of millions of dollars at grave risk should armed conflict engulf oil investments in the country.

A familiar opponent in the form of the Chinese oil company CNPC then protested the entry of OVL, and the Indian company only managed to enter Sudan thanks to prompt diplomatic action from New Delhi, helped by a preference in Khartoum to bolster the diversity of its Asian political and economic support. Nonetheless, after securing the prized oil assets of Talisman and adding other prospects to its Sudan portfolio, Indian oil interests still face the threat of renewed armed conflict as the CPA between north and south Sudan comes to an end. India is learning that the physical insecurity and political instability of conflict-prone African countries does not easily disappear.

References

BP (2009) *BP Statistical Review of World Energy*, London, BP

Calgary Herald (2002) 'Sudan's civil strife doesn't deter Indian oil explorer', 9 July

Dutta, Sanjay (2003) 'Diplomatic arm-twisting clears Sudan oil deal', *Times of India*, 14 March

Financial Express (2003) 'OVL gets okay on Sudan oil blocks', 24 August

—— (2006) 'ONGC, BHEL, VIL foul of CalPERS', 19 May

Financial Times (2003) 'ONGC pursues Sudan expansion', 16 September

Government of India (2003) 'India-Sudan, Joint Statement', press release, 22 October, New Delhi, Ministry of External Affairs

—— (2005) 'Joint statement of India and Sudan', press release, 8 June, New Delhi, Ministry of External Affairs

Government of Sudan, Ministry of Finance and National Economy (2009) 18 November, www.mof.gov.sd/ accessed 18 November 2009

Haggett, Scott (2003) 'Out of Africa: Talisman closes the book on Sudan', *Calgary Herald*, 13 March

Hindustan Times (2005) 'Sudan for bigger Indian investment', 7 June

International Petroleum Finance (2003) 'ONGC makes progress in Sudan', March

Jopson, Barney (2010) 'Japan group eyes oil pipeline plan', *Financial Times*, 4 March

Lewis, Mike (2009) 'Skirting the law: Sudan's post-CPA arms flows', *Small Arms Survey*, Geneva

Moro, Leben N. (2008) 'War and peace transition' in *Oil, Conflict and Displacement in Sudan*, DPhil thesis, Oxford University, Oxford

Oil and Gas Journal (2003) 'ONGC seeks to be global oil and gas player', February

Outlook (2002) 'Gift of the Nile', 1 July

Patey, Luke A. (2007) 'State rules: oil companies and armed conflict in Sudan', *Third World Quarterly*, vol. 28, no. 5, pp 997–1016

—— (2009) 'Against the Asian tide: the Sudan divestment campaign', *Journal of Modern African Studies*, vol. 47, no. 4, pp. 551–73

—— (2010) 'Crude days ahead? Oil in Sudan after the Comprehensive Peace Agreement', *African Affairs*, vol. 109, no. 437, pp. 617–36

Small Arms Survey (2009) 'Conflicting priorities: GoSS security challenges and recent responses', no. 14

Times of India (2002) 'Petronas to hit ONGC's overseas investment plan', 18 December

Varcoe, Chris (2003) 'Sudan sale to close in March', *Calgary Herald*, 1 February

Vyas, Neena (2003) 'Kalam calls for greater Indi-Sudan cooperation', *The Hindu*, 21 October

Wall Street Journal (2007) 'China can do more on Darfur', 7 October

Part 3
A wider picture of India–Africa partnership

10

The rhetorics and rituals of 'South-South' development cooperation: notes on India and Africa

Emma Mawdsley

Introduction

Most accounts of India's development cooperation with different African countries focus on the historical and ideological contexts for their bilateral relations, the institutions and modalities of India's development cooperation, and the extent to which these relations complement or are mismatched with India's current foreign policy and commercial agendas. Analysts have examined the relative significance of India's development cooperation in specific sectors and countries, the responses of other donors to India's presence, the definitions and reporting of India's development cooperation, the changing strategic imperatives driving Indian aid, and the changing geographical distribution of its development cooperation efforts (DN 2003; Price 2005; Agrawal 2007; Jobelius 2007; Singh 2007; Chanana 2009; Mawdsley 2010; Sinha 2010). Although usually overshadowed by interest in China, India's development cooperation efforts are also analysed as part of the wider emerging interest in the 'emerging donors' (Grim and Harmer 2005; Jerve 2007; McCormick 2008; Woods 2008).

In this volume, the chapter by Fantu Cheru and Cyril Obi sketches out the main elements of Indian development cooperation, while other authors, including Sanusha Naidu and Simona Vittorini and David Harris, also make pertinent observations.

This chapter seeks to do something different. Using insights developed from anthropological theories of reciprocity and social relations between states, it critically evaluates the discourses and practices of Indian development cooperation. It examines the contrast between dominant 'western' constructions of the moral underpinning of foreign aid (principally that of 'charity'), to that articulated by India and other southern development cooperation partners (principally that of 'solidarity' and 'mutual benefit'). The chapter asks what social relations these differently constructed 'moralities' assert, but also what they respectively conceal.

Before starting, I need to make an emphatic caveat. The arguments in this short chapter are set up around the two highly stylised categories of 'western donors' and 'southern development cooperation partners'. Evidently this binary is based on a very broad resolution indeed, which, while a useful means to chart out a wider argument, does not capture the differences within and across both groups of development actors. I am acutely aware of risks and shortcomings of this simplification, and although I suggest that it is a useful device to advance a rather original argument, I recognise the necessity of, and welcome, more nuanced, country-level analyses to test and critique the propositions made here.

The chapter starts by outlining 'gift theory', an idea that originated in anthropology and which has travelled far and wide to other disciplines and contexts. It then briefly recounts how gift theory has been deployed in order to critically evaluate western foreign aid. While concurring with the insights and arguments of several theorists, I observe that, to date, these analysts have tended to overlook the wide range and growing number of southern development partners. What is interesting about this omission is that these commentators are particularly critical of the unequal, hierarchical social relations that are established between states as (western) 'donors' and (low-income) 'recipients' through the transfer of (apparently) unreciprocated 'charity', as western aid is overwhelmingly morally framed. Many southern development partners, in contrast, explicitly and adamantly reject and resist this hierarchy, insisting on more 'horizontal' relations of partnership, and a different construction of what is 'ethical' between states. Does this mean that they rightfully escape the criticisms that are made of western foreign aid through the lens of gift theory? And even if so, does gift theory offer a useful perspective on the social bonds established through South–South development cooperation? The chapter takes up this interesting question, and critically evaluates the discursive claims articulated and performed by the southern donors, with a particular emphasis on India–Africa relations. It concludes by appraising the notion and symbolic importance of reciprocity – the positioning of 'recipient' African countries as sites of opportunity and mutual benefit.

Foreign aid and the gift

In 1924 the French anthropologist Marcel Mauss published *The Gift*, launching a set of ideas that have been profoundly influential and fruitful in stimulating debates in a range of fields. The essence of Mauss's landmark essay is that the act of giving creates a social bond between giver and receiver. According to Mauss, there are three components to this: giving (which initiates a social bond); receiving (because to refuse would not just be to renounce the gift, but also the social relationship); and reciprocating (to demonstrate in return one's own honour, wealth and standing). It is the *social function* of gift giving that distinguishes it from two other forms of resource allocation: economic exchange (simultaneous commercial transactions – straightforward buying and selling) and redistribution (social or political entitlements transferred from the ruler/state to subjects/populations).

A key feature of the 'the gift' is that it must be conducted as voluntary, disinterested and free, even as it sets an obligation at some future point to reciprocate in some form. This means that there is an inherent ambivalence in gift giving – it is *performed* as 'free', but the social bond that is created relies on the unvoiced expectation of eventual return. For example, if you buy a drink for a friend or colleague, you don't ask them for money or immediately and explicitly secure their agreement that they will buy the next one, but it is what you would reasonably expect at some undetermined point in the future. And in buying, receiving and reciprocating a drink, particular social relations are being established. In formulating his arguments, Mauss drew upon the cultures of the indigenous peoples of the American Pacific Northwest coast, amongst others, and especially the potlatch – festivals in which the central ritual was the provision of feasts that expressed and symbolised the redistribution of wealth. Leaders and clans demonstrated their status not by amassing wealth, but by the extent to which they shared it, gave it away, or even, in some spectacular cases, destroyed it.

A number of authors have drawn upon these anthropological theories of reciprocity in analyses of official foreign aid from the 'North' to the 'South'. Tomohisa Hattori (2001), for example, argues that the grant element of official (bilateral and multilateral) foreign aid should be categorised as a gift. It is not an economic exchange or the outcome of rights-based redistribution. However, unlike gifts between relative equals, this gift is unreciprocated – unlike loans, grants are not paid back: they appear to be exempt from the obligation to return something to the giver. Here Hattori turns to another anthropologist, Marshall Sahlins (1972), who finesses Mauss's arguments with a greater attentiveness to power.

Sahlins argues that when the norms of reciprocity are indefinitely suspended, the social relationship that is created and maintained by gift giving is one of superiority and inferiority, rather than the competitive and/or friendly giving-receiving-reciprocating circulation between relative equals. According to Hattori, official foreign aid clearly exhibits the features of Sahlins' 'negative giving': it reflects a condition of significant material inequality between donor and receiver; and it makes a (supposed) virtue of (apparently) unreciprocated giving. Hattori argues that western foreign aid establishes a highly unequal social relationship between states – being a donor confers a symbolic superiority in the order of nations, while being a recipient symbolises inferiority. Being permanently on the receiving end of the aid relationship without (apparently) offering anything in return for such charity other than gratitude acts to demean the recipient.

The French social theorist Pierre Bourdieu (1977, 1990) adds further to gift theory by exploring the acquiescence of some recipients in their 'symbolic domination', proposing their active complicity in maintaining an unequal social order. He asserts that persistent unreciprocated receiving allows social inequality to be naturalised as the normal order of things, effectively helping legitimate it.

Although Hattori's analysis of the post-1945 foreign regime

aid from the perspective of gift theory includes some discussion of the Soviet Union, his empirical focus is otherwise on the dominant western donors. Interestingly he notes, although does not elaborate on the fact, that China and India are exceptional among the recipient countries in also being donors, to which in his 2003 paper he adds South Korea, Taiwan and oil-exporting Arab countries as states which are also in transition from recipients to donors.

Ilan Kapoor (2008) also draws on gift theory as well as post-colonial theories of nationalism and Lacanian psychoanalysis, in his powerful critique of western foreign aid. He asserts that the dominant 'moral' framing of western foreign aid within the public and policy arenas is that of charity to the less fortunate (notwithstanding the recent turn to the language of 'partnership' in policy circles, something which many critics argue is a rather shallow claim). However, Kapoor argues that this construction of foreign aid as free and generous sits at odds with (and helps obscure) the multiple ways in which it actually acts to serve donor interests while extracting a price from its recipients. This includes tied aid, loan repayments, conditionalities that suit western investors and traders, and support for donor foreign policy objectives, notably national security. Furthermore, Kapoor argues that the symbolic work performed by foreign aid produces the sense of a unified, virile and generous nation. Foreign aid, he suggests, allows the visible display of apparent generosity – the creation of heroic figures such as relief camp workers; the branded sacks of grain being dispensed – while negative impacts, self-interest and payback are obscured.

Like Hattori, Kapoor scrutinises the gap between the symbolic claims and performance of aid as free and the realities of its leverage. Interestingly for the analysis here, Kapoor also observes the growing presence of a range of southern development cooperation partners, including India, China, Egypt and Brazil, and spends some time analysing the way in which they are excluded from what he sees as the clan-like Development Assistance Committee (DAC), a powerful forum of (mostly western) OECD donors. Kapoor argues that the DAC's donor classification is 'selective and insular, effectively discriminating against non-western and southern donors' (Kapoor 2008, p. 89). But even as Kapoor draws attention to these non-western donors he continues to focus on Occidentalist nationalism and foreign aid, asserting the role of aid in maintaining a moral ordering of the superior West and the inferior southern recipients of its largesse. It is not clear where the (so-called) 'emerging donors' fit in to this schema – something to which I return later.

Other commentators have deployed gift theory to analyse the ideologies and practices of foreign aid in more ethnographic ways, paying attention to the etiquettes and rituals of gifting aid (see also Appadurai 1986 and Smart 1993 on the performance of the gift). For example, following Mauss, Kelly da Silva describes the extraordinary penetration of (multiple) donor rules and values in all spheres of East Timor's financial, political and judicial systems. Silva examines the ritual performances around donor gift giving, uncovering the ways in which donors construct and enact identities and relations of 'honour, alliance and precedence' (2008, unpaginated). Observing the annual meeting of donor partners, for example, she elucidates the remarkably stable ritualised etiquette through which each bilateral or multilateral donor present competed to demonstrate their generosity and 'aid virility'. Around the table each donor in turn followed the same path: stressing their praise for 'the government' (largely a client regime of their own creation), their identification of shortcomings, their generosity to date, and their commitments to future donations. This donor potlatch represents the 'condensed and expressive manifestations of this universe's symbolic repertoire and modes of functioning' (Silva 2008, unpaginated).

In a discussion that recalls Bourdieu's thoughts on the compliance of the demeaned, Silva goes on to argue that 'East Timor's biggest counter-gift to the international community has been to function as an instrument through which the values cherished by aid donors, expressed in western myths of good society, can once again be cultivated in the process of building a new national state' (Silva 2008. p.1). Its compliant recipient status allows the donors to pursue their material and geopolitical interests (for example, securing access to East Timorese resources, notably offshore hydrocarbons), but to veil this under a symbolic regime of them as generous and altruistic. Silva also mentions a number of southern development actors in East Timor and present at these meetings

(Brazil, China, Malaysia and Thailand), but does not comment on any similarities or differences with the mainstream DAC donors.

This brief outline demonstrates that theories concerning the symbolic power of foreign aid provide rich and vital insights into the social relations constructed between donors on the one hand and recipients on the other. However, analyses to date have focused overwhelmingly on the powerful donors – the DAC bilaterals, UN agencies and other multilaterals. Although there is not the space to discuss them here, R.L. Stirrat and Heiko Henkel (1997) and Benedikt Korf (2007), amongst others, have also examined western NGOs and publics through gift theory. Thus commentators have used gift theory to prosecute the dominant symbolic regime of western foreign aid: that it is free and that it is charitably inspired. Without condemning official foreign aid entirely, which would be foolish, there is no doubt that the persistence of this moral framing of official aid appears to be able to withstand a great deal of evidence to the contrary. As Dane Rowlands observes:

> Despite the consistent evidence that [western] aid allocation tends to be dominated by … political and strategic interests … there remains within the development community as a whole a sense that the true objective and motivation of development is the moral one of assisting the less fortunate. (Rowlands 2008, p.5)

How do these arguments stand up in the face of a set of donors who explicitly articulate a very different set of foreign policy and development cooperation principles which seem to deny such inequalities?

South–South development cooperation and the imaginative geographies of foreign aid

The DAC of the OECD has 24 members. Between them they account for the vast majority of official bilateral aid (between 85 and 95 per cent since the 1990s), and the DAC has assumed the role of arbiter in setting and monitoring the international rules, regulations and norms of foreign aid definitions and conduct. However, Homi Kharas identifies at least 27 non-DAC countries which are 'giving significant amounts of aid on an annual basis' (Kharas 2007, p. 7; see also Manning 2006; Kragelund 2008; Rowlands 2008), and at least 30 additional countries have given smaller amounts of aid, sometimes on a more sporadic basis, often as a result of humanitarian crises (Grimm and Harmer 2005).

Current estimates suggest that together the 'non-DAC donors' (NDDs)[1] contribute between 10 and 12 per cent of global bilateral aid, although deeply contested definitions, weak and/or unavailable data and evidence of official errors in reporting, mean these are hazardous calculations (UN ECOSOC 2008; Brautigam 2009). Amongst the most interesting and potentially important of these non-DAC donors are a range of southern countries, from emerging powers like China, India and Brazil, to pivotal regional states like South Africa, to smaller but economically dynamic states like Thailand.

Despite the long-standing nature of some South–South development cooperation, and at times its reasonably substantial contributions to global overseas development aid, until recently most southern actors were largely overlooked and ignored by academics and policymakers engaged in development. Clemens Six (2009) suggests that the neglect of the non-western donors is powerfully revealing about the psychology and representational regime of development in the West. He argues that these development actors represent a challenge to the dominant aid paradigm by transgressing the cultural categories and social hierarchies that the dominant aid system acts to symbolise and maintain: in other words, who gives and who receives. We might add that these ruptures are not only produced through the provision of South–South aid, but also the refusal to accept aid from the North. On the subject of India's decision to refuse external assistance after the 2004 tsunami, for example, Ole Bjerg states:

> By refusing these gifts India refused once again to enter into the subordinate role of a hopeless developing country dependent on foreign benevolence. Instead the refusal is the expression of a newly gained Indian self-consciousness of strength and independence. (Bjerg 2005, p. 17)

It seems then, that western imaginative geographies of foreign aid have been built upon ignorance and even the active obscuring of the presence and activities of a substantial range of non-western donors. However, this is a situation that has changed sharply, and these states are now an increasingly visible part of the aid landscape. This has been largely driven by China's rise, and to a lesser extent other emerging economies. Various initiatives are now emerging within the traditional centres of the development industry in response to the issue of the non-DAC donors (Grimm and Harmer 2005; UN ECOSOC 2008).

Although some of the non-DAC donors are keen to collaborate and move closer to the DAC community, notably many of the 'new' European states, others are cautious about aligning with the 'mainstream'. According to Rowlands, Brazil and South Africa are more open to cooperation with DAC, but even here: 'Though less reticent [than China and India], Brazil remains wary of such arrangements, and takes care to ensure that it is not simply re-establishing older hierarchical relations wherein it plays a subordinate role to a traditional donor' (Rowlands 2008, p.16).

As I noted in the introduction to this chapter, most analyses of the various non-DAC donors have focused on their economic and political implications for recipient countries, and for international trade, investment and development standards and regulations. In this chapter I build on the work of those theorists who have used gift theory to critically evaluate western foreign aid by asking what it might reveal about South–South foreign aid. Where possible I illuminate the argument with reference to India's development cooperation activities in Africa.

Post-colonial politics and the gift in South–South development cooperation

The southern development partners vary in their histories of aid and cooperation as recipients and donors, the absolute and relative size of their contributions, their aid institutions and modalities, their economic and political positioning within international and regional regimes and institutions, and in their cultural repertoires and discourses of development and humanitarian aid. Moreover, individual donors are not unitary or uniform actors, but complex, contingent, and sometimes contradictory assemblages of different actors, institutions and interests, engaged in dynamic and differentiated relationships with their different partners.

As noted above, the arguments set out here are inevitably highly generalised and the need for country-specific studies should be evident. With this caveat in mind, I argue that we can identify a broadly shared symbolic regime of South–South development cooperation, including that of India. Its characteristic features are:

- The assertion of a shared experience of colonial exploitation, post-colonial inequality and present vulnerability to uneven neoliberal globalisation, and thus a shared identity as 'third world' nations
- Based on this shared experience, a specific expertise in appropriate development approaches and technologies
- An explicit rejection of hierarchical relations between states, and a strong articulation of the principles of respect, sovereignty and non-interference
- An insistence on win-win outcomes of South–South development cooperation and mutual opportunity.

Coded or explicit within each of the characteristics outlined above is a view of the recipient being willing and able to offer counter-gifts in return – in other words, a notion of reciprocity. The gift is performed and conducted as one that is reciprocated, through material returns (such as access to resources) and the provision of investment and market opportunities, as well as esteemed diplomatic ties. This is morally positioned not as eroding true charity – compromising the gift – but in fact as morally better, as recipients maintain their honour and dignity.

As we shall see, this symbolic regime is propagated through statements, speeches and declarations, to some extent through modalities and practices, and also in the ritualised performances of respect and equality in various high-level meetings and forums. What is immediately striking, of course, is the (apparent) contrast to the DAC/western donors. Table 10.1 sets up a generalised binary scheme to highlight this although, needless to say, it grossly simplifies the complexities and differences within and between these two problematic categories of development actors.

Table 10.1 The symbolic claims of western and South–South development actors

Western donors	South–South development cooperation partners
Charity	Opportunity
Moral obligation to the unfortunate	Solidarity with other third world countries
Expertise based on superior knowledge, institutions, science and technology	Expertise based on direct experience of pursuing development in poor country circumstances
Sympathy for different and distant others	Empathy based on a shared identity and experience
The virtue of suspended obligation, a lack of reciprocation	The virtue of mutual benefit and recognition of reciprocity

Let us look then at how donors such as India enact and assert this symbolic regime. To start with, most resist the terminology of 'donor-recipient' and even that of 'foreign aid', contaminated as they are by dominant western/DAC associations (Woods 2008). India refers to 'development cooperation', while Brazil talks in terms of 'horizontal cooperation'. A more controversial construction of aid is articulated by Hugo Chavez, who explicitly positions Venezuelan aid to other Latin American countries as a tool of the 'Bolivarian Revolution', through which he aims to contest US hegemony in the continent. South Africa articulates its role as 'contributing to the African Renaissance', locating itself as an organic part of the greater whole, to which it gives, but from which it can expect reciprocal benefits.

The symbolic claim that emerges from this language of horizontal rather than vertical relations is that of mutual opportunity. China and India, for example, couch their development cooperation in terms of the benefits it brings not only to their recipients, but also to themselves – drawing attention not just to what they give, but what they get in return. So, Senegal, Zambia, Ghana and others are not just the objects of charity or humanitarian compassion, but places that can redeem their honour and status by providing resources, investment opportunities and markets for China and India in return. This foregrounding of mutual benefits establishes the receiver's ability to reciprocate, and therefore the status this affords. In gift theory, the social bond this creates and maintains is one of honourable equality rather than the inferiority that is naturalised over time by the endless cycles of (supposedly) unreciprocated aid, which as radical critics of aid point out, is in any case far from free.

This language of development cooperation is part of a broader contemporary discourse of South–South solidarity, which remains heavily inflected by the language and principles of the Non-Aligned Movement (NAM) and the solidarity of the third world. Of course, now as in earlier decades, the rhetoric of mutual self-respect can be easily dismissed as idealistic and naive: profound differences rapidly arose between different NAM members, and the cracks soon started to show. But it is noteworthy that this language has stood the test of time, even as the membership and functioning of the NAM, not to mention the geopolitical and economic contexts within which it has evolved, have changed enormously over the past 60 years.

Julia Strauss (2009) reminds us that what matters here is not the distance between foreign policy rhetorics and realities (the NAM countries or G77 are hardly unique in this), but how rhetorics serve as legitimating devices and, in doing so, what they intend to signal and create. The rhetorics around development cooperation are not mere window dressing, a gloss over the geostrategic and commercial ambitions that truly motivate such ties. Rather, they serve as a means of persuading, symbolising and euphemising claims to particular identities and social relations.

Although not formally located in gift theory, Strauss's (2009) analysis of the legitimising languages and practices deployed by China in its official relations with Africa exemplifies the argu-ments made in this chapter. Strauss observes the way in which a particular suite of historical events and relations (or rather, sanitised and heroic versions of them) has been elevated to a stable narrative that is repeatedly invoked in the opening rituals and ceremonies of official meetings. Intriguingly, this narrative includes idealised accounts of China's engagement with Africa during the Maoist era. What is striking, says Strauss, is the fact that within China the Maoist period is a subject to be avoided, even repudiated. In contrast:

> China's current official and semi-official statements and rep-
> resentations of China–Africa relations self-consciously and
> deliberately situate current Africa policies and initiatives in a
> distinguished lineage of principled relations, even when the
> actual links are at best tenuous and the substantive content
> radically transformed … The PRC continues to trumpet its past
> 50-odd years of involvement in Africa as positive, progressive
> and grounded in the eternal and principled truths of non-inter-
> ference, mutual benefit, unconditionality, and special friend-
> ship and understanding towards Africa. (Strauss 2009, p. 228)

Interestingly then, although these claims to sturdy 'all-weather'
friendship, shared exploitation and ongoing unfairness con-
sciously stand in sharp contrast to the West's dominant rhetorical
motifs, they share a certain projection of 'goodness'. Strauss's
findings suggest that, like the West, the Chinese also project onto
Africa a certain purity of involvement, if with very different sets
of cultural signifiers and constructions of what constitutes virtue.

India too repeatedly mobilises a set of sanitised historical refer-
ents in its official pronouncements on development cooperation.
When visiting different African countries or regional institutions,
for example, ministers and other dignitaries will unswervingly
start with the ancient trade ties of the Indian Ocean, move to
shared colonial oppression, recall Gandhi's initiation into political
and social activism in South Africa, and invoke Nehru's commitment to African independence and autonomy (see Luke Patey's
comments on the president of India's recent visit to Sudan in this
volume, for example). In a recent visit to Mauritius, India's urbane
UN representative Shashi Tharoor exemplified the content and
tone of dozens of official speeches:

> The India–Africa partnership has deep roots in history. Linked
> across the Indian Ocean, we have been neighbours and partners
> for thousands of years … The advent of the Europeans and
> the colonial period disturbed these interactions but could not
> disrupt them. Later, both India and Africa shared the pain of
> subjugation and the joys of freedom and liberation. Satyagraha,
> non-violence and active opposition to injustice and discrimina-
> tion were first used by Mahatma Gandhi on the continent of
> Africa … Nehru was also a firm believer and practitioner of the
> principle of Afro-Asian solidarity. (Tharoor 2009)

Although all this is indeed the case, more complex and contested histories (the role of Asians as lower level officials in the imperial machinery; Gandhi's neglect and sometimes problematic views of black Africans; Idi Amin's expulsion of Asians in 1972) are excised from these warm accounts of naturalised solidarity and shared identity. The performative work of these declarations is to symbolise difference from the West, respect for partners, and the shared benefits of greater interaction, while obscuring more uncomfortable past and present realities.

These rhetorics of friendship and equality are given expression in the ritualised performances that surround events like the India–Africa summits, as well as high-level meetings and delegations. The red carpet is literally rolled out, and every effort made to enact and convey respect, while underlining the dignity and sovereign presence of the 'partner' nations. It would be hard to miss the difference with the West in the performance of egalitarian solidarity.

Finally, India and other southern development cooperation partners foreground claims to expertise based not on inherently culturally superior institutions, science or technology, but on their own domestic challenges and experiences. Brazil, for example, asserts its know-how in issues such as combatting urban violence and youth gangs, literacy programmes, and HIV/AIDs awareness and prevention initiatives in slums (de Sousa, n.d.). India highlights its ability to develop Triple A technology (affordable, available, adaptable), and in both development assistance and the commercial arenas contrasts this to the often unsuitable models and provision coming from the North.

By highlighting these assertions of subaltern expertise, and grounding development assistance in shared experiences and challenges, southern development partners such as India aim to assert a distinct position for themselves in the foreign aid arena. This type of narrative appears to stand in sharp contrast to the dominant western theme of benevolence and charity – and of course to more critical interpretations of the West's neo-imperialist exploitation of the developing world.

So, if this is what the southern partners might be trying to symbolise and signal, what then might such symbolic repertoires seek to 'euphemise', in Hattori's formulation, or obscure?

What gets obscured in these symbolic claims?

I suggest there are three issues to explore here. First, and hardly surprisingly, like all donor states, national self-interest drives much of the decision making about development cooperation, including the choice of recipients and its nature and conduct. This is not necessarily a problem – indeed, it can easily be construed as a strength of post-colonial development relations. As Six argues: 'Precisely because China, India and other southern donors act in an interest-oriented manner and, for historical reasons, cannot apply the same pseudo-emancipatory rhetoric as the western development paradigm does, we should consider their rise as a unique chance for real progress towards serious partnership' (Six 2009, p. 1109).

I agree with Six here, but although win-win relations are perfectly feasible under this dispensation, such mutually beneficial outcomes are not always the case. Southern development partners have and will continue to prioritise their own interests when seen as necessary, even if these might conflict with those of their partner countries. Whereas the West deploys a symbolic regime of charity and benevolence to obscure this truth, the southern development partners invoke the rhetoric of solidarity and shared identities to do the same.

Moreover, the assertions of 'win-win' outcomes are founded on a simplistic construction of national interest, whether of donor or recipient. No southern development actor of which I am aware has confronted the inherently contested and dislocating nature of development, or even more fundamentally, the class divides fostered by global neoliberal capitalism (Prashad 2007). Building roads, developing raw materials and modernising agriculture will bring benefits to many, but it will also bring costs, particularly to indigenous peoples, small farmers, forest-reliant people and the poorest. The vision of development that is articulated by India is unabashedly capitalist and modernist – economic growth equates to development. The uneven social and economic consequences of development are obscured beneath a symbolic regime of striving nations, which are seeking to contest the inequalities and injustices within the international hierarchy of states. The contested sub-national politics of development are concealed in this account of win-win relations and third world solidarity. India's own development path has been enormously successful and impressive in many ways, but it has come at tremendous environmental and social costs, and it has disproportionately rewarded a minority, while excluding or even exploiting the majority (see also Naidu, this volume).

Second, the repetitive invocation of solidarity that arises from a shared colonial–post-colonial identity and common experience acts to diminish acknowledgement of the ever-widening differences within the global South. The emerging powers – Brazil, India, China, Mexico, South Africa and others – have complex relationships with the poorer and smaller countries of the rest of the G77. As Raphael Kaplinsky and Dirk Messner (2008) document in the case of the Asian drivers (China and India), the direct and indirect impacts of their growing economic and political clout, as well as their changing industrial profiles, can be complementary to some sectors and interests in the rest of the global South. Their economic growth is raising the price of many resources and raw materials; they are providing more affordable goods and services for consumers; and their political clout is helping them to stand up to the G8 in various global forums. The rise of the G20 as the world's premier forum for economic decision making is testament to the strength of the rising powers.

However, interests also clash – the small island states of the Pacific and certain countries of sub-Saharan Africa might have very different positions to Brazil and India on climate change, for example. Lesotho and China are in competition for textile manufacturing jobs and investment. The emerging powers have diplomatic interests in maintaining G77 unity, but they do not and cannot represent the interests of the world's poorest countries (or the rather different issue of the world's poor, as noted above), and the larger ones might find the G20 provides more opportunities and openings, and in doing so, will perhaps pull away from the G77. South–South development cooperation is couched in a symbolic regime of shared identities and interests, but this conceals, or at least euphemises, profound differences in identities and interests that also exist.

Third, southern development actors are not always immune to the aura of national superiority that donor status seems to confer.

181

Amongst a complex mix of motivations and incentives it seems clear that southern donors, like their western counterparts, seek to augment a sense of national virility, in Kapoor's words, through their development assistance activities. In some cases, southern actors reinforce the social hierarchies that they purport to reject. For example, a number of commentators have noted India's susceptibility to locate its growing role as a donor (and its decision in 2003 to ask most of its own donors to leave) in a triumphal and aggrandising narrative of increasing global status. Although many welcome the adjustment that western powers will increasingly have to make in response to the rise of India (and others), smaller nations in Asia and beyond may be less enthused. Writing in *Economic and Political Weekly* (2003), the unnamed author argues that India needs to be aware that it is opening itself up to the same criticisms it has often directed at its own major donors in the past. Although the rhetoric and modalities might appear to avoid the inequalities and humiliations that accompany the unreciprocated gift, India and others might not always avoid the association of aid giving with superiority. Similar to the earlier schema, Table 10.2 is highly simplified, but aims to illustrate the argument here.

Table 10.2 What the symbolic regimes of western and South–South development actors obscure

Western donors	South–South development cooperation partners
Commercial and geopolitical self-interest	Commercial and geopolitical self-interest
Hegemony	The challenge to hegemony
National superiority	National superiority
Inadequate responses to the structural causes of gross inequality	Growing differences in interests between the 'third world' states
Foreign aid that continues to embody neo-imperialistic perspectives and relationships	Development cooperation that primarily serves class based/elite interests in both donor and recipient countries

Conclusion

I have argued that the discourses and performances of South–South development cooperation are not just a superficial veneer over the 'real' geopolitical and commercial strategies that motivate them, but are essential to understanding the social relations and identities between states that they seek to create and those they seek to obscure in their constructions of themselves and their partners.

Different elements of western foreign aid have been subject to close critique through the lens of gift theory, allowing analysts to demonstrate the ways in which the symbolic properties of foreign aid work to assert benevolence and generosity within the dominant moral framing of aid as charitable, while obscuring more exploitative, hierarchical and self-interested relations. These are exactly the social relations that the southern development partners claim to avoid, a position that finds expression in the rhetorical and performative regimes they enact. However, just as the declarations of the Non-Aligned Movement could not withstand the realpolitik of regional rivalries and cold war interference, the language of solidarity that clothes South–South development cooperation cannot entirely obscure the differences between the larger emerging economies, such as Brazil, China, India and others, and with the lower income countries of the global South.

Moreover, in celebrating national virility through their transition from recipient to donor, India and other southern donors can sometimes act to reinforce the social hierarchy of nations; while it is clear to all commentators that – just like the western donors – national self-interest (however constructed by elites) is a major driving force behind development cooperation. The insights of gift theory allow us a stronger analytical purchase on the symbolic realm of Indian development cooperation, to complement the more materialist analyses. In particular, it allows us to recognise that the discourse of reciprocity (expressed as 'win-win' and mutual benefit, and the construction of African and other partner countries as places of opportunity in return) should not necessarily be seen as demonstrating a failure of morality. Some critics of southern development cooperation argue that they are insufficiently 'charitable', and deficient when it comes to moral or ethical motivations for aid. But I suggest that gift theory reminds us of the virtue of reciprocity – maintaining, as it does, social relations of honour, dignity and status. As Mary Douglas says in her introduction to Mauss's famous essay (Mauss 1990), we know that charity is a Christian virtue, but it wounds. Southern donors actively attempt to avoid this discursive positioning of their development cooperation: something that many western donors could learn from. But just like western donors, southern development partners are in pursuit of their own interests, and their symbolic claims should be equally subject to critical evaluation as those of the western donors.

Note

1. Finding the right term for the various development assistance partners around the world who are not members of DAC is extremely challenging. They include a vast spectrum of countries, with different historical and ideological experiences (including as recipients and donors), and different political positionings in the world today (including in relation to the international aid architecture. Although 'non-DAC' partners might be accurate, the residual nature of the category tends to keep DAC as the normative centre of bilateral donors. It also perhaps implies too much coherence in DAC. I use the term here, but with caution.

References

Agrawal, S. (2007) 'Emerging donors in international development assistance: the India case', IDRC, http://www.idrc.ca/uploads/user-S/12441474461Case_of_India.pdf, accessed 18 February 2011

Appadurai, A. (1986) *The Social Life of Things: Commodities in Cultural Perspective*, Cambridge, Cambridge University Press

Bjerg, O. (2005) 'To give or not to give: ethics after the tsunami', in Nordic Institute of Asian Studies (NIAS) *The Tsunami and its Social and Political Implications*

Bourdieu, P. (1977) *Outline of a Theory of Practice*, tr. Nice, R., Cambridge, Cambridge University Press

—— (1990) *The Logic of Practice*, tr. Nice, R., Cambridge, Polity Press

Brautigam, D. (2009) *The Dragon's Gift: The Real Story of China in Africa*, Oxford, Oxford University Press

Chanana, D. (2009) 'India as an emerging donor', *Economic and Political Weekly*, 21 March, pp.11–14

DN (2003) 'Aid: old morality and new realities', *Economic and Political Weekly*, June 14

Economic and Political Weekly (2003) 'Aid: old morality and new realities', 14 June

Grimm, S. and Harmer, A. (2005) 'Diversity in donorship: the changing landscape of official humanitarian aid: aid donorship in Central Europe',

HPG background paper, September

Hattori, T. (2001) 'Reconceptualising foreign aid', *Review of International Political Economy*, vol. 8, no. 4, pp. 633–60

—— (2003) 'The moral politics of foreign aid', *Review of International Studies*, vol. 29, pp. 229–47

Jerve, A.M. (2007) 'Asian models for aid: is there a non-western approach to development assistance? Summary record of seminar held in Oslo, December 2006', http://www.cmi.no/publications/file/2767-asian-models-for-aid.pdf, accessed 18 February 2011

Jobelius, M. (2007) 'New powers for global change? Challenges for international development cooperation: the case of India', FES Briefing Paper 5, Berlin, March

Kaplinsky, R. and Messner, D. (2008) 'Introduction: the impact of Asian drivers on the developing world', *World Development*, vol.36, no. 2, pp. 197–209

Kapoor, I. (2008) *The Postcolonial Politics of Development*, London and New York, Routledge

Kharas, H. (2007) 'The new reality of aid – The Brookings Blum roundtable', 1 August, http://www.brookings.edu/-/media/Files/rc/…/08aid_kharas.pdf, accessed 12 February 2011

Korf, B. (2007) 'Antimonies of generosity: moral geographies and post-tsunami aid in Southeast Asia', *Geoforum*, vol. 38, pp. 366–78

Kragelund, P. (2008) 'The return of the non-DAC donors to Africa: new prospects for African development', *Development Policy Review*, vol. 26, no. 5, pp. 555–84.

Manning, R. (2006) 'Will "emerging" donors challenge the face of international cooperation?', *Development Policy Review*, vol. 24, no. 4, pp. 371–83

Mauss, M. (1990) *The Gift*, tr. Hall, W.D., London and New York, Routledge

Mawdsley, E. (2010) 'The Non-DAC donors and the changing landscape of foreign aid: the (in)significance of India's development cooperation with Kenya', *Journal of Eastern African Studies*, vol. 10, no. 1

McCormick, D. (2008) 'China and India as Africa's new donors: the impact of aid on development', *Review of African Political Economy*, vol. 115, pp. 73–92

Prashad, V. (2007) *The Darker Nations: A People's History of the Third World*, New York, New Press

Price, G. (2005) 'Diversity in donorship: the changing landscape of official humanitarian aid: India's official aid programme', HPG background paper, Overseas Development Institute (ODI)

Rowlands, D. (2008) 'Emerging donors in international development assistance: a synthesis report', Ottawa, International Development Research Centre Report

Sahlins, M. (1972) *Stone Age Economics*, Chicago, Aldine

Silva, K.C. da (2008) 'AID as gift: an initial approach', *Mana*, no. 4

Singh, S.K. (2007) 'India and West Africa: a burgeoning relationship', Briefing paper, Chatham House Africa Programme

Sinha, P. (2010) 'Indian development cooperation with Africa', in Cheru, Fantu and Obi, Cyril (eds) *The Rise of China and India in Africa*, London and Uppsala, Zed Books and The Nordic Africa Institute.

Six, C. (2009) 'The rise of postcolonial states as donors: a challenge to the development paradigm, *Third World Quarterly*, vol. 30, no. 6, pp. 1103–21

Smart, A. (1993) 'Gifts, bribes and *guanxi*: a reconsideration of Bourdieu's Social Capital', *Cultural Anthropology*, vol. 8, no. 3, 385–408

Sousa, S.-L.J. de (n.d.) 'Brazil as a new international development actor, South–South cooperation and the IBSA initiative', http://www.nsi-ins. ca/english/events/DAW/2_de%20Sousa.pdf, accessed 24 March 2010

Stirrat, R.L. and Henkel, H. (1997) 'The development gift: the problem of reciprocity in the NGO world', *Annals of the American Academy of Political and Social Science*, no. 554, pp. 66–80

Strauss, J. (2009) 'The past in the present: historical and rhetorical lineages in China's relations with Africa', in Strauss, J. and Saavedra, M. (eds) 'China and Africa: emerging patterns in globalisation and development', *The China Quarterly,* Special Issue, no. 9

Tharoor, S. (2009) 'India–Africa: partners in development', address by Minister of State Dr Sashi Tharoor, University of Mauritius, 3 November, http://meaindia.nic.in/, accessed 27 July 2010

United Nations Economic and Social Council (UN ECOSOC) (2008) 'Background study for the development cooperation forum: trends in South–South and triangular development cooperation', April

Woods, N. (2008) 'Whose aid? Whose influence? China, emerging donors and the silent revolution in development assistance', *International Affairs*, vol. 84, no. 6, pp. 1205–21

11

India's security concerns in the western Indian Ocean

Alex Vines

Introduction

Although India regards the western Indian Ocean as its backyard, among the coastal and island countries that make up its African arc, it has historically only really regarded its relationship with Mauritius as a strategic partnership, cooperating with others primarily through South–South initiatives such as the Non-Aligned Movement (NAM), the Indian Ocean Rim Association for Regional Cooperation (IOR-ARC), and further ad hoc economic efforts led by the Indian private sector. During the past few years, however, India has deepened security and diplomatic cooperation with the Seychelles, South Africa, Madagascar and Mozambique as Sino-Indian rivalry hots up and its concern about piracy grows. This chapter charts an evolving relationship between India and other countries of the African Indian Ocean rim and looks at the factors inducing changes (see also Vines 2010).

Increasing strategic importance

On 16 December 1971 the United Nations General Assembly adopted a resolution declaring the Indian Ocean 'for all time as a zone of peace'. The basis for this had been laid at the Non-Aligned Summit in Lusaka in 1970. India supported these efforts, but it is clear that they were a product of the geopolitical environment and the superpower rivalry dominating the world at the time (Braun 1983). The introduction of nuclear issues into the region complicated matters further, and no progress was made on creating the Indian Ocean as a zone of peace by the time the UN Committee set up to implement the General Assembly resolution was dropped in 1998 (Press Trust of India 1998).

By 1997 India's policy makers believed that the 'meetings of the Ad Hoc Committee have shown that they more often add to the problems than they resolve them and they do not contribute to an effective dialogue. It is suggested that a better option may be to bury the dead and start anew' (Press Trust of India 1998). In 1997 just after the launch of the IOR-ARC, Inder Kumar Gujral, then Indian minister of external affairs, said: 'By virtue of its geographical position, India has a natural interest in maintaining the Indian Ocean as a region free from military rivalries. The Indian Ocean rim initiative with which we have been associated since its inception aims at bringing together countries with a shared objective' (Government of India 1997).

However, security cooperation within the framework of the IOR-ARC was not part of India's immediate vision. India is wary of Pakistani, US and particularly Chinese military influence, which has led to the increasing significance of the African Indian Ocean rim states in recent years (Campbell 2003). Mauritius has regularly supported India among the African Indian Ocean rim, from selective membership of IOR-ARC to defence (Campbell 2003).

A significant Indian diaspora live in the western Indian Ocean particularly in Mauritius (68 per cent of population – some 800,000 people), La Réunion (about 220,000 or 30 per cent of the total population), Kenya (80,000), Tanzania, (50,000), Madagascar (25,000), Mozambique, (21,000), Seychelles (around 6 per cent of population) and South Africa (1.2 million). During the past decade the Indian government has sought to engage with non-resident Indians (NRIs), including through the issue of Person of Indian Origin (PIO) cards. In January 2006, the Indian government also introduced the Overseas Citizenship of India (OCI) scheme to allow a limited form of dual citizenship to Indians, NRIs and PIOs for the first time since independence in 1947. It is expected that the PIO card scheme will be phased out in coming years in favour of OCI.

Because of geographical proximity, but also in response to this large diaspora, India has its most comprehensive diplomatic presence in eastern Africa and the western Indian Ocean, with embassies or high commissions in Kenya, Tanzania, Mozambique, South Africa, Seychelles, Madagascar and Mauritius and a consulate general in Réunion.[1] Even so, surprisingly, given its growing strategic importance, India covers much of this region through defence attaches based in Kenya and South Africa, and its diplomatic presence remains thin, under-resourced and understaffed compared with China.[2]

Since it was published in 2004, India's maritime doctrine has shaped the country's policy in the Indian Ocean. It asserts that all 'major powers of this century will seek a toehold in the Indian Ocean region' and envisages an ambient naval presence from the Strait of Hormuz to the Strait of Malacca (Berlin 2006). As a response to Somali piracy this doctrine was updated in 2009 to provide for responses to such challenges (Chatham House 2010). The Indian airforce also sees an arc of interest from Malacca to Suez and has been purchasing aircraft to permit it to engage in contingency operations.

Indian naval planners assume that the US military presence on Diego Garcia of the Chagos Islands (British Indian Ocean Territory) is complementary, allowing the Indian navy to focus their efforts elsewhere; as does the French naval base at Port de Galets on La Réunion, which hosts the second largest permanent navy deployment in the Indian Ocean (a fleet of small patrol boats, two frigates and two P400 class patrol vessels).

The French Comoros island of Mayotte also maintains a small French naval base, which might explain partly why India's diplomatic efforts in the Comoros Islands are thin. However, the United States is encouraging India to beef up its naval efforts in the Indian Ocean, because it finds its naval assets increasingly overstretched. India, on occasion, conducts joint naval exercises with the French Indian Ocean fleet from La Réunion.

Unlike western efforts, Chinese diplomatic and economic expansion in the Indian Ocean is watched particularly closely by India. China is increasing its access to global ports and airfields, and developing special diplomatic relationships from the South China Sea to the Arabian Gulf. The state-owned China Harbour Engineering Company, through a $198 million Chinese loan, helped Pakistan complete Phase I for its deep-sea port at

Gwadar, just 72km from the Iranian border at the mouth of the strategic Strait of Hormuz, a major conduit for global oil supplies (Ramachandran 2006).

China's efforts in Sri Lanka have also alarmed New Delhi. At Hambantota, China is building a $1 billion port that the media has reported to be a refuelling and docking station for its navy, as it patrols the Indian Ocean and protects China's supplies of Saudi oil. Ever since Sri Lanka agreed to the plan, in March 2007, China has given aid, arms and diplomatic support to Sri Lanka. India has found itself sidelined, to its obvious irritation. 'China is fishing in troubled waters', Palaniappan Chidambaram, India's then home minister, warned in April 2009 (Page 2009). China denies it is building a port for its navy and its officials say that India was approached initially by the Sri Lankan government to invest in this project, but declined.

The significance of the Indian Ocean to India's economic development and security is immense. Most of India's trade is by sea and nearly 89 per cent of India's oil arrives in this manner. India – soon to become the world's fourth largest energy consumer, after the US, Japan and China – is dependent on its oil for roughly 33 per cent of its energy needs, 65 per cent of which it imports. Its coal imports from Mozambique are to also increase substantially in coming years, adding to the coal that it is already importing from other Indian Ocean countries, such as South Africa, Indonesia and Australia (Kaplan 2009). The five-day official visit to India of Mozambique's president, Armando Guebuza, in September 2010 – his first trip to a foreign country outside Africa after his re-election in 2009 – followed Mozambique's award of two coal acreages in Moatize to Coal India Ltd in late 2009. The Indian Ocean is India's main supply line for energy and trade. Avoiding disruption in the sea lanes of communication in the Indian Ocean is vital for India's economy.

The Indian Ministry of Shipping estimates that $50 billion of Indian imports and $60 billion of exports pass through the Gulf of Aden. Prime Minister Manmohan Singh emphasised this at a joint press conference with Mozambique's President Armando Guebuza in New Delhi in September 2010, stating: 'It is our common mutual interest to ensure the safety and security of sea lanes of communication in the Indian Ocean' (*The Hindu* 2010). For this reason India wants to see if the IOR-ARC can be revitalised through its presidency in 2011.

India is enlarging its navy. With 155 warships, it is one of the world's largest and it expects to add three nuclear-powered submarines and three aircraft carriers to its arsenal by 2015. As it expands, senior Indian navy officials believe that they are in direct competition with China and that India's near-country hegemony is being challenged. This is most visible in the Seychelles and Mauritius. New Delhi was particularly alarmed that Chinese President Hu Jianto ended his tour of eight African states in early 2007 by visiting the Seychelles (*Times of India* 2007). Symbolically, in March 2007 ten members of China's communist youth league arrived in the Seychelles.

Increasing Chinese activity in the Seychelles resulted in India signalling its concern to Beijing when Pranab Mukherjee, the External Affairs Minister, indirectly warned the Chinese that 'we have a strong stake in the security and stability of these waters, which is linked to energy security, since a large percentage of Asian oil and gas are shipped through the Indian Ocean' (Abdi 2007). The Chinese appeared to have ignored Indian sensitivities again in February 2009 when the Chinese President's four-nation African tour concluded in Mauritius. It is clearly not accidental that Hu's two trips to Africa are ending in Indian Ocean island states that maintain close ties to India.

Hu's visit to Mauritius was the first ever by a Chinese head of state, during which a $260m loan for the expansion of the international airport and the completion of a Chinese $730m special economic zone were announced. This special economic zone is the largest ever single injection of foreign capital into the island and it is hoped it will be a gateway into African markets, creating 40,000 jobs and generating exports of up to $200m annually (*China Daily* 2009). Such Chinese economic penetration will strengthen India's resolve to protect its security and military presence in the western Indian Ocean.

India has defence agreements in place with the Seychelles and Mauritius. India agreed on its defence cooperation with Seychelles through a memorandum of understanding for India to patrol her territorial waters when in 2003 then vice president Bhairon Singh Shekhawat visited the islands in 2003.

In February 2003 an anticipated Chinese move in a similar direction was pre-empted by Admiral Arun Prakash, the Indian naval chief, gifting the INS *Tarmugli* to the Seychelles Coast Guard for regular surveillance of the coastal areas of the island nation (it became Coast Guard Ship *Topaz*).[3] The Indian navy considered the request from the Seychelles so urgent that it decided to pull the ship out of its own fleet barely three years after commissioning (Mohan 2009). India seconds one coast guard adviser and has also gifted a few helicopters to the Seychelles and Indian navy ships routinely visit the islands.

In November 2001, a contingent of the Indian army's special forces and the Indian air force conducted a joint exercise with the Seychelles People's Defence Force (SPDF), including training in airborne and anti-terrorist operations, situating them as a response to the 9/11 terrorist attacks in the United States. The Indian air force dispatched two AN-32 transport aircraft to participate in the exercise and an airborne exercise in the Praslin Islands was part of the programme. An Indian official at the time said the Seychelles was vulnerable to regional, political and economic 'manipulative pressures and military threats, besides internal subversion and sabotage' (Kumar 2008). In 2003, INS *Investigator* transported military stores (small arms and ammunition), gifted by India, to the SPDF (Kumar 2008).

The Indian government took a further step to strengthen the island-nation initiatives when in September 2005 it created a new defence ministry office headed by a two-star admiral (Berlin 2006). High-level visits have also been frequent, and have included a visit in 1981 by then Prime Minister Indira Gandhi, and a visit by Seychellois President James Alix Michel to India in 2010. During this visit, India committed $5 million assistance to the Seychelles for defence related projects, and agreed to provide one new Dornier and two Chetak helicopters from Hindustan Aeronautics Ltd for maritime surveillance. Prior to delivery, India would provide an in-service Dornier aircraft and promised additional Indian naval visits to conduct surveillance and hydrographic surveys.

Security cooperation between India and Mauritius dates back to 1974 when India handed over a naval ship AMAR for coastal surveillance. Under a 1974 agreement, Indian defence officers (from the Indian air force and navy) are sent on secondment with the national coast guard and the helicopter squadron of the Mauritius Police Force (MPF). In 2001, India provided Mauritius with an interceptor patrol boat, CGS *Observer*, on lease for five years. India has also funded the repairs of Mauritius' flagship, CGS *Vigilant*. In addition under the India Technical and Economic Cooperation (ITEC) programme, training facilities in Indian defence establishments are provided to the MPF. India is also the largest supplier of defence equipment to Mauritius, which in 2004 bought a Dornier 228 maritime surveillance aircraft from Hindustan Aeronautics Limited (Kumar 2008). In a bid to further strengthen their defence ties, in July 2010 India signed a memorandum of understanding (MoU) with Mauritius to provide it one offshore patrol vessel paid by a grant and credit line.

Since early 2003, India has been patrolling the exclusive economic zone of Mauritius (Berlin 2006). Indian naval ships *Delhi* and *Trishul* of the western fleet called in 2005 at Port Louis on a goodwill visit and naval visits from 2009 became more regular in response to the threat posed by Somali piracy.

The Indian navy has also provided Mauritius and the Seychelles with hydrographic cooperation. In 2006, the INS *Sarvekshak* carried out hydrographic surveys of Port Louis harbour and the Agalega islands, following the signing of an MoU in 2005. India provided Mauritius with the first ever chart of the Agalega islands. The Indian navy has also conducted similar surveys for the Seychelles in 2003 and 2006. The National Hydrographic School at Goa trains hydrographers from both these island states (Kumar 2008). India's expertise has been sought by the International Hydrographic Organisation (IHO) to establish a marine electronic highway in the seas along Africa's east coast to aid sailors in navigation. The highway would extend from South Africa to the Mozambican port of Nacala, and then to the Comoros and to Adabara in the Seychelles (Press Trust of India 2009).

With China building deep-water ports to its west and east, and increasing Chinese arms sales going to Indian Ocean states, Indian naval planners fear being encircled. Beijing has sought naval links with the Maldives, Seychelles, Mauritius and Madagascar, and New Delhi is concerned that China wants to control vital sea lanes of communication between the Indian and Pacific Oceans through a 'string of pearls strategy'.

A response has been India's first listening post on foreign soil, which began operations in northern Madagascar in July 2007. New Delhi has apparently rented land for $2.5m from the Mauritius government in order to construct a radar surveillance station with high-tech digital communication systems to watch shipping movements.[4] India has further been in discussions with the Mauritian government in 2010 about a long-term lease of the two Agalega islands, which would officially serve as a high-end tourist resort. In strategic terms Agalega could serve as a small yet significant base on the path between India and the important shipping lane of the Mozambique Channel on the southeast coast of Africa (Forsberg 2007).

A cat-and-mouse-game reminiscent of the tussle between the US and Soviet navies during the cold war happened in February 2009 when Indian submarines, maritime reconnaissance aircraft and warships tracked, 'buzzed' and photographed two Chinese destroyers and a supply ship as they made their way to join international anti-piracy patrols off Somalia (Pandit 2009). The Chinese media claimed that their navy forced up an Indian kilo class submarine that had been seeking to 'fingerprint' the two Chinese destroyers. Both the Indian and Chinese governments have denied this, but Indian officials admit that such cat-and-mouse surveillance games are normal and what is unusual is that on this occasion the press reported this tussle (Chellaney 2009).[5]

Indian military ties have also been growing with other African Indian Ocean rim states. In late 2004, the Indian air force conducted a combined air-defence exercise with its South African counterpart. This was the first ever combined air exercise by India in Africa with six Mirage-2000s, with the help of two Il-78 aerial tankers and two Il-76 transports, carrying personnel and supplies to South Africa via Mauritius. India and South Africa also conducted combined naval drills off the African coast in June 2005 and, in association with Brazil, off Cape Town in May 2008 and in August 2010.

India's president also visited Tanzania in 2004, which led to an agreement for increased training of Tanzanian military personnel in India and more frequent calls by Indian warships at Tanzanian ports. Relations have also expanded with Mozambique. India provided joint patrols off the Mozambique coast during the Africa

Union summit in Maputo in 2003 and has provided this service again in 2004 for a World Economic Forum meeting.[6]

A defence agreement was signed in 2006 for the Indian navy to organise regular patrols off Mozambique's coast and to supply it with arms and services for defence purposes (India Public Information Bureau 2006). In May 2008, two vessels, the INS *Mumbai* and INS *Karmukh* docked in the Mozambican ports of Nacala and Maputo on goodwill visits.

In July 2008, following an Indian Ocean Naval Symposium, India sent four of its warships from its western naval command to the Red Sea and the East African coast on a two-month deployment with INS ships calling at Mombasa, Dar es Salaam, Madagascar and Mauritius. According to an Indian naval official:

> With India's economic interest in West Africa and Asia region increasing, Navy will be playing its diplomatic role by visiting more ports all along the coast of eastern Africa, touching the Horn of Africa … Most of the navies in eastern Africa are small in size compared to the Indian Navy. What we would be aiming during these interactions is to give them the confidence that India would come to their aid whenever there is a need, considering that we have enough experience in all aspects of operations, be it military, diplomatic, policing or benign. (India Defence 2008)

Four Indian warships again deployed to western Indian Ocean waters in August 2010 for naval exercises with the navies and coast guards of Tanzania, South Africa, Seychelles and Mauritius and port calls to Réunion and Mozambique.

Anti-piracy and counter-terrorism operations and evacuation

Piracy and counter-terrorism also increasingly feature in India's naval interest in the western Indian Ocean rim, although this is spreading to threaten shipping off India's southwest coast, which has resulted in the Indian navy launching, in December 2010, Operation Island Watch for intensive patrolling of Indian waters. Profound societal problems in Somalia and the associated regular acts of piracy off its coast have made its waters the most dangerous in the world for merchant shipping and in 2010 some 67 ships had been hijacked off Somalia and 714 sailors were held for ransom. Indian ships are not immune. In January 2006, an Indian dhow, the *Delta Ranger*, was overtaken in international waters by Somali pirates armed with rocket-propelled grenade launchers and AK-47 rifles, but was saved by the US warship *Winston Churchill*, which was in the vicinity, seized control of the vessel and detained the pirates.

These pirates were transferred to Mombasa and later sentenced to seven years imprisonment although Indian anti-piracy legislation was not in place and in 2011 is still in draft stage. Not long after this incident an Indian commercial vessel and its 35 crew were hijacked by Somali gunmen in March 2006 (Ramachandran 2006). Attacks on shipping with Indian nationals involved increased. The Indian navy therefore increasingly sought cabinet approval to engage in anti-piracy operations off the Somali coast but failed to obtain it.

It took the hijacking on 15 September 2008 of the Hong Kong-flagged chemical tanker MT *Stolt Valor* with its 18 Indian crew members to get the Indian government to approve a naval deployment (Ministry of Defence 2008). The government's decision was also a pre-emptive action to avoid noisy scenes expected from a debate on piracy scheduled in parliament soon thereafter and a response to a ruling by the Supreme Court of India that ordered the government to be very quickly more transparent and forthcoming with information in its dealings with relatives of those on hijacked vessels (*Times of India* 2008).

The decision to deploy also followed a high-profile campaign by Seema Goyal, the wife of the captain of MT *Stolt Valor*. She became the point person for the hijacked crew and provided the Indian media with daily reports from Somalia about their plight. Later, she moved to New Delhi to keep the crew's plight in public view, organised peace marches, threatened a hunger strike and met Rahul Gandhi, the Congress general secretary (*Times of India* 2008).

The Indian navy deployed a warship in the region from 23 October 2008. The frigate, INS *Tabar*, began patrolling the pirate-infested waters off Somalia on 2 November. It was also augmented in November 2008 in the Gulf of Aden by the deployment of a larger destroyer, the INS *Mysore*, which carries two Sea

King helicopters on board. Somalia also added India to its list of states permitted to enter its territorial waters, extending up to 12 nautical miles from the coastline, in an effort to discourage piracy.

An Indian naval official confirmed in a letter to the defence ministry that: 'We had put up a request before the Somali government to play a greater role in suppressing piracy in the Gulf of Aden in view of the United Nations resolution. The TFG [Transitional Federation Government] government gave its nod recently' (*Thaindian News* 2008). This letter reached the ministry on 19 November 2008, a day after the INS *Tabar* stopped a pirate attack and sunk an alleged pirate mother ship in the Gulf of Aden. India indicated that it was considering deploying four more warships in the region in 2009 following the May Indian elections and that 'our main concern will remain ships under Indian flag to deter piracy and instil confidence in the shipping community. The main role will remain patrolling and surveillance' (*Economic Times* 2008).

Negotiations for the release of the *Stolt Valor* merchant ship from pirate control was complex. It took several months and the Indian defence ministry said it could not intervene in the hostage crisis because it had occurred in Somali territorial waters. However the Indian minister of shipping, road transport and highways defended the lack of direct action, explaining that 'the entire issue was complicated by the fact that the ship owner was Japanese, flag Hong Kong, Charter Norwegian and the crew mainly from India'. New Delhi set up an inter-ministerial coordination team, involving Pranab Mukherjee, the then minister of external affairs, the Ministry of Defence and a delegation led by Captain Mohan, chairman of the National Shipping Board, which visited Japan in late October 2008 (*Economic Times* 2008). On 16 November 2008 a $1.1 million ransom payment was paid ($6 million had been originally requested) (Aneja 2008).

Indian sailors continued to be taken hostage in 2009 and 2010, such as the three Indian sailors on board the MV *Alpha Manyara* fishing trawler, who were seized by pirates on 9 January 2009. Indian navy chief Admiral Sureesh Mehta assured action would be taken saying 'We will do anything to rescue the Indian sailors taken hostage by Somali pirates off the Kenyan coast' (*Indian Express* 2009).

Responding to a distress call from the Indian-flagged MV *Premdivya* on 12 February 2009, the US navy arrested nine more suspected pirates off the coast of Somalia – the second capture in two days. The Indian vessel sent a distress call to all ships in the area reporting that she had been fired upon by a small skiff, and suspected pirates were attempting to board. A US navy helicopter crew was launched from the USS *Vella Gulf* and fired two warning shots at the small aggressor boat. A navy boarding team was then launched to investigate the skiff's crew and found rocket-propelled grenades and other weapons on board the small craft, according to navy officials. The suspected pirates were taken aboard the USS *Vella Gulf*, processed and subsequently handed over to the Kenyan authorities (*News India-Times* 2009).

The INS *Nirdeshak*, along with a French warship and Spanish frigate, also intercepted and arrested nine pirates as they tried to hijack an Italian cruise liner in the waters of the exclusive economic zone off the Seychelles. The pirates were handed over to the Seychelles. The INS *Nirdeshak* is a hydrographic survey ship, equipped with a Chetak helicopter, interceptor boats and carries a 40mm Bofors gun on board. The Indian navy now regularly patrols the Seychelles economic zone after the island nation requested anti-piracy assistance.

The Indian navy was also quietly deployed in early January 2008 during the height of the post-election political crisis in Kenya in case the situation deteriorated to the point that evacuation of Kenyan NRIs was necessary. The Indian government had announced that urgent visas could be issued to needy individuals. The call for an immediate rescue operation was officially rejected because Indian officials correctly assessed that PIOs were not being targeted and feared that any public talk of evacuation could render Kenyan Indians more vulnerable in the unrest, as well as put a strain on bilateral relations (*Business Standard* 2008). With memories of India's failure to intervene in support of East African Asians in 1968 and 1971 from Kenya and 1972 from Uganda, the Indian navy wanted to be ready in case it became politically expedient to engage in a civilian evacuation mission, as it did in Beirut in 2006 with the assistance of four Indian navy ships. It is interesting to note the extent to which the projection of Indian naval capacity globally resonates with nationalist sentiments within the country.

The Indian navy has sought to develop a maritime military block comprising of littoral states of the Indian Ocean, known as the Indian Ocean Naval Symposium (IONS). This would include 33 countries ranging from South Africa to Australia and would not exclude Pakistan (although China and the US have been excluded thus far). The maiden symposium of this initiative in February 2008 in India attracted senior participation, with the exception of Bahrain, Comoros and Pakistan. According to Indian officials the IONS aims to 'increase maritime cooperation among participating navies/maritime agencies by providing a forum for discussion of maritime issues, both global and regional, and in the process generate a flow of information and opinion between naval professionals leading to common understanding and possible agreements on the way ahead' (*Financial Express* 2008). The IONS is also a response to the fact that, although India is a member of the nine-nation South Asia Regional Port Security Cooperative, maritime issues are not adequately covered by this body or within the IOR-ARC, although India is looking at how it might revive the IOR-ARC under its presidency in 2011.

Conclusion

India's western Indian Ocean rim strategy is deepening and, unlike in other parts of Africa, is not simply commercially led, but is underpinned by India's 2004 maritime doctrine and a response to growing Sino-Indian rivalry. New Delhi maintains a special relationship with Mauritius because of its strong population base of Indian origin, but also because it is the largest offshore investor in India.

Chinese and Pakistan efforts in the western Indian Ocean rim are closely monitored by India, and concern about Chinese expansionism has resulted in the Indian navy seeking to deepen its defence and commercial engagement with the Seychelles, Madagascar, Mauritius and Mozambique. However, as discussed above, Indian government efforts in this region are under-resourced and constrained by bureaucracy and lack of skilled human resources to underpin this policy. It is evident that it is not deepening its political, economic and defence profile in the manner that China has done in recent years except for anti-piracy operations in the Gulf of Aden and around the Seychelles. This is not necessarily negative as China in reality is much less of an immediate threat to India than the spreading threat of Somali piracy to international shipping.

Notes

1. India had 20 ambassadors or high commissioners posted in sub-Saharan Africa in 2007. In addition to missions in all the African Indian Ocean rim countries (except Comoros) there are envoys in the Democratic Republic of Congo, Angola, Namibia, Botswana, Côte d'Ivoire, Senegal, Sudan, Uganda, Zambia, Zimbabwe, Ghana, Nigeria and Ethiopia. There is also a network of honorary consuls including in the Comoros Islands.
2. India has four defence attachés stationed in Africa, in Kenya, Nigeria, Egypt and South Africa. The defence attaché stationed in Nairobi is directly credited to Kenya, Tanzania and the Seychelles but also Somalia and Eritrea comes under his watch because the Indian High Commission in Nairobi is responsible for both countries. This office also oversees on an ad hoc basis Mozambique, Comoros, Madagascar and the Democratic Republic of Congo.
3. In 2008 the *Topaz* was refitted by India and handed back to the Seychelles in late April 2009.
4. According to an Indian official this links up with Indian navy berthing rights in Oman and navy monitoring stations also in Mauritius, Kochi and Mumbai, providing cover of the sea lanes right from Mozambique and the Cape of Good Hope to the Gulf of Oman. See *Indian Express* (2007) and *The Indian Ocean Newsletter* (2007).
5. According to reporters at the *South China Morning Post*, the General Administration of Press Publication, China's top government censor for the print media, issued new guidelines including developing a blacklist of journalists and said this 'report led to a bad impression with the public and cast a bad light on the reputation of the country and the army'.
6. The later deployment was of two Sukanya-class, offshore patrol vessels (OPV), the INS *Sujata* and INS *Savitri*.

References

Abdi, S. (2007) 'India on guard in fallout from China's missile test', *South China Morning Post*, 11 February

Aiyar, P. (2007) 'China continues to court Africa', *The Hindu*, 1 February

Aneja, A. (2008) 'Hijackers release all Indian sailors', *The Hindu*, 17 November

Berlin, D. (2006) 'India in the Indian Ocean', *Naval War College Review*, vol. 59, no. 2, p. 62

Braun, D. (1983) *The Indian Ocean: Region of Conflict or 'Zone of Peace'*, London, C.H. Hurst

Business Standard (2008) 'Kenya violence: Centre not to evacuate Indians', 4 January

Campbell, G. (2003) 'The Indian Ocean Rim (IOR) Economic Association: history and prospects', in Campbell, G. (ed) *The Indian Ocean Rim: Southern Africa and Regional Cooperation*, London, Routledge

Chatham House (2010) 'Two years on from the forum summit: the future of Africa–India engagement', conference report, Africa Programme, Chatham House, 9 April, http://www.chathamhouse.org.uk/ files/16546_0410conf_report.pdf, accessed 12 February 2011

Chellaney B. (2009) 'China's maritime chess', *DNA Newspaper,* 10 February, http://chellaney.spaces.live.com/Blog/cns!4913C7C8A2EA4A30!985.entry, accessed 12 February 2011

China Daily (2009) 'China Signs $260m airport deal with Mauritius', 17 February

Economic Times (2008) 'Somalia seeks India's help to quell piracy', 21 November

Financial Express (2008) 'India navy floats maritime military bloc', 8 February

Forsberg, S. (2007) 'India stretches its sea legs', United States Naval Institute, Proceedings 38, vol.133, no. 3

Government of India (1997) 'Defence and security in the post-cold war scenario', address by Government of India at the United Services Institution of India, 23 January

The Hindu (2010) 'India offers $500m credit line to Mozambique', 1 October

India Defence (2008) 'Indian navy to hold exercises with France, African navies', 17 August

Indian Express (2007) 'India activates first listening post on foreign soil: radars in Madagascar', 17 July

—— (2009) '"We'll take required actions for sailors" release: navy', 17 January

The Indian Ocean Newsletter (2007) 'India inaugurates a monitoring station in Madagascar', 28 July

India Public Information Bureau (2006) 'MoU for military cooperation', April, http://mod.nic.in/samachar/april1-06/h3.htm, accessed 12 February 2011

Kaplan, R. (2009) 'Centre stage for the 21st century: power plays in the Indian Ocean', *Foreign Affairs*, 1 March

Kumar, R. (2008) 'Peace uplift for Africa', *Africa Quarterly*, vol. 48, no.1, p. 75

Ministry of Defence, (2008) 'Indian naval warship deployed in Gulf of Aden', 16 October, Press Information Bureau Government of India

Mohan, C. (2009) 'Sino-Indian rivalry in the western Indian Ocean', ISAS Insights, no.52,

News India-Times (2009) 'United States navy helps Indian ship, captures pirates off Somalia', 27 February

Page, J. (2009) 'Chinese billions fund battle against Tamil Tigers', *The Times*, 2 May

Pandit, R. (2009) 'Indian sub stalked China warships?', *The Times of India*, 6 February

Press Trust of India (1998) 'UN may drop "peace zone" proposal for Indian Ocean', 30 April

—— (2008) 'India begins naval games with France, Africa', 17 May

—— (2009) 'India to join marine highway project in Africa', 24 March

Ramachandran, S. (2006) 'Delhi all ears in the Indian Ocean', *South Asia*, 3 March

Thaindian News (2008) 'Somalia seeks India's help to quell piracy', 21 November, http://www.thaindian.com/newsportal/uncategorized/somalia-seeks-indias-help-to-quell-piracy_100121994.html, accessed 12 February 2011

Times of India (2007) 'China's anti-satellite test worries India', 5 February

—— (2008) 'Somalia hijacking: SC seeks report on steps taken by centre', 2 October

—— (2008) 'Ship hijack: hostage captain's wife fights on', 4 October

Vines, A. (2010) 'India's Africa engagement: prospects for the 2011 India-Africa Forum', Programme Paper: AFP 2010/01, Chatham House, December 2010, http://www.chathamhouse.org.uk/files/18076_1210vines.pdf, accessed 12 February 2011.

12

India goes over to the other side: Indo-West African relations in the 21st century

Simona Vittorini and David Harris

Despite having more poor people than the whole of sub-Saharan Africa, one could argue that India no longer inhabits the same developing world. India's new-found affluence, however unevenly spread, and its drive for resources, trade and influence has led to recent unprecedented engagements with Africa, and not just in India's traditional backyard, East Africa, but in the West of the continent as well.

Indian relations with West Africa have undergone a recent and dramatic overhaul: to India, West Africa is no longer an area of limited interest, based largely on developing world solidarity. The repercussions of this sea change are only just beginning to materialise and it is conceivable, given the historic differences, that the process in West Africa may show marked divergences from that on the other side of the continent.

Past Indo-West African relations

Indo-West African relations were based until very recently almost entirely on former Indian Prime Minister Jawaharlal Nehru's idea of Afro-Asian solidarity, mediated by its reception within different spheres of the African elite. Nehru's vision was also popular in East and southern Africa. However, instead of the immediate, if not formally endorsed, links with the Indian diaspora in the East African states of Kenya, Tanzania and Uganda, West African ties were largely a rhetorical and diplomatic relationship fostered within the Non-Aligned Movement (NAM), dating back to the Bandung Conference of 1955.

This was not entirely without effect though. Nehru strongly advocated decolonisation in Africa on the global stage and referred to Africa as a neighbour and a sister continent (*Nehru Centenary Volume* 1989). Two founding fathers of African nationalism, Kwame Nkrumah of Ghana and Chief Obafemi Awolowo of Nigeria, both West Africans, acknowledged their admiration of Indian leaders. Nkrumah visited India in 1958, just one year after Ghanaian independence and Nehru visited Lagos in 1962, two years after independence in Nigeria.

From the first days of African independence, African students began to populate universities in India, while officers of African militaries were offered places on Indian defence training courses. South–South cooperation as a practice was born. Indian teachers were sent to work in rural areas of Ghana and Nigeria, and India assisted in the establishment of the still-influential military university, the Nigerian Defence Academy at Kaduna in 1964 (Singh 2007).

However, the relationship was for a long time very limited in scope. Equally, relations, such as they were, were heavily biased toward anglophone countries. Former imperial connections through London and later the Commonwealth, language advantages and, conversely, the ties between most francophone African states and France which remained strong and required solidarity with France on the world stage, mitigated against a widening of the relationship.

Indo-West African relations today

Today, both continental and sub-regional scenarios are profoundly different. With India's annual bilateral trade figures with African countries for 2008 at around $36 billion, a 12-fold increase from a mere $3 billion in 2002, and approaching half that of China, there has been an expansion in terms of geography, magnitude and the array of India's interests in Africa. The inaugural India–Africa Summit in New Delhi in April 2008 attracted 14 African leaders.

Indian private companies are investing heavily in Africa. In addition, since 2003, when it was announced that India would accept bilateral aid from just five sources and tied aid from none, it has begun its conversion from aid recipient to aid donor. At the

2008 summit, India pledged to disburse $500 million in grants for development projects in Africa in the following five years (which have now been allocated) and to double its credit line to African states and regional groupings to $5.4 billion (Jobelius 2007).[1] Finally, at the summit in 2008, all delegates notably signed up to promote India's aspiration to a seat on the UN Security Council, part of India's quest for a re-organisation of global governance.

Although the East African connections persist, West Africa has now become a great attraction for Indian companies and the Indian government. For instance, of total Indian imports from Africa, 65 per cent now emerge from West Africa and total West African exports to India grew by 19 per cent from 2006/7 to 2007/8, and 15 per cent from 2007/8 to 2008/9 (Government of India, Ministry of Commerce and Industry 2010). Because 80 per cent of these exports come from Nigeria, mainly in the form of oil and petroleum products, some might suggest that this is essentially an oil relationship, but it certainly goes beyond that.

The total export figures from India into West Africa constituted a 42 per cent rise from 2006/7 to 2007/8, an increase which was maintained in 2008/9 in the face of the global recession (Government of India, Ministry of Commerce and Industry 2010). Although textiles, manufactured goods and machinery, and processed food and drinks constitute current exports, pharmaceuticals and the health sector, information technology, water management and education are seen by the Federation of Indian Chambers of Commerce and Industry as areas ripe to further boost Indo-Africa trade.

Indian companies are investing heavily across the anglophone-francophone borders in Côte d'Ivoire, Ghana, Liberia, Nigeria and Senegal. Indian oil firms have been awarded blocks in Nigeria and Côte d'Ivoire, while Tata buses are now being assembled in Senegal. Exim Bank India has extended lines of credit (LOCs) to Senegal, Côte d'Ivoire, Mali, Burkina Faso and Niger, which are earmarked for agri-related projects and which have supported Indian companies in securing projects in countries including Senegal.

The Techno-Economic Approach for Africa–India Movement (TEAM-9) initiative established a development cooperation package in 2004 with eight West African countries, soon to be increased to 14. Finally, to show the range in diversification of relations in West Africa, more than 3,000 Indian peacekeepers deployed as part of a United Nations mission in Sierra Leone, in which the Indian Major-General Vijay Jetley became force commander for nine months in 1999/2000; and a female Indian police unit is currently serving in Liberia. In light of this resurgent engagement across the region, we investigate two specific case studies in this chapter – Liberia and Ghana. Both are West African and anglophone, but have been chosen to demonstrate the wide variety of Indian engagement in West Africa in two states with starkly contrasting political and economic environments.

Liberia: narrow Indian investment in a war-torn country

Liberia is a small country of just 3.5 million people. The independence of a black settler Americo-Liberian pseudo-colonial state arrived as early as 1847. From this unusual beginning emerged, however, a particularly weak state with a small elite maintained in power largely through patronage and coercion. The Americo-Liberian oligarchy was ousted in a coup in 1980 by a junior officer, Samuel Doe, who being unable to control the patronage system resorted to ethnically-oriented violence.

Fourteen years of conflict and instability ensued, interrupted only by three years of relative calm when major violent incidents were limited to state-sanctioned repression under Charles Taylor. Taylor's exile in 2003 led to a two-year coalition government, which continued the pattern of gross corruption in government but held the peace deal. The intention in this very brief sketch up to the beginning of the administration of current president, Ellen Johnson-Sirleaf, is not to provide a history but to highlight the obstacles confronting the Liberian state, and its lack of legitimacy.

Johnson-Sirleaf was elected into the presidency in 2005 in a remarkably free poll (Harris 2006). However, she inherited a state that barely functions, infrastructure which is still shattered, simmering ethno-regional rivalries, and entrenched patronage and corruption. Equally, while the pre-recession economy had been growing at around 9.5 per cent, these are increases from a very low baseline. Clear technocratic actions have been taken including the shake-up of ministries, the sacking of corrupt officials, the establishment of commissions to deal with corruption, governance reform, land reform, and emergency issues such as the retraining of security bodies and the slashing of foreign debt.

Into this environment, the second largest single investor (after the Chinese deal for the western cluster of mines amounting to $2.6 billion) is ArcelorMittal (formerly Mittal Steel, an Indian company). Mittal has a franchise to extract iron ore at Yekepa near the Ivorian border, rebuild a 270km railway (the breadth of the country), and reconstruct and control the Buchanan port with investment costs that now amount to $1.5 billion. About 3,500 direct and 20,000 indirect jobs are planned.

Mittal, the biggest steelmaker in the world even before its merger, plans to almost double in size in the next 25 years, although the current recession might dent this aspiration, and half of the ore needed for that expansion was set to come from Liberia. There has, however, been a delay to the beginning of production, which had been expected in 2010, because of low ore prices and the global recession, and this might yet affect Mittal's calculations further. Although there are also more than 50 small Indian traders in Liberia and three Indian timber concessions, these are dwarfed by Mittal and the Chinese deal.

The original Mittal deal was in fact signed in the last days of the interim unelected coalition government, then renegotiated to Mittal's detriment by the newly elected administration. The August 2005 deal stipulated a $900 million investment, allowed Mittal to opt out of human rights and environmental laws, pay no tax for five years with the option of an unspecified extension, maintain control over how much royalties are paid as the agreement does not set a price for the ore, and provide $3 million to local communities (Global Witness 2006).

The renegotiated deal of December 2006 removed the exemptions from Liberian laws and tax benefits, transferred control of the railway and port back to the state, set market prices for ore, and still provided $3 million to local communities. In December 2007, Mittal raised its investment to $1.5 billion. In mid-2008, Mittal became embroiled in its first major scandal: the donation of 100 vehicles to members of the legislature purportedly to be used for agricultural purposes in their respective constituencies and counties in response to a food crisis (Liberia Government 2008). The story, whatever the veracity of its contents, neatly summarises on the one hand the considerable influence that Mittal has in Liberia and on the other the prevailing political environment in which they are investing.

Ghana: diverse Indian investment in a stable country

Ghana is a much bigger country than Liberia, comprising a population of 23 million. It has been largely stable with a slowly growing economy since the mid-1980s, despite a prior three decades of political turmoil, coups, military juntas, gross corruption and economic mismanagement following independence from Britain in 1957.

Ghana has just successfully completed its fifth election since 1992. The five elections have included two presidents stepping down according to the constitution, Jerry Rawlings in 2000 and John Kuffour in 2008. Each election has been closely contested, if not always without flaws, and there have been two turnovers of power: in 2000 Rawlings' National Democratic Congress (NDC) lost to Kuffour's New Patriotic Party (NPP) and in 2008, Kuffour's NPP lost to John Atta Mills' NDC.

Of course, the problems of the weak state are not alien to Ghana, and patronage and corruption are prevalent, but there is relative calm in Ghana's state-society and ethno-regional relations. Relatively prosperous in West African terms, GDP grew by around 4 per cent in the 1990s rising to 7.3 per cent in 2008 and dropping to 4.7 per cent in 2009. Ghana has many investors, including many from India, and offers a very different environment to that of Liberia. A huge offshore oil find was due on stream in 2010. Kuffour, at the time still in the presidency, said that the discovery of the country's first major oil deposit could turn the West African country into an 'African tiger'. 'Even without oil, we are doing so well ... With oil as a shot in the arm, we're going to fly,' he told reporters (BBC 2007).

There are a variety of Indian engagements in Ghana. Trade turnover between the two countries has increased tenfold since 2001. It doubled from $280 million in 2005–6 to $564 million in

2006–7 and almost again to $948 million in 2007–8 (Government of India, Ministry of Commerce and Industry 2010). The drop to $710 million in 2008–9 during the recession period was made up mostly by a decrease in Indian exports.

One highly ambitious plan (widely stated in the press to be a massive $6 billion investment), a tractor assembly plant established by Mahindra and Mahindra Group of India in collaboration with ZoomLion Ghana, has been commissioned in Kumasi, alongside a technology transfer centre. The tractors, with assembly plants already in three other West African states, will be customised to suit agriculture in the country (Government of India, Ministry of Commerce and Industry 2010).

There has been an increase in investments by Indian companies in Ghana in sectors such as construction, manufacturing, trading, services and tourism and in areas such as steel, cement, plastics, pharmaceuticals, ICT, agro-processing and agricultural machinery, electrical equipments and chemicals. A number of Indian companies are thus establishing a presence in Ghana.

From the public sector, Telecommunications Consultants India has an office in Ghana, and the first Indian bank, the Bank of Baroda (one with a long heritage in East Africa), started operations in Accra in 2008. The private sector is represented by such eminent companies as Tata, Ashok Leyland, Larson and Toubro, NIIT Technologies and several pharmaceutical companies, among others (Freiku 2008). India is involved in rural electrification through a LOC, the participation of an Indian company, Bilpower, and the Ghanaian section of the Pan African e-Network. Indians are now the largest foreign investor in Ghana in terms of number of projects – 11 per cent of the total from 1994 to 2007 (Indian High Commission in Ghana n.d.).

At state level, Anand Sharma, then Indian Minister for External Affairs, visited Ghana four times between 2006 and 2008. India contributed to the setting up of the India–Ghana Kofi Annan Centre of Excellence in Information and Communication Technology. The centre was jointly inaugurated by the Prime Minister of India (via video) and the president of Ghana in December 2003.

Last year Ghana also opened an impressive new presidential palace, Golden Jubilee House, financed by a $30 million LOC from the Indian Exim Bank. Much maligned by the opposition at the time, the palace was built by an Indian contractor, Shapoorji Pallonji, using Ghanaian sub-contractors and opened in the presence of Anand Sharma (BBC 2008). The palace's original price tag of $37 million has, however, reportedly increased considerably with Shapoorji Pallonji the most likely main benefactor.

Potential effects of India in Liberia and Ghana

There are, as noted before, potential economic and political repercussions in Liberia and Ghana that accompany India's growing presence and role. On an economic level, in both cases there are clearly major investments afoot. From an Indian perspective, there appears to be a level of local recruitment and training of indigenous staff with the use of local suppliers and sub-contractors, as highlighted in the Mahindra and Golden Jubilee House cases (Broadman 2006). Appropriate technology and technology transfer also appear to be important aspects, particularly in the case of the Mahindra tractor plant. There is aid and/or soft financing shifting into previously unfashionable areas, such as rural electrification in Ghana and transport infrastructure in Liberia.

At the same time, the aid is also tied to both Indian companies and Indian projects, as exemplified in the Ghanaian electrification project, a development which is creating debate on the nature of India's African partnerships (Jobelius 2007; Mawdsley, Chapter 10 in this volume). Tied aid is of course nothing new and was once common in western deals. Moreover, it is difficult to identify what is and is not untied aid, particularly because different states and institutions define aid, soft financing and particularly LOCs, in varying fashions.

It is, though, the potential political implications which we consider to be key. Even though the neopatrimonial model of African states does not explain all politics in Africa, there is reason to believe that the overriding concerns for communalism, reciprocity and patron-clientelism (the exchange of economic resources for political support between patron and client) in the African body politic go some way to explaining the political and economic malaise on the continent (Chabal and Daloz 1999).

The colonial legacy of the weak state and strong society or, put another way, the fusing of African indigenous political structures with the colonial under-resourced and malfunctioning western-style state, led directly to the reliance of post-independence African leaders on patron-clientelism in order merely to stay in power (Migdal 1988). In effect, the adverse structural conditions, in particular the weak state, existent in most sub-Saharan African countries, severely constrain African leaders in what they can realistically achieve. Any changes to this environment, while inherently important in themselves, are also the ones that are most likely to make long-term economic differences.

The academic debate surrounding the effects of Chinese investment in Africa might then assist here in a framework for looking at its Indian counterpart. On the one hand, there are those who point towards the possibility of a brighter future. Chris Alden has noted the twin possibilities of 'an Africa without Europeans' and 'an Africa that can say no' (Alden 2005, 2008). Not only is there potential that 'accountable African governments' might look to the Chinese experience as a developing country, but they might then exert some leverage over China for their own benefit, particularly in the context of a greater number of suitors, India included (Alden 2005). There are also China's own intentions, which go beyond crude economic rationality to a need to portray itself as a major player on the global stage and whose own 'peaceful rise' will not 'jeopardise poor countries' interests (Alden and Alves 2008).

On the other hand, there is the view that China faces the same dilemmas in Africa that all foreign powers have faced. As Christopher Clapham (2006) has noted, 'African states and societies have historically proved extremely intractable to grand projects of social and economic transformation'. This would apply equally to the various Afro-socialist and Marxist transformational projects of Africa's own leaders, such as Nkrumah, Julius Nyerere and Samora Machel, as to the post-cold war western liberal conditionalities on trade and aid, all of which have had limited success. Further, as Jean-François Bayart has told us, African leaders have a long history of 'extraversion' and the use of foreign powers in their own difficult quests to place some form of control over their societies (Bayart 1993).

Although Clapham acknowledges that China's involvement in Africa will this time be much longer and deeper, he is also of the opinion that China is far more likely to conform to long-established patterns of Africa's external engagement than transform them. China has no 'project of transformation' for Africa and is in any case 'extremely unlikely fundamentally to change' the African experience (Clapham 2006).

Uniquely, India approaches Africa also as a former colony, a developing and plural country, an emerging power and a democracy. However, until such a time as India decides to become involved in its own social transformation project or democracy promotion or other such enterprise in Africa, the direct role model idea is far-fetched. It would certainly contradict decades of Indian non-interventionist foreign policy.

In any case, the staggering levels of rural and urban poverty in India, and the state-led oppression of poorer, indigenous people inhabiting mineral-rich areas, calls into question what model India might uphold. Its economic growth has indeed been spectacular, but the rewards and costs that this has entailed have been spread very unevenly. There must, though, be caveats in this notion and here we turn to the possible indirect effects, on an ideological, local and international level.

On an ideological level, there are suggestions that in a world of waning western liberal influence, African countries might be tempted by a Chinese authoritarian model of development, despite Chinese protestations that they have no such model. President Abdoulaye Wade of Senegal has already said that 'the Chinese model for stimulating rapid economic development has much to teach Africa' (Wade 2008).

Are these temptations somewhat countered by an Indian democratic model for development? In Ghana, there is already a history of attempts at authoritarian economic development, first largely unsuccessfully under Nkrumah's Afro-Socialism, then in a modified manner under various subsequent military leaders, and then relatively successfully under neoliberal economic orthodoxy with Rawlings between 1981 and 1992. This has, of course, been followed by nearly two decades of growth under democratic conditions.

The question, though, is how fragile this growth is when put under the pressures of global recession and how willing Ghanaians are to consider alternatives again if the economy begins to slide and liberalism to retrench. In Liberia, governments have historically been aligned with and taken an ideological lead from the US. Johnson-Sirleaf's government is no different and her experience in various international financial institutions has given her a strict neoliberal economic and political approach.

At a local level, if there is an expansion of local businesses and the employment of junior and senior staff by Indian companies then there is the potential for the indirect creation of alternative local economic and/or political networks. Because the Indian presence in West Africa is small, this might emerge without the complications that large-scale Chinese migration is said to cause (Haugen and Carling 2005; Dobler 2008).

At the same time, the history of foreign concession areas, of which Mittal's is possibly just the next in a long line, looms large in the Liberian economy and politics and this history has not always been a happy one. Exploitation by foreign companies, the control of receipts by elites and the creation of zones of relative prosperity all contributed to the collapse of pre-war Liberian politics.

Finally, at a governmental level, and with the concurrent re-emergence of China in Africa, there is the potential for increased African leverage in a new world of multipolarity, leverage potentially greater than that experienced under the East-West bipolar conditions of the cold war. Not only does this give African governments some muscle and choice, but provided the idea of sovereignty is maintained by the Asians, there may be more African government leeway in economic planning and attendant political decisions than has been the case under the formerly dominant western liberal agenda. This can, very importantly, be read as the possibility of some government autonomy from client forces, or at least, if more resources are in government hands with fewer strings attached, greater room to manoeuvre might be generated.

With the Ghanaian and Liberian governments claiming progressive and developmental intentions, a new-found scope to manoeuvre in both senses might be very useful. We have of course heard before claims for developmentalism in Africa with limited end results. Despite government rhetoric and indeed actions in Liberia, Johnson-Sirleaf has recently reversed her decision not to stand in the 2011 elections because she is unhappy with progress thus far. Large-scale diversions of government funds have been exposed on a frequent basis and she has sacked various ministers, including some who were seen as old and close allies.

Equally, there are dangers associated with the forthcoming oil wealth in Ghana, as previously has been demonstrated in the political difficulties of oil-rich Nigeria and Angola and diamond-rich Sierra Leone. But it is conceivable we might discover that Ghana and Liberia develop instead as politically well-managed governments. This is not seen here as good governance in a strict liberal sense, but as a relatively sustainable balance between responses to political patron-cliental demands, reform and developmental government.

It is then the prospect of a different kind of investment from India leading to indirect repercussions, and/or the addition of India to the mix of developmental ideology and multipolarity in Africa which might conceivably bring change. To support Clapham's viewpoint, neither the effects of a bipolar cold war world, nor those of a unipolar world with the injection of neo-liberal programmes appears to have fundamentally transformed African society or affected the largely neopatrimonial nature of politics. Having said that, it would be rather rash to conclude that democratisation and limited democratic consolidation have no purchase at all on the continent.

The emergence of governments with a degree of democratic legitimacy, the electoral need for these governments to deliver in a developmental as well as a patron-cliental fashion, and with the possibility that these governments can be removed, Liberia and Ghana might both have made small steps toward being 'politically well-managed' (Manor 2006).[2]

If this is the case, it is not outside the realm of possibility that multipolarity might be of benefit to a greater range of Ghanaians and Liberians beyond the elites who benefited during the bipolarity of the cold war. The need for African governments to resort to patron-clientelism to stay in power has not disappeared. Nor has Ghanaian or Liberian society been transformed. Equally, there is now a global economic downturn to consider, although there are indications that India with its relatively healthy domestic market might ride the storm better than others. The possibility, though, that patron-clientelism can be more successfully managed in a semi-democratic political arena with a paradoxically greater state autonomy, might be growing.

India in East and West Africa

In an initial reading of this somewhat speculative argument, one might assume that Indian involvement in East and West Africa might produce similar results. The Indian government and business approach is relatively homogenous on the continent, and the status and modus operandi of African governments does not throw up stark dissimilarities.

However, this would be to ignore the historical trajectories of the various East and West African states. First, on an ideological level, the likelihood of any specific state being drawn towards an Indian or Chinese developmental model is affected by history. Just as Ghana has positive and negative experiences under various types of government, and Liberia has little to show from several authoritarian and faux democracies, we could equally make an East-West comparison between Nigeria's mostly difficult encounters with military authoritarianism and Tanzania's more nuanced experience of one-party rule. In other words, the future trajectory will, to some extent, be guided by the past experience of a particular state.

Second, at a local level, West Africa has nothing like the population of Indians that live in East Africa. There is no comparable legacy of mistrust of Indians in West Africa and there are few resident Indians to take up jobs. Equally, although India cannot rely on its diaspora to broker its investments in East Africa (McCann, Chapter 6 in this volume), it has no similar community to build, or indeed hinder, its relationship in West Africa. India has reached out to all West African countries, whether anglophone, francophone or lusophone, and its engagement is new and at a huge and suddenly increased level.

Finally, there is the specific nature of particular governments. The long-standing and partially consolidated democracy of Ghana and the brand new Liberian democracy just emerging from its post-conflict, post-electoral honeymoon period offer two different political environments into which Asian investment enters. Again, there is a need for a case-by-case analysis of the pressures on and the inclinations of how to use Asian investments of individual governments on both sides of the continent.

Growing Indian-West African engagement is just one

demonstration of shifting global, and more particularly South–
South geographies, emerging in the 21st century. In this case, the
question is whether this shift is creating a new political arena: an
environment unseen before in Africa, where democratic semi-
consolidation appears alongside huge Indian and Chinese investment and potentially much greater African international leverage.

Notes

1. Although Jobelius estimates that a calculation based on items in the 2006
   Indian budget suggests total Indian overseas development assistance was
   already $300 million for just that year, sources, he says, are 'approximate
   and contradictory' and have generally led to underestimates.
2. James Manor's ideas of 'post-clientelism' or 'clientelism-plus' in state-
   level Indian elections, which he also applies to Ghana and Zambia, are
   useful here.

References

Alden, C. (2005) 'Leveraging the dragon: toward "An Africa that can Say
No"', eAfrica – Electronic Journal of Governance and Innovation, February
—— (2008) 'An Africa without Europeans', in Alden, C., Large, D. and Soares
de Oliviera, R. (eds) China Returns to Africa: A Superpower and a Continent
Embrace, London, Hurst
Alden, C. and Alves, A.C. (2008) 'History and identity in the construction of
China's Africa policy', Review of African Political Economy, vol. 35, no. 115, p. 43
Bayart, J.F. (1993) The State in Africa: The Politics of the Belly, London,
Longman
BBC (2007) 'Ghana "will be an African tiger"', 19 June, http://news.bbc.
co.uk/1/hi/world/africa/6766527.stm, accessed 4 November 2008
BBC (2008) 'Ghana unveils presidential palace', 10 November, http://news.
bbc.co.uk/1/hi/world/africa/7720653.stm, accessed 2 December 2008
Broadman H.G. (2006) Africa's Silk Road: China and India's New Economic
Frontier, Washington, World Bank
Chabal, P. and Daloz, J.P. (1999) Africa Works: Disorder as Political Instrument,
Bloomington, IN, Indiana University Press
Clapham, C. (2006) 'Fitting China in', August, Brenthurst discussion paper,
Brenthurst Foundation
Dobler, G. (2008) 'Solidarity, xenophobia and the regulation of Chinese
businesses in Namibia', in Alden, C., Large, D. and Soares de Oliviera,
R. (eds) China Returns to Africa: A Superpower and a Continent Embrace,
London, Hurst
Export-Import Bank of India (2006) 6 July, http://www.eximbankindia.com/
old/press060706.html, accessed 8 November 2008
Freiku, S.R. (2008) 'Mahindra tractor assembly plant commissioned
in Kumasi', Ghanaian Chronicle, 21 October, http://allafrica.com/
stories/200810210991.html, accessed 4 November 2008

Global Witness (2006) 'Heavy Mittal?', October

Government of India, Ministry of Commerce and Industry (2010) http://commerce.nic.in/eidb/default.asp, accessed 20 March 2010

Harris, D. (2006) 'Liberia 2005: an unusual African post-conflict election', *Journal of Modern African Studies*, vol. 44, no. 3, pp. 375–95

Haugen, H.O. and Carling, J. (2005) 'On the edge of the Chinese diaspora: the surge of baihuo business in an African city', *Ethnic and Racial Studies*, vol. 28, no. 4, pp. 639–62

India High Commission in Ghana, http://www.indiahc-ghana.com/, accessed 8 November 2008

Jobelius, Matthias (2007) 'New powers for global change? Challenges for the international development cooperation. The case of India', March, FES briefing papers

Liberia Government (2008) 'Mittal dealings: President Sirleaf defends Arcelormittal vehicle donation', press release, 1 November, http://allafrica.com/stories/200811031165.html, accessed 4 November 2008

Manor, J. (2006) 'The changing character of the Indian state', Waheeduddin Khan memorial lecture, Centre for Economic and Social Studies, Hyderabad

Migdal, J. (1988) *Strong States and Weak Societies*, New Jersey, Princeton University Press

Nehru Centenary Volume (1989) New Delhi, Oxford University Press, http://www.anc.org.za/ancdocs/history/solidarity/nehru-africa.html, accessed 9 July 2008

Singh, S. (2007) 'India and West Africa: a burgeoning relationship', Chatham House, April, p. 3

Wade, Abdoulaye (2008) 'Time for the west to practise what it preaches', *Financial Times*, 24 January

Index

ACBF *see* African Capacity Building
   Foundation
ACCZ *see* Association of Chinese
   Corporations in Zambia
AfDB *see* African Development Bank
Africa Export-Import Bank
   (Afreximbank) 23
African Capacity Building
   Foundation (ACBF) 60
African Development Bank (AfDB)
   23
African Union (AU), India relations
   25
Aga Khan hospitals 134, 136
Agalega islands 193, 194
AGOA *see* United States, African
   Growth and Opportunity Act
Alpha Manyara 197
Amin, Idi 115, 141
Angola 18
anti-colonial struggle, India–Africa
   relations 14, 50, 114–16, 141, 204
Anyona, George 143
Apollo group 21, 125, 134, 135
AquaSan 38
ArcelorMittal 31, 35–7, 44n1, 56,
   207–8
Ashok Leyland 209
Asian Africans 146
Association of Chinese Corporations
   in Zambia (ACCZ) 102
AU *see* African Union
AwaaZ 7, 140–52
Awolowo, Obafemi 204

Bank of Baroda 116, 209
Bhagat, B.R. 116
Bharati Airtel Telecommunications
   57, 108, 110, 117

Bilpower 209
Bindra, Sunny 149, 150
Bjerg, Ole 173
Bourdieu, Pierre 169
BRIC countries (Brazil, Russia, India
   and China) 1, 44, 50
Burkina Faso 19
Bush, George W. 54

California Public Employees'
   Retirement System (CalPERS)
   160
Canada, Sudan oil 154–5, 156
CCIPT *see* Chinese Centre for
   Investment Promotion and Trade
Chad 19, 40
Chagos Islands 189
Chandra, Atul 158
Chavez, Hugo 176
China
   Africa relations 2–3, 5, 30–1, 34,
      60, 112, 211–12
   competition with India 12–26,
      44, 49–50, 95–103, 191–2,
      199–200
   diaspora in Africa 99–103
   entrepreneurs in East Africa 6,
      88–104
   Indian Ocean presence 189–94
   Sudan oil involvement 157–9
   textile and clothing trade 75–6
   trade with Africa 55–6, 88–9
China National Petroleum
   Corporation (CNPC) 154, 156,
   157, 160, 163
Chinese Centre for Investment
   Promotion and Trade (CCIPT)
   102–3
Chipata Cotton Company 98

Choudhary, Prashant 100
CII *see* Confederation of Indian
    Industries
Clapham, Christopher 211–12, 214
clothing industry *see* textile industry
CNPC *see* China National Petroleum
    Corporation
cold war 14, 51–2
colonialism, end of 52, 141
COMESA *see* Common Market for
    East and Southern Africa
Common Market for East and
    Southern Africa (COMESA) 58–9
Comoros Islands 189
Confederation of Indian Industries
    (CII) 21, 57, 110
Côte d'Ivoire 18, 19
cotton production, India 74

DAC *see* Development Assistance
    Committee
defence agreements 43, 191, 195
democracy, India–Africa relations
    24, 25–6, 44, 212–14
Democratic Republic of Congo 63
Deng Xiaoping 14
Deora, Murli 18–19
Desai, Manilal Ambalal 147–8
development assistance
    gift theory 168–72
    Indian in Africa 16–21, 40–2,
        60–1, 166–84
    non-DAC donors 173–4, 184n1
    South–South cooperation 172–84
Development Assistance Committee
    (DAC) 170–1, 172–3
Development Bank of Zambia 23
developmental ideology 210–14
diamonds 33
diaspora
    business networks 99–103
    Chinese in Africa 91–4

Indian Ocean states 188
Indians in Africa 3, 6–7, 38–9, 63,
    114–16, 140–52
Diego Garcia 189
diplomatic relations 23–5, 188–9,
    200nn1,2
Doe, Samuel 206
Douglas, Mary 184
drug production 61, 62
dukawallahs 6, 92, 104

e-network *see* Pan-African
    e-Network
EACA *see* Eastern Action Club of
    Africa
EASSY *see* East African Submarine
    Cable
East Africa
    Chinese and Indian
        entrepreneurs 6, 88–104
    Indian involvement 215–16
East Africa Indian National
    Congress 141
East African Development Bank 22,
    59
East African Submarine Cable
    (EASSY) 38
East Timor 171
Eastern Action Club of Africa
    (EACA) 143–5
Eastern and Southern African Trade
    and Development Bank 22, 59
Economic Community of West
    African States (ECOWAS) 19,
    24, 58
ECOWAS *see* Economic Community
    of West African States
Egypt 18
entrepreneurs, Chinese and Indian
    6, 88–104
EPZs *see* export processing zones
Equatorial Guinea 19

Escort 21
Essar group 39, 102, 108, 117, 121
Ethiopia 59
European Union (EU), India
    relations 62
export processing zones (EPZs),
    Kenya 73, 80
Export-Import (Exim) Bank of India
    16, 21, 22–3, 33–4, 58–9, 110, 205

family businesses, Chinese 93–4
FDI *see* foreign direct investment
Focus Africa Programme 19, 58–9
foreign aid, gift theory 168–72
foreign direct investment (FDI) 73,
    84, 88
Fortis 21
Fouress International 103

G20 181
G77 181
Gabon 18
Gandhi, Indira 51
Gandhi, Mahatma 30
Garang, John 154
geopolitics 42–4, 51–3
Ghana
    e-network 59
    Golden Jubilee House 209–20
    Indian investment 19, 34, 208–14
gift theory 167, 168–72
globalisation, South–South relations
    30, 38
GNPOC *see* Greater Nile Petroleum
    Operating Company
Goyal, Seema 196
Greater Nile Petroleum Operating
    Company (GNPOC) 154–5, 159
Gregory, Robert 142
guanxi networks 99, 102
Guinea Bissau 19
Gujarati merchants 90–1

Gujral, Inder Kumar 188
Gulf of Guinea, oil resources 18–19

Hamid Ansari, Mohammad 64
Hattori, Tomohisa 169–70
healthcare
    e-network 137–8
    East Africa 95–6
    Kenya 128–30, 133
    medical tourism to India 125–39
    Tanzania 95, 96, 128–32
    see also pharmaceutical
        companies
Hu Jianto 191
hydrographic cooperation 193

IBSA *see* India, Brazil, South Africa
IDSA *see* Institute of Defence Studies
    and Analyses
independence movements 52,
    114–15, 141, 204
India
    Africa policy 60–5, 108–23,
        210–16
    competition with China 12–26,
        44, 49–50, 95–103, 191–2,
        199–200
    development assistance to Africa
        16–21, 40–2, 60–1, 166–84
    diaspora in Africa 3, 6–7, 38–9,
        63, 99–103, 140–52
    diplomatic relations 23–5, 188–9,
        200nn1,2
    economic liberalisation 31–2
    energy supply 15, 18–19, 35–6,
        53–4, 190
    financial policy 58–9
    foreign policy 14–15
    future of Africa relations 25–6
    geopolitics 42–4, 51–3
    history of Africa relations 90–1,
        92, 113–16

maritime policy 16, 189
medical tourism 125–39
navy 191, 195, 196–7, 198–9
nuclear programme 54
private sector 21–3, 56–7
Sudan oil involvement 153–63
textile industry 72–9, 82–5
trade with Africa 15, 33–4, 54–8, 70–1, 205, 208–9
West Africa relations 203–16
India Africa Diamond Institute 25
India–Africa Forum Summit, First (2008) 20, 25, 43, 58, 103, 110, 204–5
India–Africa Forum Summit, Second (2011) 57
India Africa Institute of Educational Planning and Administration 25
India Africa Institute for Foreign Trade 25
India Africa Institute of Information Technology 25
India, Brazil, South Africa (IBSA) group 42–3, 50
India–Ghana Kofi Annan Centre of Excellence in Information and Communication Technology 209
India Infrastructure Development Fund (Mauritius) 38
Indian Chambers of Commerce and Industry (FICCI) 25
Indian Ocean, Indian security interests 7, 16, 187–200
Indian Ocean Naval Symposium (IONS) 199
Indian Ocean Rim Association for Regional Cooperation (IOR-ARC) 43, 187, 188, 191, 199
Indian Technical and Economic Cooperation (ITEC) Programme 18, 41, 60, 117, 159, 193
Indian Telecom Industries 21

Industrial Development Bank of Kenya 59
InfoSys 31
Institute of Defence Studies and Analyses (IDSA) 49–50
IONS *see* Indian Ocean Naval Symposium
IOR-ARC *see* Indian Ocean Rim Association for Regional Cooperation
Iran, in Africa 3
Ismail, Mustafa Osman 158–9
ITEC *see* Indian Technical and Economic Cooperation

Jaitley, Arun 158
Japan, in Africa 3
Jeevanjee Gardens (Nairobi) 143
Jetley, Vijay 206
Johnson-Sirleaf, Ellen 36, 113, 206–7, 213

Kalam, Abdul 131, 159
Kalapaaru Power Transmission Ltd 22
Kamai Engineering Corporation 104
Kanabar, Rajani 131, 132
KANU *see* Kenya African National Union
Kapila, Achhroo Ram 149
Kapoor, Ilan 170
Karaturi Networks 117
KEC International 103
Kenya
    anti-colonialism 141, 142–4
    business networks 100
    Chinese entrepreneurs 97
    defence agreements 43
    export processing zones (EPZs) 73, 80
    healthcare 128–30, 133
    India relations 113–23, 198

Indian diaspora 6–7, 39, 114–16, 140–52
Indian investment 116–21
textile industry 6, 70–85, 97
Kenya African National Union (KANU) 116, 118, 146, 147
Kenya Petroleum Refineries 108
Kenya Social Congress 143
Kenyan Asians 146
Kenyatta, Jomo 117–18, 141
Kibaki, Mwai 118, 123
Kirloskar Brothers Limited 21, 56, 102
Konkan Railways 21
Kuffour, John 208

Larson and Toubro 209
Lesotho 40
Li Changcheng 93
Liberia, Indian investment 36, 113, 206–8, 210–14
Libya 18
lines of credit (LOC) 14, 16–17, 22, 33–4, 58–9, 205
Lions Club International 131, 132, 134
Lundin 155

Machakos Protocol 155
Machel, Samora 211
Madagascar, security issues 16, 43, 193, 194
magazines, Kenya 140–52
Maharaj, Omkara 100
Mahindra and Mahindra 21, 209, 210
Makokha, Wanjohi 149
Malaysia
in Africa 3
Sudan oil 154–5, 157–9
Mali 19
Maliti, Tom 144, 151

Mangat, J.S. 142
manufacturing sector, Indian investment 37
Mashuli Gashmani Ltd 103–4
Mauritius
Chinese presence 191
defence agreements 43, 191
e-network 59
Indian investment 57
investment in India 38
security cooperation 188, 192–3
Mauss, Marcel 168
Mayotte 189
medical sector see healthcare
medical tourism, Africa to India 125–39
Mehta, Sureesh 197
MFA see multi-fibre arrangement
mineral resources, Indian investment 36–7
Mittal 19, see also ArcelorMittal
Moi, Daniel arap 117–18, 141
Mozambique
coal resources 190
India defence relations 43, 194–5
Mukherjee, Pranab 191
multi-fibre arrangement (MFA) 75, 77–9
Mumbai, medical tourism 125–7
Mutahi, Wahome 148

Naik, Ram 158
Namibia 40, 63
National Christian Council of Kenya, Community and Race Relations project 142
Nehru, Jawaharlal 14, 30, 51, 110, 114–15, 203–4
NEPAD see New Partnership for Africa's Development
New Partnership for Africa's Development (NEPAD) 20, 24, 59

Nextcell 38
Nigeria
    Indian farmers 63
    Indian investment 56
    oil resources 18–19, 35–6
Nigerian National Petroleum
    Corporation (NNPC) 19
NIIT Technologies 209
Nirdeshak 198
Nkrumah, Kwame 204, 211
NNPC *see* Nigerian National
    Petroleum Corporation
Non-Aligned Movement (NAM) 14,
    51, 110, 177, 187, 203–4
nuclear programme, India 54
Nyerere, Julius 130, 211

Odinga, Raila 118–19
OECD *see* Organisation for
    Economic Cooperation and
    Development
Oil and Natural Gas Corporation
    (ONGC) 21
    Videsh Limited (OVL) 18, 35, 54,
        153–63
oil resources
    Africa 18–19, 35–6, 53–4
    Sudan 3, 7, 18, 153–63
Okumu, John Sibi 149
ONGC *see* Oil and Natural Gas
    Corporation
Operation Island Watch 195
Orange Democratic Movement
    (ODM) 119
Organisation for Economic
    Cooperation and Development
    (OECD) 17, 23
Overseas Citizenship of India (OCI)
    scheme 188
OVL *see* Oil and Natural Gas
    Corporation, Videsh Limited

Pabari, Dipesh 151
Pan-African e-Network 19–20, 41,
    42, 59, 137–8, 209
Pan-African Stock Exchange 25
Pant, Apa 114
Party of National Unity (PNU)
    (Kenya) 118, 119
Patel, Zarina 142–52
Pattni, Kamlesh 118
peacekeeping missions 24, 206
Person of Indian Origin (PIO) cards
    188
Petronas 154–5, 156, 157–8, 160
pharmaceutical companies 61, 62, 95
    see also healthcare
Pinto, Pio Gama 149
piracy, Indian Ocean 16, 189, 195–8
PNU *see* Party of National Unity
post-colonialism 210–11
Prakash, Arun 192
Premdivya 198
Prince Aly Khan Hospital 126, 134,
    135
private sector, Indian in Africa 21–3,
    56–7

Raha, Subir 156, 158
Rail India Technical and Economic
    Services (Rites) 21, 22
railways 21–2
Rajan, Zahid 142–52
Ramrakha, Priya 147
Ranbaxy Laboratories 56
Rao, S.R. 22
Rawlings, Jerry 208
Republic of Congo 40
Réunion 189
Rowlands, Dane 172
Russia, in Africa 3

SADC *see* Southern African
    Development Community

Sahlins, Marshall 169

Sanghi 117

SCAAP *see* Special Commonwealth African Assistance Programme for Africa

scramble for Africa, new 6, 12–13, 15, 26, 34, 44, 51, 64, 113

security issues, Indian Ocean 7, 16, 187–200

Senegal 19

Seychelles 43, 191–2

Shah, Ajay 118

Shah, Madhukant 144

Shapoorji Pallonji 210

Sharma, Anand 64, 209

Sharma, R.S. 160

Shelby hospital 135–6

Sheth, Pranlal 148

Sierra Leone 24, 206

Silva, Kelly da 171–2

Singh, Lakhvir 145

Singh, Makhan 150

Singh, Manmohan 31, 43, 60, 190

Singh, Rao Inderjit 43

Sino-Indian War (1962) 116

Six, Clemens 173, 180

small and medium enterprises (SMEs), Chinese and Indian 89–104

social relations, development cooperation 167–8

Somali piracy 16, 189, 195–8

South Africa
    e-network 59
    India defence cooperation 194
    India relations 24–5, 57
    Indian diaspora 63

South Atlantic 3/West Africa Submarine Fibre Optic Cable (SAT-3/WASC) 38

South–South relations 38, 51, 109, 166–84, 216

Southern African Development Community (SADC) 24

Special Commonwealth African Assistance Programme for Africa (SCAAP) 18

SPLA/M *see* Sudan People's Liberation Army/Movement

Sri Lanka, Chinese interests 190

Stolt Valor 196–7

Strauss, Julia 177–8

structural adjustment programmes (SAPs) 73, 129, 133

Sudan
    civil war 154, 160–1
    Comprehensive Peace Agreement (CPA) 161
    Darfur conflict 160–1
    oil resources 3, 7, 18, 34, 153–63

Sudan People's Liberation Army/Movement (SPLA/M) 154, 155, 162

Sudapet 155

Talisman Energy 154–5, 156, 158–9

Tanzania
    healthcare 95, 96, 128–32
    India defence relations 194

Tata Group 21, 31, 37, 56, 96, 117, 205, 209

Taylor, Charles 206

TEAM-9 *see* Techno-Economic Approach for Africa–India Movement

Techno-Economic Approach for Africa–India Movement (TEAM-9) 19, 41, 59, 65n3, 205–6

telecommunications, Indian companies in Africa 57, 108

Telecommunications Consultants India Ltd 20, 209

textile industry
    Chinese 97–8

India 73–9
    Kenya 6, 70–85, 97
    trade competition 75–9
Tharoor, Shashi 64, 178
tourism, medical 125–39
Toyota Tsusho Corporation 162
trade
    India and Africa 15, 33–4, 54–8,
        70–1, 205, 208–9
    textile and clothing 75–9

Uganda
    Chinese industries 96–7
    Indian entrepreneurs 100–1
    Indian investment 34
United Arab Emirates, in Africa 3
United Nations (UN), peacekeeping
    missions 24
United Nations Security Council,
    India's bid for membership 23,
    25, 41, 159, 205
United States (US)
    African Growth and Opportunity
        Act (AGOA) 6, 71, 73, 77, 79,
        81, 82, 84
    clothing imports 77–9, 82–3
    Indian Ocean security 189

Sudan involvement 160
uranium exploration 54

Vedanta Resources 36, 56, 102
Vidyarthi, Girdhari Lal 146–7
Vidyarthi, Shravan 147
Visram, Sugra 149
Voice of EACA 144–5

Wade, Abdoulaye 212
West Africa, Indian relations 7–8,
    203–16
West African Development Bank
    22, 23
Wockhardt hospital 126, 135
World Trade Organisation (WTO),
    Doha Development Round
    Negotiations 61

Zain 57, 108, 110
Zambia
    copper resources 36
    foreign investment 34
    Indian investment 37, 56
    textile industry 97–8
Zuma, Jacob 57

From Citizen to Refugee: Uganda Asians Come to Britain

Mahmood Mamdani

2011
paperback £15.95
978-1-906387-57-0

In *From Citizen to Refugee*, republished with a new introduction by the author and with contemporary photographs, Mahmood Mamdani explores issues of political identity. This gripping personal account of the Asians' last days in Uganda following their expulsion in 1972 interweaves an examination of Uganda's colonial history with the subsequent evolution of post-independence politics.

Arriving in overcast London, Mamdani joins compatriots in a refugee camp. 'It was the Kensington camp, and not Amin's Uganda, which was my first experience of what it would be like to live in a totalitarian society.' Mamdani's story, as pertinent as when first published, will be familiar to refugees and those seeking asylum in Britain today.

Chinese and African Perspectives on China in Africa

Edited by Axel Harneit-Sievers, Stephen Marks and Sanusha Naidu

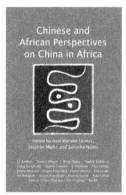

2010
paperback £16.95
978-1-906387-33-4

The deepening engagement of China in Africa has led to debates about the evolving nature of this relationship. Yet the analysis has largely focused on interactions between states, with little attention on the growing dialogue between Chinese and African civil society organisations. These essays, written by African and Chinese scholars and activists, explore the interaction between non-state actors and argue that the future of Africa–China relations rests on including such voices.

This book assesses patterns of investment, legal cooperation, effects on the environment, trade, aid and labour links, questions of peace, security and stability, the African Union response, possible regulatory interventions and the future strengthening of the dialogue between Chinese and African civil society organisations.

China's New Role in Africa and the South

Edited by Dorothy Guerrero and Firoze Manji

China's global expansion is usually talked about from the viewpoint of the West. These essays, by scholars and activists from China and the global South, provide diverse views on the challenges faced by Africa, Latin America and Asia as a result of China's rise as a global economic power. Chinese aid, trade and investments – driven by the needs of its own economy – present both threats and opportunities for the South, requiring an analysis that goes beyond simplistic caricatures of 'good' and 'evil'.

2008
paperback £16.95
978-1-906387-26-6

'... important new perspectives on this emerging issue within international relations.'

Johanna Jansson, *The China Monitor*,
Centre for Chinese Studies, Stellenbosch University

African Perspectives on China in Africa

Edited by Firoze Manji and Stephen Marks

2007
paperback £11.95
978-0-9545637-3-8

China's involvement in Africa has provoked much discussion. Is China just the latest exploiter putting its own economic interests above environmental or human rights concerns? Or is China's engagement an extension of 'South–South solidarity'? Does China's involvement enable African countries to free themselves from debt and conditionality? Or is Africa swapping one tyranny for another? Lost in the discussion have been the voices of African analysts and activists. They are heard in these essays demonstrating that there is no single 'African view' about China in Africa.

'This book is an interesting and easy read, granting the reader access to an enriching debate and opening new questions.'

Tania Adam, Centre d'Estudis Africans, Barcelona

· ·

CPSIA information can be obtained
at www.ICGtesting.com
Printed in the USA
LVOW04s0005290716
498256LV00018B/135/P